American foreign policy

MANCHESTER
1824

Manchester University Press

American foreign policy

Studies in intellectual history

Edited by *Jean-François Drolet and James Dunkerley*

Manchester University Press

Published by Manchester University Press
Altrincham Street, Manchester M1 7JA
www.manchesteruniversitypress.co.uk

British Library Cataloguing-in-Publication Data is available

ISBN 978 1 5261 1650 5 hardback
ISBN 978 1 5261 1652 9 paperback

First published by Manchester University Press in hardback 2017

This edition first published 2020

Typeset by Out of House Publishing

Contents

Notes on contributors

Duncan Bell is Reader in Political Thought and International Relations at the University of Cambridge. He is the author of *The Idea of Greater Britain: Empire and the Future of World Order, 1860–1900* (Princeton University Press, 2007) and *Reordering the World: Essays on Liberalism and Empire* (Princeton University Press, 2007), as well as assorted edited books, including *Uncertain Empire: American History and the Idea of the Cold War* (co-edited with Joel Isaac, Oxford University Press, 2012).

Jean-François Drolet is Senior Lecturer in Politics and International Relations at Queen Mary University of London. He is the author of *American Neoconservatism: The Politics and Culture of a Reactionary Idealism* (Columbia University Press, 2011) and has published numerous articles on questions of ideology, violence and culture in international political thought and the history of ideas. He is presently in the process of completing a monograph on Nietzsche and political thought.

James Dunkerley is Professor of Politics at Queen Mary University of London. Between 1998 and 2008 he was Director of the University of London's Institute for the Study of the Americas. Amongst his books are: *Power in the Isthmus: A Political History of Modern Central America* (Verso, 1988); *Political Suicide in Latin America* (Verso, 1994); *The United States and Latin America: The New Agenda* (co-edited with Victor Bulmer-Thomas, Harvard University Press, 1999); *Americana: The Americas in the World around 1850* (Verso, 2000).

David Milne is Senior Lecturer in American Political History at the University of East Anglia. He is the author of several journal articles on the diplomatic history and intellectual history of American foreign policy. His first monograph *America's Rasputin: Walt Rostow and the Vietnam War* (Hill and Wang, 2008) was reviewed to acclaim. David's current project explores the different ways in which humanities and social science graduates approach foreign policy-making.

Tracy B. Strong is Distinguished Professor in Political Science at the University of San Diego, emeritus, and Professor of Political Theory and Philosophy at the University of Southampton. He is the author of several books including *Friedrich Nietzsche and the Politics of Transfiguration* (currently in its third edition, University of Illinois Press, 2000), *The Idea of Political Theory: Reflections on the Self in Political Time and Space* (University of Notre Dame Press, 1990) and *Jean-Jacques Rousseau and the Politics of the Ordinary* (second edition, Rowman & Littlefield Publishers, 2002). His most recent book is *Politics Without Vision: Thinking without a Banister in the Twentieth Century* (University of Chicago Press, 2012, winner of the David Easton Prize, 2013). He is currently working on a book on music, language and politics in the period that extends from Rousseau to Nietzsche, as well as a conceptual history of American citizenship, for which he is the recipient of a Leverhulme Fellowship.

Jeremi Suri is Mack Brown Distinguished Professor for Global Leadership, History, and Public Policy at the University of Texas at Austin. He is the author of several books on American foreign policy and American intellectual history including *Liberty's Surest Guardian: American Nation-Building from the Founders to Obama* (Simon and Schuster, 2011), *Henry Kissinger and the American Century* (Harvard University Press, 2009) and *Power and Protest: Global Revolution and the Rise of Détente* (Harvard University Press, 2005).

Vibeke Schou Tjalve is a senior researcher at The Danish Institute for International Studies (DIIS), Copenhagen. She is the author of *Realist Strategies of Republican Peace: Morgenthau, Niebuhr and the Politics of Patriotic Dissent* (Palgrave, 2008) as well as numerous journal articles on American history, identity, religion and security. Among her recent publications are '(Neo)Republican Security Governance: US Homeland Security and Politics of Shared Responsibility' (2013) *International Political Sociology* 7:1 (with Karen Lund Petersen) and 'Reviving the Rhetoric of Realism: Politics and Responsibility in Grand Strategy' (2015) *Security Studies* 24:1 (with Michael C. Williams). She is currently involved in a project on American Realism and the Rise of the Right with Michael C. Williams.

Michael C. Williams is Professor in the Graduate School of Public and International Affairs at the University of Ottawa. He is the author (with Rita Abrahamsen) of *Security Beyond the State: Private Security in International Politics* (Cambridge University Press, 2011), *The Realist Tradition and the Limits of International Relations* (Cambridge University Press, 2005) and

Culture and Security: Symbolic Power and the Politics of International Security (Routledge, 2007). He is also the editor of several books, including *Realism Reconsidered: The Legacy of Hans J. Morgenthau in International Relations* (Oxford University Press, 2007). He is currently involved in a project on American Realism and the Rise of the Right with Vibeke Schou Tjalve.

Acknowledgements

This volume of essays is the product of a two-day international workshop held at Queen Mary, University of London (QMUL) in June 2014. The book brings together scholars from the sub-fields of international relations, political theory, history and US foreign policy analysis to propose different ways of thinking about the intellectual history of modern American foreign policy. Our aim has been to go beyond the usual account of US foreign policy in terms of a synthesis of – or duel between – liberal idealism and realist materialism. The essays in this volume draw attention to the more nuanced and multifaceted set of concerns, concepts and rationalities of government that have marked the theory and practice of American foreign policy since the late nineteenth century. To this end, the book is organised around some of the key themes and practices that have shaped the ways in which we have come to think about US foreign policy over the years, and it looks at the work of intellectuals who have written both in support of and critically about US foreign policy in various geographical and historical contexts. The authors were invited to participate not simply for their prestige in the field but also because they come from North America as well as the UK, reflecting distinct academic traditions, political perspectives and expressive styles. Correspondingly, the reader will not find in this book a clear analytical consensus, still less a single, bounded interpretation. However, we hope that the range of perspectives will stimulate research and debate in new as well as revisionist directions.

The editors would like to thank all the authors for their generous collegiality. We are also indebted to Bryan Mabee, Michael Cox and Bryan Schmidt for valuable inputs made during the course of the project. We are particularly grateful for contributions made at the workshop by Luca Tardelli, John A. Thompson, Ray Kiely and David Williams. The project as a whole owes much to the understanding and warm support of Adam Fagan, Head of the School of Politics and International Relations at QMUL. The final preparation of the manuscript was greatly assisted by the precision and professionalism of Sue Serra Iamamoto.

James Dunkerley

Introduction: thinking about America in the world over the longer run

> For all their bragging and their hypersensitivity, Americans are, if not the most critical, at least the most anxiously self-conscious people in the world, forever concerned about the inadequacy of something or other – their national morality, their national culture, their national purpose. This very uncertainty has given their intellectuals a critical function of special interest. The appropriation of some of this self-criticism by foreign ideologues for purposes that go beyond its original scope or intention is an inevitable hazard. But the possibility that a sound enterprise in self-correction may be overheard and misused is the poorest of reasons for suspending it.[1]

There are, perhaps, times in political history when public reflection, the role of ideas and the life of the mind seem less well starred than others. If so, the middle months of 2016 in the North Atlantic world offered a distinctly depressing constellation. From the extraordinary purveyance of spectral evidence and attractive falsehoods in the campaigns for the US presidency and the UK membership of the European Union to the awful massacres perpetrated on continental Europe in the name of religious zealotry, much of the 'global North' looked and felt darkened by a pall of militant anti-intellectualism of a type so vigorously deconstructed by Richard Hofstadter half a century earlier. And yet, when reviewed even superficially, much of the rhetoric, many supposed 'facts' and a great deal of the ostensible reasoning related to the 'rest of the world'. This included those considerable portions of planetary space occupied by people of Muslim faith, the population of Mexico, refugees from war-torn Syria and other victims of the 'War on Terror', which persisted after a dozen years even if its title had been disowned by the administration of Barack Obama, who signally failed to close down the extra-territorial detention and punishment camp in Guantánamo Bay, Cuba.

In the United States a spate of killings of African Americans – some in their place of private worship; others in public by officers of the state – raised acute issues about the very parameters of citizenship that predated the era of Civil Rights and revived views on race associated with the pre-Civil War republic. The impact of killings depicted so vividly by contemporary telephony brought into the twenty-first century visceral sentiments and conceptual constructions associated with an era of human bondage. And that reaction was not just inside the United States; it was amply registered in the world abroad. In Great Britain, a state that had gone to war in 1939 in defence of the territorial integrity of Poland, citizens of the latter country became prime targets of a xenophobic campaign concocted with appreciable appetite and minimal disguise by a section of the political elite supported by a powerful yellow press. One Member of Parliament, Jo Cox, who in the campaign for the referendum on Britain's membership of the European Union had deployed a language of solidarity and unity more redolent of North America than England, was assassinated.

The immediate impression was of a bewildering interaction of 'post-truth politics' and 'collective memory', conducted in a hybrid manner that exploited popular sentiment and sought to strengthen state managerialism. What once, in a firmly Protestant register, used to be denoted a lie had become 'Bullshit', knowingly and purposefully untrue, almost designed to be reinforced by rebuttal and fortified by falsification.[2] In this regard the trajectory of Donald Trump far exceeded that of, say, Barry Goldwater, in a stream of vulgar assertions that did not stop at the seashore, but teased the ruler of Russia and abused the people of Mexico in a manner that requires recourse to the ideas of Nietzsche and Foucault as much as those of Diderot for its proper understanding. Simultaneously, Boris Johnson, the lead vocalist of the 'Brexiteers' in the UK, and a man vainly proud of his classical education, ratcheted up such tendentious associations on matters domestic and international – Turkey's impeding membership of the EU was his preferred artifice – that he seemed set for a positively Ciceronian fate, only to be appointed Foreign Secretary upon a victory that was possibly as consequential as Britain's loss of its thirteen North American colonies in 1783.[3]

These were the ugly politics of the political elite, but they bore down heavily on the everyday lives and world visions of each populace at large. At the time of the US Republican Party Convention majorities in several 'rustbelt' states, formerly proletarian and safely mortgaged members of 'the middle class' embraced an *enragé* denial of the extended inequities foisted upon them by the neoliberal elite against which Trump so angrily and artlessly inveighed. That political class was, in turn, temporarily flummoxed by a proven liar who repeatedly assailed his opponent as 'Lyin' Hillary', so that the Democrats increasingly relied upon ethnic identity to do their ideological heavy-lifting for them, whilst a rump of 'Vichy Republicans' simply disowned the more base invective. With the signal exception of Trump's criticism of North Atlantic Treaty Organization (NATO) partners, they stopped well short of that fabled salt-water bipartisanship on foreign policy. Only some Republican Party foreign policy specialists, such as Robert Kagan, whose work Obama much admired, were brave enough to become public turncoats.[4]

The term 'isolationism' was widely heard anew in 2016, and in a national and international context comprehensively distinct to that of the 1930s. 'Populism' seems too superficial a term to capture such a phenomenon. Yet the 'Washington Consensus', so associated with free market restructuring of Latin American economies in the 1980s and the 'pink tide' anti-American backlash of the early twenty-first century, was also applied in key ways to the US domestic economy. When screened for long-standing national tropes, the Trump election campaign of 2016 is usefully compared with that of 1998 by Hugo Chávez in Venezuela. Their rhetoric, indicting the lords of misrule and heralding the armies of deliverance, offers reward to an international history of ideas.

Alexis de Tocqueville, writing in the 1830s, believed that foreign affairs were an intrinsically aristocratic pursuit: 'Foreign affairs demand scarcely any of those qualities which are peculiar to democracy; they require, on the contrary, the perfect use of those in which it is deficient … A democracy can only with great difficulty regulate the details of an important undertaking, preserve it in a fixed design, and work out its execution in spite of serious obstacles.'[5]

Personal interest and practical experience, however, are rather distinct from intellectual capacity. For Thomas Jefferson, serving as American minister in pre-revolutionary Paris, the matter was less hierarchical: 'State a moral case to a ploughman and a professor. The former will decide it as well, and often better than the latter, because he has not been led astray by artificial rules.'[6]

Perhaps, indeed, the dichotomy between 'intellect' and 'common sense' is too starkly drawn in times of crisis? Certainly, the debate over US foreign policy at the end of the second Obama term was as modulated as could be expected with such low levels of cooperation between the executive and a Republican-controlled congress. The latter made little headway in impugning the nuclear agreement with Iran, despite breaking all protocol in providing Israeli Prime Minister Netanyahu a platform for bitter criticism of US policy. Equally, Obama's restoration of diplomatic relations with the communist regime in Havana excited far less outrage than might be expected after forty years of Cold War quasi-blockade and a vociferous émigré community in the politically vital states of Florida and New Jersey. Congress alone had control of the future of the trade embargo, but even there significant Republican sectors responded to corporate interests that sought access to a market out of which the United States had shut itself, rather like Jefferson and Madison had done with Europe during the Napoleonic conflict.

There was next to no popular concern about Obama's visit to Hiroshima in May 2016, when he repeated his call for the voluntary surrender of nuclear weaponry. As we will see, assessing the balance between continuity and rupture in US foreign affairs is a matter of considerable importance and interpretative controversy, even when periodisations familiar to the popular mind are involved. In 2016 very few recalled that US public opinion in August 1945 had been strongly in favour of yet further bombing. Equally, the nativist instincts reflected and ignited by the Trump campaign had plenty of precedents, not least in the elective ignorance of the 'Know-Nothings' of the 1850s who sought to 'purify' Anglo-American society by halting Irish and, remarkably, German immigration.[7]

For Hofstadter, it was McCarthyism that 'aroused the fear that the critical mind was at ruinous discount in this country'. Writing a decade after McCarthy's fall – tellingly triggered by a call to 'decency' made on television not unlike those made about Trump's invectives against the parents of the late Captain Humayan Khan – Hoftstader came to a plausibly modulated conclusion: 'The greater part of the public, and a great part even of the intelligent and alert public, is simply non-intellectual; it is infused with enough ambivalence about intellect and intellectuals to be swayed now this way and now that on current cultural issues.'[8]

'The intellectual' and intellectuals in public life

All the contributors to this book are intellectuals, but they all also hold academic positions. Academics, of course, don't always fulfil the common desiderata for 'independent' and informed reflection on public life, and, as Jefferson's declaration shows, 'intellectual' serves equally well as adjective and noun. None the less, for the modern age Christopher Hitchens had a point when he adopted the term 'public intellectual' as a 'term that expresses a difference between true intellectuals and the rival callings of "opinion maker" or "pundit", especially as the last two are intimately bound up with the world of television'.[9]

Like many others, Hitchens traces the dismissive or abusive connotations of 'intellectual' back to the Dreyfus affair of the 1890s, even as he noted in 2008 that the species had become such an object of 'celebrity' that rankings were regularly being published.[10] *Foreign Policy* in that same year listed a 'Top 100', provoking Russell Jacoby, arguably the originator of the term 'public intellectual', into a renewal of his view that the traditional role of an independent thinker orientated to the mainstream public had become marginalised by escalating academic specialism and attachment to Marxism, the rise of the internet and the expansion of African American and female intellectuals. In a sign of the waspishness that often obtains in such circles, Jacoby noted that the 'decline of public intellectuals correlates with the rise of Richard Posner'. Posner, a judge on the US Court of Appeals for the Seventh Circuit, had recently published *Public Intellectuals: A Study in Decline*, which did a great deal of counting itself (of citations and website hits) as well devoting much space to the 'Jeremiah School' with an affinity for cultural pessimism (Lasch; Himmelfarb; Putnam; Bork; Kristol).[11]

Here the politics is pretty close to the surface. For Hitchens, the 'decline' in Posner's title owed much to the fact that his choice of top intellectual was Henry Kissinger. Posner himself is not greatly interested in politics, still less foreign policy, but his own least favourite intellectual appears to be Noam Chomsky:

> [T]he most influential figure in modern linguistics and probably in cognitive science as well. In book, pamphlet, lecture and interview, he repeatedly denounces the United States for violent, lawless, repressive, and imperialistic behavior as black as that of Hitler's Germany ... Not that Chomsky's dozens of books and pamphlets contain no useful interesting information and interesting half-truths, as when he calls Theodore Roosevelt a 'racist fanatic and raving jingoist'. But the tone and the one-sidedness of this characterization are all too typical.[12]

Hitchens had an indirect response to this:

> An intellectual need not be one who, in a well-known but essentially meaningless phrase, 'speaks truth to power'. (Chomsky has dryly reminded us that power often knows the truth well enough.) However, the attitude towards authority should probably be sceptical, as should the attitude towards utopia, let alone heaven or hell. Other aims should include the ability to survey the present through the optic of a historian, the past with the perspective of the living, and the culture and language of others with the equipment of an internationalist.[13]

Meeting even these provisional requirements is a tall ask, and it was not one that Hitchens himself always managed. For Tony Judt, a historian at New York University, Hitchens was one of 'Bush's Useful Idiots' (along with Michael Walzer of Princeton; Todd Gitlin of Columbia; Michael Ignatieff of Oxford, Cambridge and Harvard) for supporting the military response to the 11 September 2001 terrorist attacks as 'liberal hawks'. Not unlike Posner, Judt made a backward-looking analogy:

> Like Stalin's western admirers who, in the wake of Khrushchev's revelations, resented the Soviet dictator not so much for his crimes as for discrediting their

Marxism, so intellectual supporters of the Iraq War ... in the North American liberal establishment ... have focused their regrets not on the catastrophic invasion itself (which they all supported) but on its incompetent execution. They are irritated with Bush for giving 'preventive war' a bad name.[14]

Some of the discussion in David Milne's chapter on Paul Wolfowitz suggests that this polemic might usefully be seen in a wider context – one, for instance, in which successful Western military intervention and the notable absence of it (or significant liberal calls for such) during the Rwandan genocide could be cast as a renovated anti-fascism (Hitchens) and the supersession of interests by human rights (Ignatieff).[15]

One prior step in this history – a history that might possess something of a 'tradition' – adduced by Judt was the full-page advertisement in the *New York Times* of 26 October 1988 rebuking President Reagan for treating the term 'liberal' with opprobrium. Signed by sixty-three prominent writers, businessmen and intellectuals (including Daniel Bell, J. K. Galbraith, Felix Rohatyn, Arthur Schlesinger Jr, Irving Howe and Eudora Welty), the petition upheld liberal principles as 'timeless. Extremists of the right and of the left have long attacked liberalism as their greatest enemy. In our own times liberal democracies have been crushed by such extremists.'

Nor, as we have seen, was the stage left to the 'centre'. In 1967, during the darkest moments of the Vietnam War, Irving Kristol and Noam Chomsky pitched openly antagonist claims from right and left as to the role of American intellectuals and foreign policy. For Kristol:

> No modern nation has ever constructed a foreign policy that was acceptable to its intellectuals ... It is among American intellectuals that the isolationist ideal is experiencing its final, convulsive agony ... since there is no way the United States, as the world's mightiest power, can avoid such an imperial role, the opposition of its intellectuals means that this role will be played out in a domestic climate of ideological dissent that will enfeeble the resolution of our statesmen and diminish the credibility of their policies abroad.[16]

Perhaps Kristol had been goaded by a piece published by Chomsky that February in *The New York Review of Books*, where he argued:

> Intellectuals are in a position to expose the lies of governments, to analyse actions according to their causes and motives and often hidden intensions. In the Western world, at least, they have the power that comes from political liberty, from access to information and freedom of expression ... Arthur Schlesinger, according to the *Times*, February 6, 1966, characterized our Vietnamese policies of 1954 as 'part of our general program of international goodwill'. Unless intended as irony, this remark shows either colossal cynicism, or the inability, on a scale that defies measurement, to comprehend elementary phenomena of contemporary history ... The long tradition of naiveté

and self-righteousness that disfigures our intellectual history … must serve as a warning … as to how our protestations of sincerity and benign intent are to be interpreted.[17]

Such exchanges must have exasperated Daniel Bell, a co-signatory of the 1988 petition and author of a 1960 essay 'On the End of Ideology', which, resting on the notion of 'post-industrialism', contended that sensible people should now eschew social dreaming and focus on practical, technical issues. Anticipating Francis Fukuyama's 'End of History' by a couple of decades, Bell's maximalist optimism might usefully be seen as a Cold War endorsement of the core conviction that, in all its timeliness, liberalism was no ideology. However, subsequent developments almost inevitably condemned him to the kind of jeremiads that justified Jacoby and Posner's depiction of intellectual decline. By 1992 Bell was declaiming:

> There is no longer any intellectual center in the United States. And, for that matter, very few intellectuals remain, if by intellectuals one means those socially unattached individuals devoted solely to the search for truth … The United States today is a *bourgeois society but not a bourgeois culture* … The *culture* of the United States today is permissive in its ethos (especially on moral and sexual issues) and modernist in its willingness to accept new and innovative and trendy expressions in the arts and literature. It is, to use the phrase of Lionel Trilling, an 'adversary culture', in opposition to the prevailing societal attitudes.[18]

Bell rejected Kristol's notion of a 'new class', an intellectual stratum of elites from the media, universities and publishing, as being a conceptual muddle rather than a cogent category. However, responsive to the role of agency and the evidence of change, he admitted Kristol's wry definition of a neoconservative as 'a liberal who has been mugged by reality'.[19]

Few of the thinkers mentioned above engaged directly in consultancy over foreign policy, still less serving in official state and government positions to advise and promote ideas. Aside from the obvious case of Kissinger, Schlesinger is the most prominent 'in-and-outer' moving between the academy and government, serving as speechwriter for the Democratic presidential candidate Adlai Stevenson (arguably the most 'intellectual' person to gain that nomination) and then the Kennedy administration, where his role in the Bay of Pigs invasion was understandably criticised by Chomsky. Other names who rose to prominent public positions in foreign policy formulation during the first decades of the Cold War – either going on from university posts or retiring to them – include George Kennan, Paul Nitze, Dean Rusk, McGeorge Bundy and Walt Rostow. Less publicised were members of the RAND Corporation – the think-tank run by the air force – and the

'May Group' at Harvard's Kennedy School of Government – which made a detailed analysis of the Cuban Missile Crisis – studied by Bruce Kuklick.[20]

Perry Anderson has identified a similar set of bodies for the contemporary period: the Council on Foreign Relations; Kennedy School at Harvard; Woodrow Wilson Center, Princeton; Nitze School, Johns Hopkins; Naval War College; Georgetown University; the Brookings and Carnegie Foundations, among many others: 'Think-tanks, of central importance in this world, dispense their fellows from teaching; in exchange they expect a certain public impact – columns, op-eds, talk-shows, best-sellers – from them; not on the population as a whole, but among the small, well-off minority that takes an interest in such matters.'[21]

Moreover, we should recognise that policy as formulated and enunciated in office can be very different to policy as implemented on the ground, especially overseas, and in many more ways than indicated by Chomsky's partisan perspective. Well before the information overload of the internet, primary source material (often with allied 'feedback loops') from the field emanated not only from the Central Intelligence Agency (CIA), State Department and the military but also Peace Corps organisers, missionaries, anthropologists, urban planners and a range of professionals either formally on foreign service, seconded to the federal government or simply open to debriefing on their research. On occasion, particularly in the case of anthropology, this caused controversy at home.[22]

The problem of continuity and rupture

In his assessment of the work of Walter Russell Mead, Anderson identifies a problem that extends well beyond this particular author – the extent to which modern or current US policy might be explained by the past, and how direct or interrupted such a lineage of origin might be. Anderson adeptly synthesises Mead's explanation as to why the US was free of European traditions of geopolitical realism and much more attached to the policy drivers of economic interest and moral calling: 'the policies determining these ends were the product of a unique democratic synthesis: Hamiltonian pursuit of commercial advantage for American enterprise abroad; Wilsonian duty to extend the values of liberty across the world; Jeffersonian concern to preserve the virtue of the republic from foreign temptations; and Jacksonian valour in any challenge to the honour or security of the country.'[23]

The first two elements might be characterised as elite preferences, the third one of intellectual inclination and the final one more related to folk ethos, something close in tone to the populism that dismayed de Tocqueville and the Republican opponents of Donald Trump. More important than this, though, for Perry Anderson is the deceptive smoothness of the single-surname associations: 'Analytically ... it rests on the *non-sequitur* of an equivalence between them, as so many contributors to a common upshot ... the reality is that of the four traditions, only two have had consistent weight since the Spanish American Conflict; the others furnish little more than sporadic supplies of cassandrism and cannon-fodder.'[24]

Although more variegated, Mead's genealogy suffers from a similar flaw as that identified by Ian Tyrrell in the highly influential work of Louis Hartz, 'where the liberal "fragment" derived from Europe's more complex social structure determines the nature of political debate. The fragment becomes frozen and loses its dialectical relationship with other fragments to produce a self-perpetuating "tradition". All major political and ideological developments can be explained in terms of such a national pathology.'[25]

Dorothy Ross advances an alternative explanation for the nature of the American polity that is methodologically richer than Hartz's, because it contains more than one variable and they can be supposed to vary over time:

> [T]he consensual framework of American politics that developed in the late 18th and early 19th centuries formed out of the intersection of Protestant, republican, and liberal ideas around the idea of America. Inscribed in the national ideology were not only liberal market values, but Protestant and republican ambivalence towards capitalist development and historical change. It created not a stable liberal consensus, but a continuing quarrel with history.[26]

A similarly tripartite approach to explaining the arc of US foreign policy over the history of the republic has been proposed by David C. Hendrickson, who deploys the familiar markers of union, nation and empire to symbolise ideas of internationalism, nationalism and imperialism that have interacted throughout the ages, albeit in differing strengths. Hendrickson's method is based on a *pointilliste* narrative, and so is more allusive than rigid. It may still be too determinist for Tyrrell's taste, but it addresses three familiar grand narratives of US foreign policy: a post-Second World War multilateral constitutional system (or union) led for the world by America; the United States as a realist and exceptionalist nation making instrumental alliances for the purposes of security; and the United States as an empire with dependents, protectorates and satrapies, either on account of the need for unbridled capitalist expansion or through a civic culture 'enthralled by the use of force'.[27]

Hendrickson's account ends with the US entry into the Second World War and so is focused on providing a kind of 'pre-history' of more familiar modern and contemporary debates and practices. He sees all of these are being raised in the debates of 1787 and 1788 over the Constitution, and brings something of the sensibility of an 'originalist' to the discussion of US foreign policy. This, though, does not impede him from challenging some favourite received beliefs:

> Far from being indifferent to the security problems that have drawn the anxious attention of internationalists in the Twentieth Century, Americans were obsessed by them from the American Revolution to the Civil War. They did not enjoy the alternative of withdrawing from 'the state system' because they were squarely in the middle of one. This condition helps explain why their 'domestic' discourse was filled throughout with language of a decided internationalist tenor, why there emerged doctrines of the balance of power, of intervention (and non-intervention), of the equality of states, of defense against aggression. That the greatest war in Western Civilization from 1815 to 1914 was fought in North America gives some idea of the conflict that lay embedded within the American union.[28]

In short, at least until 1865, think of the United States itself in international as well as national terms.

Space is not the only variable that deserves reconsideration; time can also usefully be reviewed in terms of direction and inference. When after the Cold War Fukuyama pronounced 'the end of history', he was in one sense simply restating a traditional motif, for, as Ross notes, 'in classical republican discourse, time is the enemy of the life of the republic, the bearer of decay and usurpation'.[29] During the Cold War itself, this negativity was encased in an existential claim of the highest order, as vividly explained by Anders Stephanson:

> Whereas the Soviet Union, representing (it claimed), the penultimate stage of history, was locked in a dialectical struggle for the final liberation of mankind, the United States *is* that very liberation. It is the end; it is already a world empire, it can have no equal, no dialectical Other. What is not like the United States can, in principle, have no proper efficacy. It is either a perversion or, at best, a not yet.[30]

A state of perfection knows no race, but where did it come from? Here there are some variations in the familiar voicings of what we might term the exceptionalist historiography, both 'intellectual' and more popular. According to Ross, after the War of 1812, which put an effective end to open Anglo-American enmity (if not cultural recrimination):

> American writers often linked their national history to the account of Anglo-Saxon liberty developed in England. American self-government was attached to a continuous inheritance that went back to the Teutonic tribes that vanquished Rome. Its institutions were carried by the Saxons to England, preserved in Magna Carta and the Glorious Revolution, and planted in the colonies, where it reached its most perfect form in the American Revolution and Constitution.[31]

These proclaimed ethnic qualities of national descent were certainly present before the Revolution and readily accepted by a white population that was perhaps 80 per cent of British origin. They were still more sharply projected in the nineteenth century, with liturgical Protestantism being overtaken by an evangelical 'Manifest Destiny', which in the 1840s justified westward movement at the expense of peoples to be declared inferior in the voice of science from the 1870s.[32] As Andrew Saxton has argued, racism is, amongst other things, a theory of history.[33]

Yet if the ascription of inferiority continued apace, the claimed virtues of the Anglo-Saxon/Teutonic/Caucasian bloodline had to be mediated in the face of rising immigration. As shown in the case of Andrew Carnegie discussed here by Duncan Bell, such virtues were to be energetically upheld into the twentieth century (and would, of course, reinvigorate trans-Atlantic discourse once the United States entered both World Wars). None the less, even before the Spanish–American War of 1898 the triumphalist fission of vertical descent was being leavened by the virtues of fusion, with the term 'melting pot' placed centre-stage by Israel Zangwill's 1908 play of that name.[34]

These were the identity politics of what we might term the dominant bloc, and they did little or nothing to alter what W. E. B. du Bois termed the international colour line. Indeed, until very recently the academic discipline of international relations displayed a massive deficit with respect to racism, and yet just two years after Zangwill's play opened the *Journal of Race Development* was founded, mutating into the *Journal of International Relations* in the wake of the Second World War. As Robert Vitalis has recently shown, there existed a vibrant school of black analysts of international politics at Howard University in the inter-war years, when their conceptual innovations (such as Raymond Leslie Buell's 'complex interdependence' of 1925) suffered from 'the norm against noticing': 'As far as I have been able to determine … in the 1920s and 1930s no white international relations scholar argued on either principled or pragmatic grounds for the restoration of black citizenship right, the dismantling of Jim Crow in the United States, and self-governance, let alone independence, for the colonies.'[35]

Several decades later, decolonisation had advanced and black African diplomats were being accredited to Washington. The scandals caused by their expulsion from the still segregated diners on Maryland's Route 40 threatened to undermine all pretence at republican universalism, spoiling the Kennedy administration's 'soft power' outreach to the Third World. The essence of the contradiction was neatly captured by Secretary of State Dean Rusk: 'Let me say with a Georgia accent, that we cannot solve this problem if it requires a diplomatic passport to claim the rights of an American citizen.'[36]

Precisely because of the 'norm against noticing', the historical interaction between religious belief, intellectual outlook and international politics was the subject of much greater mainstream academic controversy, not least in the twentieth-century debates over the influential interpretations of Vernon Parrington and Perry Miller.[37] Few would dispute the fact that in the colonial era religious ideas travelled as fast as any other by dint of advanced institutional support, or that key amongst such experiences was 'The Great Awakening' of the 1730s and 1740s and the doctrinal propositions of Jonathan Edwards. An intellectual history of America prior to the mid-nineteenth century must place Puritan theology close to its core. At the same time, any supposed lineage from Edwards through to, say, Billy Graham, has to pass through the era of Transcendentalism and the veritable force-field exercised by Reinhold Niebuhr (a telling influence on Obama), as well as the arrival of the non-Protestant diasporas on the continent.

For Andrew Preston there has been a significant deficit in the understanding of US foreign policy from a religious perspective. He suggests that this might be explained by partisanship and advocacy (even if quite similar foreign policies have been pursued by presidents of distinct denominations); secularisation; and the empirical and methodological challenges presented by these barely cognate fields. The putative separation of politics from religious faith, and the lack of an American war specifically to extend the Christian faith, have also acted as disincentives. 'Why do they hate us?' was not such a frequently posed question before 11 September 2001, and it cannot be addressed without a much greater appreciation of the sacred than US social science has habitually embraced.[38] Even Perry Anderson notes that: 'America would not be America without faith in the supernatural. But for obvious reasons this component of the national ideology is inner-directed, without much appeal abroad, and so now relegated to the lowest rung in the structure of imperial justification.'[39]

Finally, when reviewing these ideational ancestries and any allied path dependencies over 250 years, we do need to be mindful of what J. R. Pole rightly called the 'inelegant' term of 'presentism', which is not just teleology but also condescension.[40] It is worth noting, for instance, that the State Department was nowhere mentioned in the original Constitution, and that when James Madison took its helm in 1801 his staff amounted to no more than one chief clerk, seven clerks and a messenger. Even a quarter of century later – after the 'Monroe Doctrine' had proclaimed Washington's refusal to countenance new European colonies in the Western hemisphere – Henry Clay had less than double Madison's establishment to support correspondence with just fourteen US ministers, two claims agents and 110 honorary consuls overseas. The Department's principal tasks were issuing passports and sea-letters, and compiling lists of passengers entering the country.[41] The population was less than thirteen million, and the electorate in the first popular vote for the presidency (1824) was 356,000 – all white males. The entire armed forces of the republic on its fiftieth anniversary were one-third the size of the Mexican army. Even at the outbreak of the Civil War, the US Army numbered a little over sixteen thousand men, with 183 of its 198 companies stationed on 79 posts on the Indian frontier. It was not until 1912 that all of continental territory west of the Mississippi had achieved statehood.[42] Through to the 1880s the United States enjoyed what C. Vann Woodward called 'free security' courtesy of the Royal Navy, funded by the British taxpayer.[43] Notions of 'full spectrum dominance', so unremarkable in the second half of the twentieth century, would have been utterly incomprehensible in the Age of Reconstruction.

Even closer to the present, the extent and pace of change can be disconcerting. Although the US economy overtook that of the UK in the 1880s, and by 1913 its output exceeded that of the UK, France and Germany combined, the real 'quantum jump' took place during the Second World War.[44] Between 1938 and 1945 gross national product (GNP) doubled, so that at the end of hostilities, when nearly a third of GNP was devoted to defence, the US economy was three times larger than that of the USSR and five times that of the UK, and accounted for half of global industrial output. This economic superiority did not continue to accelerate at the same rate, but post-war institutional 'deepening' certainly did not revert to the status quo ante. Between the presidencies of Truman and Reagan the staff of the White House multiplied tenfold; today the staff of the National Security Council is over two hundred – four times that in 1990. Since 1960 the budget of the CIA has risen tenfold, to over US$44 billion.[45]

In terms of the academic domain in which ideas about America in the world are taught and debated, the pattern of growth has been equally impressive but rather differently paced. In 1890, when the frontier was declared closed and the total population was 63 million, Frederick Jackson Turner obtained one of only 149 PhD degrees awarded by US universities, which issued 15,500 BAs. In 1950, at the end of the first post-war student cycle, 432,000 first degree and 6,600 PhDs were awarded (population 151 million). By 2009 1.6 million students were graduating with a first degree and 67,000 with a PhD out of a population of 307 million. It cannot, of course, be assumed that the quality of ideas relates directly to the number of people receiving them, but the range of spread in both absolute and relative terms is not an insignificant factor.

To the Wisconsin School and beyond

The temptation offered by David Hendrickson to consider the sections of the Antebellum Republic as treating each other as if they were foreign, for our purposes, is best seen as a corrective against easy teleological attribution. None the less, there are some significant precursors to note beyond the putative lines of descent from Hamilton and Jefferson.

Addressing the Phi Beta Kappa Society at Harvard in August 1837, Emerson exhibited impatience with the mental inertia of Jacksonian America, looking forward to an age 'when the sluggard intellect of this continent will look from under its iron lids and fill the postponed expectation of the world with something better than the exertions of mechanical skill'.[46] Yet the following year it was only after much popular agitation that he penned a protest letter – 'hated of me' – to President Van Buren about 'this tragic Cherokee business', describing the prosecution of the Native Americans in Georgia as 'like dead cats around one's neck'.[47] Thoreau was younger and more resolute, refusing to pay taxes that might fund the Mexican War ten years later, and paying with his liberty for a few hours. In his final years Gallatin denounced that same war with resonant authority and to no effect. On the other hand, George Bancroft, fabulously wealthy author of a ten-volume history of the United States, was not only a fervent Jacksonian, which made him something of a pariah in Massachusetts, but also served as Secretary of the Navy and issued the orders for the taking of Veracruz. Bancroft's history never entered the nineteenth century; but if it had done, his depiction of the Revolution may even have been exceeded: 'The heart of Jefferson in writing the declaration ... beat for all humanity ... and ... astonished nations, as they read that all men are created equal.'[48]

So, well before the Civil War something of a pattern of intellectual criticism of and support for government policy existed in both high and low registers. However, it would be hard to disagree with Robert Beisner that Gilded Age 'anti-imperialism' was 'never a movement before 1898'.[49] The expansionism that discomforted Emerson was territorial: the peoples removed from their traditional lands had been in a form of 'domestic dependency' and, however imperfectly respected, treaties had been signed with them. In an argument that Perry Anderson picks up approvingly from Franz Schurmann, there is a qualitative difference between expansionism and imperialism, with the former exciting limited intellectual disapproval and extensive popular support, not just in the latter half of the nineteenth century but also through the first decades of the twentieth century:

> Expansionism was the step-by-step adding on of territory, productive assets, strategic bases and the like, as always practised by older empires, and continued

by America since the war through a spreading network of invasions, client states and overseas garrisons on every continent. By contrast 'imperialism as a vision and doctrine has a total, world-wide quality. It envisages the organisation of large parts of the world from the top down, in contrast to expansionism, which is accretion from the bottom up'.[50]

Following through with this logic, Anderson identifies a 'crystallisation' in the 1940s of an American World Order that had hitherto been developed only within regional enclaves (the Caribbean archipelago) or essayed in unsuccessful fashion on a world scale (by Woodrow Wilson). In this he draws on a second important argument from Schurmann – that such a universalism could only secure both international compliance and domestic endorsement through its modelling on the New Deal of the 1930s: 'What Roosevelt sensed and gave visionary expression to was that the world was ripe for one of the most radical experiments in history: the unification of the entire world under a domination centred in America.'[51]

This view, which explicitly repudiates the notion that US imperialism was 'the natural outgrowth of a capitalist world market system which America helped to revive after 1945', goes against the grain of much critical historiography, especially that emanating from within the United States.[52] It is not that free enterprise was a minor element in the 'wider arc of American power projection', but that it – rather like religion – could not be a central leitmotif, and the underlying reason for this is that the logics of state and capital, which arise from distinct origins, are different. It is one thing to attribute either the general needs or precise turns of foreign policy to some 'capitalist logic', and it quite another to see these, from the early twentieth century onwards, as realised within 'the monochrome ideological universe in which the system is plunged: an all-capitalist order, without a hint of social democratic weakness or independent organisation by labour'.[53] However, an extra element in the US foreign policy lexicon and imagination did emerge in the post-war period – the increasingly vital profile of 'security'. Here Anderson agrees with both Schurmann and John Thompson that security evolved – principally though the continuous exaggeration of threats – into an entire ideology: 'Masking strategies of offence as exigencies of defence, no theme was better calculated to close the potential gap between popular sentiments and elite designs.'[54]

Of course, that is not a congenial appraisal for many liberal analysts, whether this is because it seems to diminish the role of ideas *tout court* or because it shares none of the ideational traffic of US foreign policy as enunciated, practised and often interpreted, or because it does not provide great granularity of explanation between specific decisions and broad objectives.[55] From a more radical perspective, it deviates from what has become known as the 'Wisconsin School', which has more recently been associated with the work of William Appleman Williams from the late 1950s. Further back stands Frederick Jackson Turner, who offered sociological explanations for the distinctiveness of US development and civic culture in rejection of the 'germ thesis' of his PhD supervisor Herbert Baxter Adams which promulgated a genealogical descent from Teutonic civilisation of the type noted by Dorothy Ross. The progressive alternative lineage stems from the 1890s, with the Battles of Wounded Knee and San Juan Hill bracketing that decade as apparent instances of a closing territorial expansionism and an opening saltwater imperialism. The year 1898 – the year of the Spanish–American War – is very extensively taken as a watershed in American foreign policy and a landmark in its role as a Great Power/Empire.

Here, though, historians need to be mindful of the calibrations between events and processes. Turner provided more of an allusive than tightly illustrated bridge in his influential 'The Significance of the Frontier in American History' (1893). That essay attributed US social, developmental and political strength to the experience of its westward expansion, which increasingly severed (white settler) communities from enervating European ideas and institutions:

> According to Turner, the West was a place where easterners and Europeans experienced a return before civilization when the energies of the race were young. Once the descent to the primitive was complete, frontier communities underwent an evolution which recapitulated the development of civilization itself, tracing the path from hunter to trader to farmer to town. In that process of descent and revolution – as the frontier successively emerged and vanished – a special American character was forged, marked by fierce individualism, pragmatism, and egalitarianism.[56]

Initially voiced in rejection of European 'entanglement', this positive isolationism was later converted by Turner into a confident internationalism, even after the failure of Wilson's efforts at Versailles: 'The nation which [Washington] founded has become a great nation – so great that the question turns upon whether its economic and moral force is not strong enough to impress an American system and American ways upon Europe rather than to submit to fear from the influence of Europe upon itself.'[57]

If the frontier experience had progressively freed you from Europe at home, now it has closed, such a history may – or even must – enable you to repeat the experience overseas. Who better to illustrate this essentially romantic thesis than Theodore Roosevelt, whose roughness was Jacksonian, whose corollary was Hamiltonian and whose domestic progressivism promoted a Jeffersonianism for the industrial era? Yet William Jennings Bryan, Teddy Roosevelt's near-contemporary and Democratic opponent, shifted within months of enthusiastically seeking service in the war against Spain in the spring of 1898 to a vociferous critique of imperialism in the summer of 1900. Drawing down not just Jefferson's repudiation of 'conquest' but also the distinctive reaction and treatment of the peoples of Cuba, liberated in a matter of days across the narrow strait from Florida, and those of the Philippines, who resisted swapping one imperial master for another across thousands of miles of ocean, Bryan underscored the difficulties of declaiming grand universal ideals for a complex and variegated world:

> The right of the Cubans to freedom was not based upon their proximity to the United States, nor upon the language which they spoke, nor yet upon the race or races to which they belonged. Congress by a practically unanimous vote declared that the principles enunciated at Philadelphia in 1776 were still alive and applicable to the Cubans. Who will draw a line between the natural rights of the Cubans and the Filipinos?[58]

Robert Dallek makes the key point that popular enthusiasm for the war against Spain in Cuba was couched not just in the jingoism of the yellow press but also in a widespread popular support for a speedy and triumphant national liberation.[59] Two years later, however, sixty thousand troops were required to contain the Filipino revolt, British operations in the Boer War had demonstrated the exceptionally high cost of maintaining contested colonial rule, and Mark Twain had provided an eloquent counterblast to supremacist sentiment, whether derived from the founding scriptures, a Teutonic heritage or the frontier personality: 'Shall we? That is, shall we go on conferring our Civilization upon the peoples that sit in darkness, or shall we give those poor things a rest? Shall we bang right ahead in our old-time, loud, pious way, and commit the new century to the game; or shall we sober up and sit down and think it over first?'[60]

How to uphold such a view three generations later in the unforgiving depths of the Cold War? William Appleman Williams, whose register was more modulated than Twain's, lacked a significant popular resonance for his conviction that, 'In expanding its own economic system throughout much of the world, America had made it very difficult for other nations to retain their economic independence'.[61] In *The Tragedy of American Diplomacy* (1959) Williams identified the origins of this 'Open Door imperialism' in John Hay's 1900 'Open Door Notes' requiring imperial China to guarantee US access to its markets, but his thesis did not rest just on economic factors – still less did it attribute policy solely to material determinants – instead folding this into a *Weltanschauung* (a definition of the world combined with an explanation of how it works). Andrew Bacevich has summarised that as consisting of several elements: a tendency to equate anti-colonialism with opposition to empire as such; an insistence that American values are universal values; a self-serving commitment to the principle of self-determination; a penchant for externalising evil; a reflexive predilection for demonising adversaries; a belief that the American economy cannot function without opportunities for external expansion; a steady if unacknowledged drift towards militarisation; and an unshakeable confidence in American exceptionalism and American beneficence.[62]

Just as Turner before him, Williams's influence did not stop at the covers of his own books; the post-war Wisconsin School retained a significant presence into the post-Cold War era through the work not just of the maverick solder-intellectual Bacevich but also that of long-term academic specialists such as Walter LaFeber, who modulated Williams's claims and enhanced his sourcing while also maintaining his scepticism, especially with regard to what was by the 1990s becoming known as 'liberal interventionism' and increasingly being associated with Woodrow Wilson's Princeton.[63]

Unsurprisingly in the aftermath of McCarthyism and during the years immediately preceding the Vietnam War, Williams's work was treated as emanating from more radical, even Marxist, principles than he actually held. As Paul Buhle puts it, 'Williams's puncturing of the myth of the Open Door as the passage-way to world democracy has never been improved upon – and never been forgiven.'[64] However, his corpus, which includes the equally controversial and unreferenced *Contours of American History* (1961), was, like Turner's, subjected to the severe and often telling academic criticism that truly influential works inevitably attract.[65] For some, his definitions were mechanistic, his view of humanity static and his approach to policy excessively rationalistic.[66] For others, such as Robert Tucker, '[t]he reader is never quite clear – because Williams is never quite clear – whether America's institutions necessitated expansion or whether America has been expansionist out of mistaken conviction that the well-being ... of these institutions required constant expansion.'[67]

Still others, including John Thompson, argued that his perception of continuous 'expansion' was not borne out by reliable economic evidence and was more a 'semantic sleight of hand' conducive to an overly deterministic approach.[68] That, though, might be more palatable if, as some did, one takes Williams's *The Tragedy of American Diplomacy* more as a manifesto or 'passionate essay' than a monograph.[69]

In some ways the enduring radicalism of Noam Chomsky may be seen as a Massachusetts extension of the Wisconsin School – not least in that it is immensely more popular amongst students than academics, but also because he continuously repudiates the 'doctrinal language' of 'economic freedom'. Having served for decades as an industrious paint-stripper of official US rhetoric, Chomsky has been widely ignored within the field of international relations. According to Ronald Osborn, this is because, although he is the consummate 'left realist' with state power at the very heart of his understanding of the world, he rejects mainstream realism's refusal to apply to state behaviour the ethical considerations that obtain for individual human beings.[70]

Moreover, unlike Morgenthau, Carr and Niebuhr, with whom Osborn and Mark Laffey bracket Chomsky, he is essentially uninterested in theorising about international politics. At one level we could explain this by the weight of the tasks of persuading his audience of the demands of moral equivalence:

> No one would be disturbed by an analysis of the political behaviour of the Russians, French or Tanzanians, questioning their motives and interpreting their actions in terms of long-range interests, perhaps well concerned behind official rhetoric ... We are hardly the first power in history to combine material interests, great technological capacity, and an utter disregard for the misery and suffering of the lower orders.[71]

So far, so unremarkable; John Mearsheimer could scarcely dissent. However, Chomsky is not simply outside the guild; he positively spurns its pretensions: '[W]orld affairs are trivial: there's nothing in the social sciences or history or whatever that is beyond the intellectual capacity of an ordinary fifteen year old. You have to do a little work, you have to do some reading, you have to be able to think, but there's nothing deep – if there are any theories around that require some special kind of training to understand, then they've been kept a closely guarded secret.'[72]

In fact, Chomsky could never be part of this academic community, not just because of its incapacity to build on Thucydides or Machiavelli, but because in his understanding the great bulk of the intelligentsia forms a vital component of the prevailing power structure: 'Norms are established by the powerful, in their own interests, and with the acclaim of responsible intellectuals. These may be close to historical universals. I have been looking for exceptions for many years. There are a few, but not many.'[73]

There is, none the less, one area where Chomsky has sought to provide more inflection than allowed for by the portrait of hard power and intellectual collaborators – a model of propaganda. In his work *Manufacturing Consent*, co-authored with Edward Herman, five 'filters' are identified as variables in shaping media output: corporate ownership and common interests; media reliance on advertising; elite sources for stories; assiduous official 'spinning' of controversial news; and – the book appeared in 1988 – the importance of 'anti-communism as a control mechanism'.[74]

If these features appear a good deal less controversial nearly thirty years after they were first published, there is also something rather less fatalistic in Chomsky's appreciation of popular protest against the 'War on Terror', which he appeared to distinguish from that over Vietnam that had so animated his writing in the 1960s:

> In the international arena, the President and a reactionary circle of advisers pressed forward with plans that are novel at least in the brazen arrogance with which they are proclaimed: notably the doctrine of preventive war, which accords them 'the sovereign right to take military action' at will to control the world and destroy any challenge they perceive. The doctrine was enunciated in the National Security Strategy of September 2002, which aroused many shudders around the world and within the foreign policy elite at home. The declaration coincided with a drumbeat of propaganda for a war that would establish the doctrine as a new 'norm of international practice' and even law. The drive for war elicited popular and elite protest with no historical precedent that I can recall. If relentlessly pursued, the policies might constitute a watershed in world affairs. Nonetheless, it is important to recognise that there are precedents, both of doctrine and implementation.[75]

This does not represent a complete volte-face by Noam Chomsky, but it does suggest that there exists rather more space for understanding foreign policy in terms of history and ideas than indicated by some of his previous declarations. The editors and authors of this book, in any event, are convinced of the validity of that endeavour.

The shape of the book

In the next chapter of this volume Jeremi Suri approaches the peculiar US vocation for nation-building on a global scale from the perspective of domestic experience. Suri uses the study of the post-Civil War South by C. Vann Woodward to provide for non-Americans a sense of the ideological interstices and remarkable longevity of this feature of American 'exceptionalism'. Writing outside of the idiom but with empathy for its constituent parts and continuities, Suri describes a deep US civic culture that celebrates self-governance, popular sovereignty and open trade on an uninterrupted continuum from home to the rest of the globe. Denied the normal components of national identity, American elite and popular cultures have, from Washington's Farewell Address of 1796 to Obama's West Point speech of 2014, sustained a form of millennial conviction to universalise domestic beliefs. These ride above the particularities of culture, geography or ethnic encounters that necessarily confront a global power and which perforce cause alterations in tactics, but rarely for any length of time the broader strategic idiom. Equally, Suri argues, the contradiction between national self-interest and the need to construct states and societies along recognisably US lines is repressed through narrow, 'unionist' perspectives. It is almost as if the American public imaginary cannot conceive of an allowable 'other', even

though the efforts at self-fashioning undeniably create a multitude of victims. Suri does not expect this deep-seated cultural reflex, which sees itself
as 'above history', to end in the short or medium term. Rather, he argues,
the contradiction between ideals and interests could be better managed in
terms of both the formulation and implementation of contemporary policy.

In Chapter 2 Duncan Bell considers the extraordinary vision of an 'Angloworld' developed in the last decades of the nineteenth century by the Scots-
American magnate Andrew Carnegie. Bell situates Carnegie's writings of
the 1880s and 1890s in the context of what he describes as 'social dreaming
on both sides of the Atlantic', both in terms of Utopian literature and in
those of more politicised theses current in elite intellectual circles: 'democratic war' (H. G. Wells and William James); 'empire peace' (J. A. Hobson
and D. G. Ritchie); and 'racial peace'. Carnegie's energetic prospectus for a
fusion of the United Kingdom with the United States under a shared republican ethos and institutionality owed much to his conviction that the English-
speaking peoples constituted a single race, which was a critical category in
his political thinking. However, Carnegie never specified in detail the form of
polity he proposed. Moreover, always happy to be identified as a 'dreamer',
he was no ordinary follower of fashion. He viewed migration positively,
opposed the Spanish–American War and wished to see Canada incorporated
into the United States. Equally and perhaps more predictably for an indus-
trialist, he placed great importance on the new technologies that were effectively shrinking the world. One by-product of this was that 'dreamworlds'
no longer enjoyed such spatial imagination but needed a greater 'temporali-
sation' by being placed into the future. Carnegie's debt to Spencer, as well
as the expansive confidence of the last quarter of the American nineteenth
century, meant that he could disparage popular theological justifications of
Empire whilst himself holding a providentialist belief founded on the Anglo-
Saxons as agents of progress and the fount of human perfectibility.

Since the 1990s the German jurist and political theorist Carl Schmitt
(1888–1985) has been read both as a mediated source of intellectual influence on the American political establishment and as a vehicle for radical
criticism of this same establishment. In Chapter 3 Jean-François Drolet
offers an analytical reconstruction of Schmitt's interpretation of American
foreign policy on the backdrop of this apparent paradox in the reception
of his legacy in America and Europe. Drolet's analysis engages with a wide
range of well-known and less-well-known texts, in which Schmitt reflects on
some of the key pronouncements and moments in the history of US foreign
policy. This includes the Monroe Doctrine and its 'Roosevelt Corollary', the
rise and fall of the League of Nations, the Nuremberg Trials, the Truman
Doctrine and America's modernisation initiatives in the Third World. While
working his way through these studies, Drolet draws particular attention

to the philosophical prisms through which Schmitt came to conceptualise the relationship between technology, political violence and 'values' in the formulation of American foreign policy during the second half of the twentieth century. Although this is a somewhat more sinuous path to Schmitt's international political thought, it provides an understanding of his antagonism towards America that goes beyond the atavistic nostalgia of his own politics, and generates apposite insights into the webs of confused categories concerning war, space and historical time hardwired in the normative fabric of the so-called 'American century'.

Vibeke Schou Tjalve and Michael C. Williams reflect in Chapter 4 on one of the most persistent and controversial themes in the intellectual history of US foreign policy: American exceptionalism. But the exceptionalism under investigation here is not the familiar account inspired by a mixture of early modern Puritan theology and nineteenth-century expansionist myths of Manifest Destiny. Rather, their main concern is with a second strain of exceptionalism that took shape during the first half of the twentieth century, in response to a series of political crises triggered by a variety of phenomena such as the rise of mass society, bureaucratisation, atomisation, secularisation, social differentiation and changes in modes of economic production. In this later form, what is exceptional was the ability of American institutions to cope with the political, economic and socio-cultural challenges that led to the backlash against liberal modernisation in European states during the 1930s and 1940s. The main thesis that the authors then proceed to develop is that the origins and evolution of the American realist tradition must be reinterpreted in the context of this second exceptionalist moment in US history. Although realists are best known for their uncompromising criticisms of traditional, self-indulgent myths of American exceptionalism, Tjalve and Williams argue that a closer contextual reading of post-Second World War realist studies will reveal that their authors in fact held far more ambivalent attitudes towards the exceptionality of the American experience. Through an engagement with the paradigmatic writings of Hans Morgenthau, they show that realist warnings against the pitfalls of messianic accounts of American exceptionalism were predicated on a sophisticated understanding of the limitations and exceptional strengths of America's pluralist democracy.

The political theorist Tracy B. Strong revisits intellectual debates over the origins of the Cold War in Chapter 5. He reminds us that interpreting a historical event of such magnitude demands not only that we pay close attention to the multiplicity of causal mechanisms coming into play, but that we also leave plenty of room for accidents and contingencies. Accordingly, Strong sketches out the political and conceptual dimensions of the main domestic and international factors that are deemed to have led to the emergence of the Cold War, providing a fresh account of how the different pieces interact with one another, and emphasising the key moments of indeterminacy and uncertainty that are often ignored in the mainstream literature. Through a close analysis of debates and developments within the American Left during the early to mid-1940s, he shows that the dynamics in American society during this tumultuous period were much more complex than is usually assumed; it was also sufficiently diverse to have made other geopolitical outcomes highly conceivable. While the Cold War may have been structurally over-determined, it was by no means inevitable. Strong maintains that this was also the general perception within the decision-making community on both sides of the political spectrum in the United States until at least 1946 or so. In the end, the policy path chosen by the United States was determined in great part by the ideational frameworks that were on offer at the time to make sense of an otherwise highly confusing set of events. Herein lies the historical importance of 'strategist-intellectuals' like Henry Luce, Henry Wallace, George Kennan and Paul Nitze.

Some twenty years after its initial publication, Samuel Huntington's *Clash of Civilizations* has never gone out of print or lacked a controversial reception. As a core interpretative text of the immediate post-Cold War period, it acquired an almost infamous status amongst liberal circles on account of a perceived melange of cultural essentialism, conservative realist thinking and a confidently negative appraisal of world trends. Huntington's subsequent publication of *Who are We?* in 2004 picked up on the final 'Western' chapters of *Clash of Civilizations* and seemed to confirm a strong nativist and pessimistic substrate to his work. In Chapter 6, James Dunkerley reviews the initial, often critical reception of *Clash of Civilizations* and seeks to explain why the text has continued to enjoy such widespread attention. He agrees with the view that, alongside Francis Fukuyama's *The End of History* and John Mearsheimer's *The Tragedy of Great Power Politics*, it forms part of a distinct 'moment' following the collapse of the USSR and the complex challenges of the United States becoming, at least transiently, a 'unipolar power'. However, he also identifies the continued salience of the text in Huntington's often adept assessment of regional political trends, even when these are entirely divorced from his underlying civilisational thesis. That empirical relevance was fortified by the 11 September attacks which served to reanimate debate over the book's most controversial passages on the Muslim world as well as Huntington's category of 'fault-line states'. At the same time, the author's indefatigable capacity for qualifying or retreating from bold *ex cathedra* pronouncements made him a target for a wide range of academic and policy commentators opposed to both neo-conservatism and mainstream realism, with which Huntington remained associated.

The study of foreign policy and international relations often takes ideas as being rigid and fully formed, and assigned to individuals and categories of school, without paying much attention to the processes by which they change calibre and gain or lose traction. In Chapter 7 David Milne provides a politico-intellectual biography of Paul Wolfowitz from 1969 until he took up service in the administration of George W. Bush, focusing precisely on the vagaries as well as the consistencies in the evolution of his thought. Many of the shifts and deepening convictions were derived, of course, form the experience of observing and implementing US policy in the latter stages of the Vietnam War and thereafter. Wolfowitz's experience as a medium-ranking official during the Carter administration was vital in terms of firming up his 'neo-conservative' credentials. But, as Milne shows, so was his failure to persuade senior Republican figures of the practicality of his 'blue skies' thinking, which almost always stood in contradistinction to the pragmatic preferences of Kissinger-style realism. As with the more cautious elements of the Carter administration, they tended to the view Wolfowitz as creating unnecessary threats; several of his efforts to develop radical policy guidelines were dispatched to the archive. Wolfowitz was indeed inclined to hawkish presumptions and kept that company in and beyond the Washington Beltway. He described himself as a 'Cuban missile crisis kid', but he did not lack intellectual curiosity or a cultural 'hinterland'. His spell as ambassador to Indonesia under Reagan provided regional specialism and existential granularity to the geo-strategic 'logic' of a Cold Warrior. Milne takes us through the phases of Wolfowitz's political evolution up to the moment of 11 September, showing that the 'War on Terror' cannot simply be attributed to the trauma of that event; there were many existing tributaries that played into the Bush doctrine, and these have not always been given the recognition they deserve.

Notes

1 R. Hofstadter, *Anti-intellectualism in American Life* (New York: Vintage Books, 1962), p. vi.
2 H. Frankfurt and M. Bischoff, *On Bullshit* (Princeton: Princeton University Press, 2005).
3 His new post meant that Johnson might well have to treat directly with Hillary Clinton, whom he had recently described as being like a sadistic nurse in a mental asylum. This was neither a lie nor 'Bullshit', but an analogy designed to amuse by virtue of its explicit repudiation of international etiquette. It thereby possessed a strong family resemblance to Trump's rhetoric. For a judicious survey of presidential deception, particularly on health and foreign policy, see R. Dallek, 'Presidential fitness and presidential lies: The historical record and a proposal for reform', *Presidential Studies Quarterly*, 40:1 (2010), pp. 9–22.

4 R. Khalek, 'Robert Kagan and other Neocons Are Backing Hillary Clinton', *The Intercept* (25 July 2016). Kagan, the author of *Dangerous Nation: America and the World 1600–1898* (London: Atlantic Books, 2006), had opposed Trump from the very start of the campaign as being ignorant and possessed of Napoleonic delusions. Kagan is married to Victoria Nuland, assistant secretary of state for European and Eurasian affairs under the Obama administration. The publicity given to her statement, 'Fuck the EU', during a phone conversation with a diplomatic colleague in 2014 over Ukraine occasioned a moment of diplomatic embarrassment, but, since it was a private call leaked by Wikileaks, it does not conform to the public vulgarities of Trump and Johnson.

5 A. de Tocqueville, *Democracy in America I* (New York: Vintage, 1990 [1835]), p. 243.

6 T. Jefferson to Peter Carr, Paris (10 August 1787) in J. Appleby and T. Ball (eds), *Jefferson: Political Writings* (Cambridge: Cambridge University Press, 1999), p. 253. Gramsci made much the same point: 'all men are intellectuals, one could therefore say; but not all men have in society the function of intellectuals.' A. Gramsci, *The Prison Notebooks: Selections* (London: Lawrence and Wishart, 1971), p. 9. For an update on this suggestive theme, see B. Kuklick, 'The plumber and the professor: Or, a primer on how to think about the war', *Diplomatic History*, 26:4 (2002), pp. 559–70.

7 For surveys that place the antebellum experience in a longer political process, see the work of D. King: *Making Americans: Immigration, Race and the Origins of the Diverse Democracy* (Cambridge MA: Harvard University Press, 2000) and *The Liberty of Strangers: Making the American Nation* (Oxford: Oxford University Press, 2005).

8 Hofstadter, *Anti-Intellectualism*, p. 19. Closer to the time, Merle Curti declared: 'McCarthyism, a particular virulent form of anti-intellectualism in the popular sense, has become an international issue.' M. Curti, 'Intellectuals and other people', *The American Historical Review*, 60:2 (1955), pp. 259–82 at p. 275. Susan Jacoby notes that it was at McCarthy's hearings in spring 1954 that the defence attorney Joseph Welch, hitherto calmly emollient in style, broke through the accusatory assumptions that prevailed: 'Until this moment, senator, I think I never gauged your cruelty or your recklessness ... Have you no sense of decency, sir, at long last?' Quoted in S. Jacoby, *The Age of American Unreason* (London: Old Street Publishing, 2008), pp. 13–14. At one level this might be deemed a question of civil manners rather than intellect, but, again, any sharp distinction can be misleading – issues of ethics are decided in many mental registers, as may be seen from the Salem trials of the 1690s through to the debates on drones in the 2010s.

9 C. Hitchens, 'How to be a public intellectual', *Prospect* (24 May 2008).

10 *Ibid.*

11 R. Jacoby, *The Last Intellectuals: American Culture in the Age of Academe* (New York: Basic Books, 1987); R. Jacoby, 'Last thoughts on *The Last Intellectuals*', *Society*, 46:1 (2009), pp. 38–44 at p. 40; R. A. Posner, *Public Intellectuals: A Study of Decline* (Cambridge MA: Harvard University Press,

2001). For a robust critique of, inter alia, Jacoby's notions of 'independence' and 'the public', see B. Robbins, 'Intellectuals in decline?', *Social Text*, 25/26 (1990), pp. 254–9.

12 Posner, *Public Intellectuals*, pp. 85–8.

13 Hitchens, 'How to be a public intellectual'.

14 T. Judt, 'Bush's Useful Idiots', *London Review of Books* (21 September 2006).

15 For a useful discussion, see M. Ryan, 'Bush's useful idiots: 9/11, the liberal hawks and the cooption of the "War on Terror"', *Journal of American Studies*, 45:4 (2011), pp. 667–93.

16 I. Kristol, 'American intellectuals and foreign policy', *Foreign Affairs*, 45:4 (July 1967), pp. 594–609 at pp. 596, 605.

17 N. Chomsky, 'The Responsibility of Intellectuals', *New York Review of Books* (23 February 1967), reprinted in expanded form in N. Chomsky, *American Power and the New Mandarins* (Harmondsworth: Penguin, 1969).

18 D. Bell, 'The cultural wars: American intellectual life, 1965–1992', *The Wilson Quarterly*, 16:3 (1992), pp. 74–107 at pp. 74.

19 *Ibid.*, pp. 79, 83. The notion of intellectuals as a new class is most closely associated with A. Gouldner, *The Future of Intellectuals and the Rise of the New Class* (New York: Seabury Press, 1979).

20 B. Kuklick, *Blind Oracles: Intellectuals and War from Kennan to Kissinger* (Princeton: Princeton University Press, 2006). See also S. M. Lipset, 'American intellectuals: their politics and status', *Daedalus*, 88:3 (1959), pp. 460–86.

21 P. Anderson, 'American foreign policy and its thinkers', *New Left Review*, 83 (2013), p. 113. Amongst the writers considered by Anderson are: Walter Russell Mead; Michael Mandelbaum and John Ikenberry; Charles Kupchan; Robert Kagan; Zbigniew Brzezinski; Robert Art; Thomas Barnett; and Richard Rosecrance.

22 For a general survey, see D. H. Price, *Cold War Anthropology: The CIA, the Pentagon, and the Growth of Dual Use Anthropology* (Durham NC: Duke University Press, 2016). In the single case of Guatemala, of keen interest to Washington throughout most of the post-Second World War era for Cold War and anti-narcotics reasons, we might distinguish the work of two anthropologists: Richard N. Adams, whose independent research in the 1950s received official support and yielded a rich ethnography, and David Stoll, who appears to have had no endorsement for his impugning of the famous account of Nobel laureate Rigoberta Menchú, which produced much scandal and little light. R. N. Adams, *Crucifixion by Power: Essays on Guatemalan National Social Structure, 1944–1966* (Austin: University of Texas Press, 1970); D. Stoll, *I, Rigoberta Menchú and the Story of All Poor Guatemalans* (Boulder: Westview Press, 1999).

23 Anderson, 'American foreign policy and its thinkers', p. 115.

24 *Ibid.* Anderson prefers a Hamilton–Wilson dyad, listing as followers/emulators of the former Clay, Webster, Lodge, Theodore Roosevelt, Hull, Acheson and George W. H. Bush, whilst the Wilsonian line includes at least F. D. Roosevelt, Truman and John Kennedy. For James Livingston, '[t]he quaint but ineradicable idea that everything in American history can be explained by references to

the differences between Jefferson and Hamilton derives from, or is validated by, this assumption [a fundamental division between agriculture and industry], as is the logical correlate that capitalism is foreign to the countryside.' J. Livingston, 'Social theory and historical method in the work of William Appleman Williams', *Diplomatic History*, 25:2 (2001), pp. 275–82 at p. 276.

25 I. Tyrrell, 'American exceptionalism in an age of international history', *The American Historical Review*, 96:4 (1991), pp. 1031–55 at p. 1036. The texts by Hartz that Tyrrell was considering were *The Liberal Tradition in America* (1955) and *The Founding of New Societies* (1964).

26 D. Ross, *The Origins of American Social Science* (Cambridge: Cambridge University Press, 1991), p. xvi.

27 D. C. Hendrickson, *Union, Nation, or Empire: The American Debate over International Relations, 1789–1941* (Lawrence: University of Kansas Press, 2009), pp. 3–4.

28 *Ibid.*, p. xiii.

29 D. Ross, '"Are we a Nation?": The conjuncture of nationhood and race in the United States, 1850–1876', *Modern Intellectual History*, 2:3 (2005), pp. 327–60 at p. 343. This has been an important motif in Dorothy Ross's work: 'Standing at the westernmost culmination of European history, the United States would not follow Europe into a historical future. American progress would be like a quantitative multiplication and elaboration of its founding institutions, not a process of qualitative change. Still pre-historicist, tied to God's eternal plan outside of history, American exceptionalism prevented Americans from developing a fully historicist account of their own history through much of the nineteenth century.' Ross, *The Origins of American Social Science*, p. 26.

30 A. Stephanson, 'Kennan: Anglo-Saxon Superiority? Realism as Desire' in N. Guilhot (ed.), *The Invention of International Relations Theory* (New York: Columbia University Press, 2011), pp. 177–8.

31 Ross, *The Origins of American Social Science*, pp. 24–5.

32 R. Horsman, *Race and Manifest Destiny: The Origins of American Racial Anglo-Saxonism* (Cambridge MA: Harvard University Press, 1981).

33 A. Saxton, *Rise and Fall of the White Republic: Class Politics and Mass Culture in Nineteenth-Century America* (London: Verso, 1990), p. 14. See also the work of E. Kaufmann, *The Rise and Fall of Anglo-America* (Cambridge MA: Harvard University Press, 2004).

34 In the early 1830s, de Tocqueville declared that there was 'hardly an American to be met who does not claim some remote kindred with the first founders of the colonies; and as for the scions of the noble families of England, America seemed to me to be covered with them'. De Tocqueville, *Democracy in America II*, pp. 173–4. Sixty years later John Fleming asked: '[w]hat about the descendants of Frenchmen, of Germans, of Slavs, and of Scandinavians, who do not admit Anglo-Saxon superiority? When, overpowered by his emotions, the average Fourth-of-July orator eulogizes the Anglo-Saxon, he does not pause to consider that the Celts and German among his audience may inquire of one another if there is any room on this continent for them.' J. Fleming, 'Are we

Anglo-Saxons?', *North American Review*, 153 (August 1891), pp. 253–6 at p. 253, quoted in P. Kramer, 'Empires, exceptions, and Anglo-Saxons: Race and rule between the British and United States Empires, 1880–1910', *The Journal of American History*, 88:4 (2002), pp. 1315–53 at p. 1324.

35 R. Vitalis, *White World Order, Black Power Politics: The Birth of American International Relations* (Ithaca: Cornell University Press, 2015), pp. 10–11. See also A. Anievas, N. Manchanda and R. Shilliam (eds), *Race and Racism in International Relations. Confronting the Global Colour Line* (London: Routledge, 2015); J. M. Hobson, *The Eurocentric Conception of World Politics: Western International Theory, 1760–2010* (Cambridge: Cambridge University Press, 2012); R. D. G. Kelley, '"But a local phase of a world problem": Black history's global vision', *The Journal of American History*, 86:3 (1999), pp. 1045–77; J. C. Parker, '"Made-in-America revolutions"? The "Black University" and the American role in the decolonization of the Black Atlantic', *The Journal of American History*, 96 (2009), pp. 727–50.

36 Quoted in P. Kramer, 'Shades of Sovereignty: Racialized Power, the United States and the World' in F. Costigliola and M. J. Hogan (eds), *Explaining the History of American Foreign Relations* (Cambridge: Cambridge University Press, 3rd edn, 2016), p. 245. This excellent essay contains a full bibliography. For a more conceptual survey of the period since 1945, see D. A. Hollinger, 'How wide the circle of the "we"? American intellectuals and the problem of the ethnos since World War II', *The American Historical Review*, 98:2 (1993), pp. 317–37.

37 See, for example, R. Hofstadter, *The Progressive Historians: Turner, Beard, Parrington* (New York: Vintage 1970); D. Hollinger, 'Perry Miller and Philosophical History' in *In the American Province: Studies in the History and Historiography of Ideas* (Baltimore: Johns Hopkins University Press, 1989); and N. Guyatt, '"An Instrument of National Policy": Perry Miller and the Cold War', *Journal of American Studies*, 36:1 (2002), pp. 107–49, which properly places Miller's ideas in an extra-academic context. For a much wider (and longer) vision, see N. Guyatt, *Providence and the Invention of the United States, 1607–1876* (Cambridge: Cambridge University Press, 2007).

38 A. Preston, 'Bridging the gap between the sacred and the secular in the history of American foreign relations', *Diplomatic History*, 30:5 (2006), pp. 783–812. See also, A. Preston, 'The Religious Turn in Diplomatic History' in F. Costigliola and M. J. Hogan (eds), *Explaining the History of American Foreign Relations* (Cambridge: Cambridge University Press, 3rd edn, 2016). Andrew Rotter makes a similar point about the disinclination of diplomatic historians to engage with the work of Edward Said, who was widely disparaged for a combination of selective illustration and expansive generalisation but who was still possessed of a sensibility necessary to a full understanding of the impact of US policies in in the Middle East: A. J. Rotter, 'Saidism without Said: Orientalism and U.S. diplomatic history', *The American Historical Review*, 105:4 (2000), pp. 1205–17.

39 Anderson, 'American foreign policy and its thinkers', p. 33.

40 J. R. Pole, 'The American past: Is it still usable?', *Journal of American Studies*, 1:1 (1967), pp. 63–78 at p. 64.

41 L. D. White, *The Jeffersonians: A Study in Administrative History* (New York: Macmillan, 1951), p. 187.

42 C. Vann Woodward, 'The age of reinterpretation', *The American Historical Review*, 66:1 (1960), pp. 1–19 at p. 4.

43 *Ibid.*, p. 3.

44 J. A. Thompson, *A Sense of Power: The Roots of America's Global Role* (Ithaca: Cornell University Press, 2015), p. 26.

45 Anderson, 'American foreign policy and its thinkers', pp. 22, 107.

46 R. W. Emerson, 'The American Scholar', available at: www.emersoncentral.com/amscholar.htm (accessed 27 August 2016). For an appreciation of the iconoclastic reach of this speech, see K. S. Sacks, *Understanding Emerson: 'The American Scholar' and His Struggle for Self-Reliance* (Princeton: Princeton University Press, 2003). Oliver Wendell Holmes called the speech 'our intellectual Declaration of Independence', and Emerson was not invited back to Harvard for thirty years.

47 Quoted in H. N. Smith, 'Emerson's problem of vocation: A note on "The American Scholar"', *The New England Quarterly*, 12:1 (1939), pp. 52–67 at p. 64. The Cherokee question had, of course, occasioned a critical conflict between President Jackson and Chief Justice Marshall since it provoked issues of constitutionality. Many more native peoples were affected by the subsequent westward movement of European Americans into territory that had not yet acquired statehood, occasioning a syllogistic exchange in the Senate of 1849 between John Calhoun and Daniel Webster:

> **Mr Calhoun:** [T]he single question is, does the constitution extend to the territories, or does it not extend to them? Why, the constitution interprets itself. It pronounces itself to be the supreme law of the land.
> **Mr Webster:** What land?
> **Mr Calhoun:** The land; the territories of the United States are part of the land.

> Quoted in J. Abboushi Dallal, 'American imperialism unmanifest: Emerson's "inquest" and cultural regeneration', *American Literature*, 73:1 (2001), pp. 47–83 at p. 47.

48 G. Bancroft, *History of the American Revolution* (1852), vol. 5, p. 330, quoted in G. A. Billias, *George Bancroft: Master Historian*, (Worcester MA: American Antiquarian Society, 2004), p. 523.

49 R. Beisner, 'Thirty years before Manila: E. L. Godkin, Carl Schurz, and anti-imperialism in the Gilded Age', *The Historian*, 30:4 (1968), pp. 561–77 at p. 564. Looking forward, Beisner found telling differences and similarities between the movements of 1898 and 1968: R. Beisner, '1898 and 1968: The anti-imperialists and the doves', *Political Science Quarterly*, 85:2 (1970), pp. 187–216.

50 F. Schurmann, *The Logic of World Power* (New York: Pantheon, 1974), p. 6, quoted in Anderson, 'American foreign policy and its thinkers', p. 21.

51 Schurmann cited in Anderson, 'American foreign policy and its thinkers', p. 21.

52 *Ibid.* Anderson does not share the strength of Schurmann's depiction of F. D. Roosevelt's commitment to a global New Deal, but does accept it as an important constitutive element. See also R. Dallek, *Franklin D. Roosevelt and*

American Foreign Policy, 1932–1945 (New York: Oxford University Press, 1979). Perry Anderson's discussion of domestic US variables that feed into foreign relations is rather truncated in this essay and best augmented by his 'Homeland', where he identifies four determinants of national politics: the historic regime of accumulation; structural shifts in the sociology of the electorate; cultural mutations of social value systems; and the aims of active minorities in the voter-bases of both national parties. P. Anderson, 'Homeland', *New Left Review*, 81 (2013), pp. 5–32.

53 Anderson, 'Homeland', p. 5.

54 Anderson, 'American foreign policy and its thinkers', p. 30. For John Thompson, 'The dramatic extension of America's overseas involvement and commitments in the past 100 years has reflected a growth of power rather than the decline of security. Yet the full and effective deployment of that power has required from the American people disciplines and sacrifices that they are prepared to sustain only if they are persuaded the nation's safety is directly at stake.' J. A. Thompson, 'The exaggeration of American vulnerability: The anatomy of a tradition', *Diplomatic History*, 16:1 (1992), pp. 23–43 at p. 43. Thompson's view on this has changed very little over the years: 'those who believed that the United States should pursue the wider goal of world order regularly argued that ... core interests were dependent upon such an order. In doing so they provided the evidence drawn upon by those historical accounts that explain the American policy in terms of those interests ... Such explanations are unpersuasive ... the dependence of America's core interests on the achievement of foreign policy objectives has always been very questionable.' Thompson, *A Sense of Power*, p. 250.

55 A variety of responses may be found in the symposium on Anderson's essay on foreign policy that was published in *Diplomatic History*, 39:2 (2015). Some of the language is bracingly energetic, and a little of it unnecessarily personal. However, he would take this as a mark of success. Just like his late comrade Peter Gowan, who long held the US-watching brief for *New Left Review*, Perry Anderson exhibits an aversion to the style of those who work within the expressive comforts of both state and university discourse, and, correspondingly, he shows an admiration for any thinker, whatever their politics, who supersedes them. This can produce an odd mix of enthusiasms, but many commentators would share Gowan's appreciation of John Mearsheimer: 'Not only is his writing refreshingly free from the cant that normally surrounds the world role of the United States, it is extraordinarily accessible: forceful, direct and clear, without a trace of the usual academic jargon'. P. Gowan, 'A calculus of power', *New Left Review*, 16 (2002), pp. 47–67 at p. 47, which reviews Mearsheimer's *The Tragedy of Great Power Politics* (New York: Norton, 2002).

56 W. Cronon, 'Revisiting the vanishing frontier: The legacy of Frederick Jackson Turner', *Western Historical Quarterly*, 18:2 (1987), pp. 157–76 at p. 157.

57 Quoted in L. E. Ambrosius, 'Turner's frontier thesis and the modern American Empire: A review essay', *Civil War History*, 17:4 (1971), pp. 332–9 at p. 337.

58 W. J. Bryan, 'Imperialism' (8 August 1900), available at http://voicesofdemocracy .umd.edu/william-jennings-bryan-imperialism-speech-text/ (accessed 27 August 2016).

59 R. Dallek, 'National mood and American foreign policy: A suggestive essay', *American Quarterly*, 34:4 (1982), pp. 339–61 at p. 346.

60 M. Twain, 'To the person sitting in darkness', *The North American Review*, 531 (1901), pp. 161–76 at p. 164.

61 W. A. Williams, *The Tragedy of American Diplomacy* (New York: Norton, 2009 [1959]), p. 15.

62 A. Bacevich, 'Afterword: Tragedy Revisited' in *ibid.*, pp. 319–20. See also the summary in A. Bacevich, *American Empire: The Realities and Consequences of U.S. Diplomacy* (Cambridge MA: Harvard University Press, 2002), pp. 23–31.

63 See, for example, W. LaFeber, *The New Empire: An Interpretation of American Expansion 1860–1898* (Ithaca: Cornell University Press, 1963). In later years such a perspective became sufficiently mainstream for LaFeber to serve as an author for the *Cambridge History of American Foreign Relations*.

64 P. Buhle, 'Williams for 2000: A Comment', *Diplomatic History*, 25:2 (2001), pp. 301–8 at p. 303. See also L. P. Ribuffo, 'What is still living in the ideas and example of William Appleman Williams? A Comment', *Diplomatic History*, 25:2 (2001), pp. 309–16.

65 According to S. Lynd, '[t]his brilliant, courageous and disappointing book has been too harshly condemned by professional historians, and too readily celebrated by radicals. It is a book both very good and very bad: so good that, with all its faults, it may prove to be the most important work by an American historian since Charles Beard's *Economic Interpretation of the Constitution*, published in 1913; yet so seriously flawed that many initially-sympathetic readers will find it difficult to read through to the end.' S. Lynd, 'Book Review: The Contours of American History', *Science and Society*, 27:2 (1963), pp. 227–31 at p. 227.

66 R. A. Melanson, 'The social and political thought of William Appleman Williams', *The Western Political Quarterly*, 31:3 (1978), pp. 392–409.

67 R. Tucker, *The Radical Left and American Foreign Policy* (Washington DC: SAIS, 1971), p. 70.

68 J. A. Thompson, 'William Appleman Williams and the "American Empire"', *Journal of American Studies*, 7:1 (1973), pp. 91–104 at p. 93. Thompson's later work is less sharply critical, but he still expresses reservations about the Wisconsin style: 'Explaining US policy in terms of … "grand strategy" neglects the extent to which the shape and limits of American actions derive from pressures generated by domestic politics. Never the less, the satisfactions and gratifications of wielding power do seem at times to have given an expansionist thrust to US policy, independent of any instrumental purpose of agenda. "Empire" is an inappropriate description of something as variable in its potency and as imprecisely defined geographically as America's influence in world politics, but the role the United States has played has given rise of an "imperial" mentality'. Thompson, *A Sense of Power*, p. 282.

69 B. Perkins, 'The tragedy of American diplomacy: twenty-five years after', *Reviews in American History*, 12:1 (1984), pp. 1–18 at p. 3.

70 R. Osborn, 'Noam Chomsky and the realist tradition', *Review of International Studies*, 35:2 (2009), pp. 351–70 at p. 359. See also, M. Laffey, 'Discerning the patterns of world order: Noam Chomsky and international theory after the Cold War', *Review of International Studies*, 29:4 (2003), pp. 587–604; E. Herring and P. Robinson, 'Too polemical or too critical? Chomsky on the study of news media and US foreign policy', *Review of International Studies*, 29:4 (2003), pp. 553–68. All these studies note the marginalisation of Chomsky's work within the academic sub-field.

71 N. Chomsky, *American Power and the New Mandarins*, quoted in Osborn, 'Noam Chomsky and the realist tradition', pp. 357–8.

72 Cited in P. Mitchell and J. Schoeffel (eds), *Understanding Power: The Indispensable Chomsky* (New York: The New Press, 2002), p. 137.

73 N. Chomsky, 'Simple truths, hard problems: some thoughts on terror, justice, and self-defence', *Philosophy*, 80:1 (2005), pp. 5–28 at p. 5, quoted in Osborn, 'Noam Chomsky and the realist tradition', p. 358.

74 Herring and Robinson, 'Too polemical or too critical?', pp. 555–6. See also, K. Lang and G. E. Lang, 'Noam Chomsky and the manufacture of consent for American foreign policy', *Political Communication*, 21 (2004), pp. 93–101.

75 N. Chomsky, 'Moral truisms, empirical evidence, and foreign policy', *Review of International Studies*, 29:4 (2003), pp. 605–20 at p. 607.

1 *Jeremi Suri*

The strange career of nation-building as a concept in US foreign policy

The people of the South should be the last Americans to expect indefinite continuity of their institutions and social arrangements. Other Americans have less reason to be prepared for sudden change and lost causes. Apart from Southerners, Americans have enjoyed a historical continuity that is unique among modern peoples. The stream of national history, flowing down from seventeenth-century sources, reaches a fairly level plain in the eighteenth century. There it gathered mightily in volume and span from its tributaries, but it continued to flow like the Mississippi over an even bed between relatively level banks.

Southern history, on the other hand, took a different turn in the nineteenth century. At intervals the even bed gave way under the stream, which sometimes plunged over falls or swirled through rapids. These breaks in the course of Southern history go by the names of slavery and secession, independence and defeat, emancipation and reconstruction, redemption and reunion. Some are more precipitous and dramatic than others. Some result in sheer drops and falls, others in narrows and rapids. The distance between them, and thus the extent of smooth sailing and stability, varies a great deal.[1]

These two opening paragraphs from C. Vann Woodward's monumental 1955 book the *Strange Career of Jim Crow* capture the simultaneous invisibility and presence of race in American history over the course of three centuries. On the one hand, the history of the United States is a continuing story of liberty, capitalism and democracy. On the other hand, the hatred and violence of racial prejudice disrupt this promising story and expose its many contradictions, limitations and inhuman costs. One can think of Barack Obama's election to the US presidency as a continuation of this pattern: a promising democratic narrative accompanied by degrading hatred and violence. For Woodward, the American South was (and it remains) the region of the country where the clash of duelling historical perspectives is most evident. In these terms, it is the region with the strangest career.[2]

Similar things can be said for the long history of American foreign policy, especially as it relates to the Global South – what geographers called the Third World a generation ago. From the American War for Independence in the late eighteenth century through to the 'War on Terror' more than two centuries later, ideas of self-governance, popular sovereignty and open trade have driven American foreign policy. These ideas underpin foundational policy statements from Washington's Farewell Address in 1796, to Woodrow Wilson's Fourteen Points in 1918, to George W. Bush's Second Inaugural Address of 2005. Each defined American principles and power as alternatives to tyranny and empire. Each anticipated a progressive world where diverse societies would come to look, at least in their political and economic organisation, more like the United States.[3]

When pressed by foreign challengers and domestic critics, the only alternative to some form of nation-building that American leaders could imagine was disaster for the United States. For Americans, a world of competing systems has always seemed perilous. Balances of power and international structures for cooperation have always appeared unreliable. That was the interpretation of the First World War shared by Woodrow Wilson and Franklin Roosevelt – the perception that continual great power competition breeds war. Wilson and Roosevelt sought to tame the wilds of the international system by making it operate in ways more like the American system, with the United States at the centre, of course. Wilson and Roosevelt sought to avoid future wars by making societies – friend and foe alike – follow basic American principles for democracy and free market exchange.[4]

As Woodward explains, the ubiquitous disappointments and deviations from principle have not diminished American resolve. Even as he withdrew US forces from two unsuccessful wars in Iraq and Afghanistan, President Barack Obama affirmed American nation-building hopes. Although he rejected unilateral American military occupations of foreign societies, President Obama remained committed to encouraging and, when necessary, forcing reforms in governments that depart from 'civil' assumptions about self-government, openness and security. This was especially the case when Americans confronted a new challenge to their vision of liberal democracy and regional stability from the Islamic State in Iraq and Syria (ISIS). The brutality of ISIS symbolised a deeper evil: extreme anti-modernism and anti-secularism fused with anti-Americanism.

In the seminal foreign policy speech of his second term, delivered at the US Military Academy on 28 May 2014, President Obama rejected 'realist' suggestions that American foreign policy should focus on core material interests and abandon its broader, more problematic ideological agenda. 'I believe', the President explained, 'that a world of greater freedom and tolerance is not only a moral imperative, it also helps to keep us safe.' President

Obama echoed his predecessors in affirming an 'indispensable' world leadership role for the United States:

> America's support for democracy and human rights goes beyond idealism – it is a matter of national security. Democracies are our closest friends and are far less likely to go to war. Economies based on free and open markets perform better and become markets for our goods. Respect for human rights is an antidote to instability and the grievances that fuel violence and terror.[5]

What a strange career for American foreign policy ideals! How can they remain so strong, even among those who see their failures in places like Iraq and Afghanistan? The criticisms of President Obama circulate primarily around the application of these ideals, not their articulation or importance.[6] Like the views of race analysed by C. Vann Woodward, the assumptions about purpose and principle in American foreign policy are sufficiently protean to bend and adjust in different times, but endure in their core influence on decision-makers. They are the basic parameters for the American global imagination. They are the bedrocks on which Americans build toward the world they expect to resemble their own.

Throughout their history and into the present, Americans have shown a remarkable (perhaps stubborn) capacity to support the frequently contradictory urges toward national self-interest and democratic transformation at the same time. Both sentiments are sincerely believed. For most leaders and citizens they are two sides of the same coin. When they obviously contradict, as in the many dictatorial regimes the United States has defended, then Americans believe the trade-off is temporary. When popular groups assert control over formerly repressive regimes, including repressive regimes the United States has supported, Americans tend to side with the revolutionaries. We saw this most recently in the 'Arab Spring' revolts of 2010–11.[7]

Contradictions between material self-interests and ideological preferences do not detract from the importance of both phenomena. It is their co-dependence as true belief, not hypocrisy, that defines the repeated idealism of American power in action. Just as nineteenth-century slave-holders seriously believed in freedom, twenty-first-century advocates of American primacy embrace democratic ideals. Contradictions reinforce faith, and they encourage an aspiration to synthesis between ideals and interests in a predicted future.

The historical teleology of American nation-building

The strange career of American international ideas includes countless debates about policy, political party and ideology, but it replicates similar 'end of history' expectations. One can read claims about an end to 'normal' history in the words of Washington, Wilson, Bush, Obama and most other American leaders. They acknowledge the messy and complex elements of past international behaviour, but they assert that the United States can transcend, improve, simplify and ultimately redeem an unsatisfactory inheritance. This is the essence of American exceptionalism – the claim to stand above history. The popularity of Francis Fukuyama's 'end of history' essay in the United States during the late twentieth century captured this posthistorical element of the American foreign policy faith.[8]

The post-historical presumption is what has led many observers to emphasise the millennial streak in American thinking. The United States has fought its wars to end all wars. It has invested in foreign societies to raise them to what Americans perceive as a mature level of development. Washington has advocated for democratic and capitalist governance as the only viable system for peace and prosperity. The keywords of 'democratisation', 'civilisation' and 'development' have recurred throughout the history of American foreign policy. They have gone together as a triad for the American vision of well-maintained nation-states in a world imperilled by disorder (anarchy) or tyranny (empire). The keywords served as building blocks and touchstones for an American-led alternative to inherited international history.[9]

American foreign policy thinking has been post-historical and decontextualised. The particularities of a specific culture, geography or ethnic mix matter only in tactics, and not as strategic goals for US leaders imagining global trends toward common nation-building. The universalism of the American project is striking in its asserted 'opportunity for all', and also in its homogeneity of expectations for the behaviour and outlook of non-American citizens. American foreign policy, in this sense, replays the Republican universalism about free institutions and labour that Northerners brought to the post-Civil War South, according to C. Vann Woodward. In both contexts – at home and abroad – American universalism has always been remarkably limited in its range of accepted opinion. It has been idealistic and inclusive, but also self-interested and incapable of addressing local diversity. Making freedom real for challenging and unique circumstances has been very difficult for Americans thinking in universal terms. Americans embrace diversity, but they seek ultimate universality. The frame for policy debate has therefore been quite narrow. That has not changed in the twenty-first century.[10]

The mechanisms producing (and enforcing) this historical teleology have differed greatly from one era to another, but a common nation-building vision has exerted strong and consistent influence on each generation of US policymakers. American leaders have imagined a legible world of nation-states like their own, emerging from empire, anarchy or other conditions in-between. Scholar David Hendrickson calls this the position of 'union', meaning a belief in the political legitimacy of government institutions that represent an identifiable nation of people in a distinct territorial setting.[11] Political scientist Daniel Deudney looks back to a longer tradition of 'republican' security theory in the classical world that, filtered through the American founders, invests authority in governing institutions that ensure order against violence (external and internal) and protect basic citizen interests.[12]

Drawing on Hendrickson, Deudney and, and others, I have argued that the experience of 'union' and 'republic' in early American history became codified in a default American repertoire for nurturing familiar-looking nation-states in foreign spaces, especially during moments of threat and uncertainty. From the American Civil War through to interventions in the Philippines, Germany, Vietnam and Afghanistan, one can see a pattern of American efforts to create national identities and modern representative states that had previously experienced deeply contested and divergent histories. American actions have almost always included military force, but they have extended into economic aid, legal advice and cultural influence as well. These nation-building efforts have produced a very mixed record, including startling successes in Western Europe and Japan after 1945, abject failures in places like Vietnam, and many results in-between.[13]

Although some American leaders (including presidents Herbert Hoover and George W. Bush) have sought to depart from this inherited nation-building programme, they have found themselves returning to this same vision when they have most needed a policy response for rising threats. Nation-building is so deeply rooted in the American psyche and political rhetoric that it re-emerges, like a comfortable and familiar song, during moments of uncertainty and confusion. Nation-building is indeed part of the national anthem: the self-proclaimed 'land of the free and the home of the brave' forged in a war against empire.[14]

Based on their own experiences at home, Americans have trouble imagining a just and stable international political order that looks like anything but their own system of governance and representation. Despite the popularity of cultural relativism and multicultural thinking, the dominant model for understanding the 'other' remains American-centred in the United States. This applies to academia as much as politics and economy. Dorothy Ross has shown how the development of the social sciences, key contributors to policy and higher education in the twentieth-century United States, drew explicitly on presumptions of American civic nationalism, democratic governance and capitalist acquisition as norms for social development.[15] Peter Novick and David Brown have extended this analysis into the development of history and other more humanistic fields of inquiry, where presentist familiarities consistently trumped 'objective' examinations of other times and places.[16]

When Americans compare themselves to others, they almost inevitably see themselves in others, rather than the other way around. This a paradox for a country composed of so many recent immigrant groups, but it shows the power of the nation's constructed civic identity. Americans cannot define themselves by blood, by language, by education, or even by material circumstances. The ethnic diversity and economic inequality of the country's population make these categories too limiting. Instead, Americans define themselves by their reverence for a set of political economic institutions and practices that compose the United States as a system of governance. Most citizens see flaws in these institutions and practices, but they hold tight to them as the sources for American greatness. That is the paradox of the Tea Party – anti-government, but triumphal about the American system. Free elections and free markets, for all their distortions, create an orderly American self-image. They are the starting points for all serious thinking about change at home and abroad.[17]

Almost by definition, then, Americans identify their political-economic history as *the* political-economic future for the world. This is a matter of faith – a national creed as deep as constitutional democracy in the American language and imagining of politics. It has a bible (the Constitution), a set of prophets (the Founders) and a high priesthood (Supreme Court justices and various legal and policy experts). Americans are pragmatic profit-seekers, but they are, more fundamentally, faithful believers in a Second Coming of their own Founding Moment around the world. They re-enact this faith with every domestic election and every foreign intervention – moments when the words of the Founders and their assumptions about nation-building are newly espoused, even in the most inopportune circumstances.[18]

The American promotion of a particular nation-building vision, at home and abroad, connects different periods and people in American history. The national creed is deeply and widely held, often advanced by traditional outsiders – including Henry Kissinger and Barack Obama – whose own place in American society is contested. It gives them belonging. It also excludes others – and that is C. Vann Woodward's point about the 'strange career'. The ideals of democracy and nation-building that define an alternative American political agenda for social improvement have repeatedly justified the use of force and the deprivation of local rights. This phenomenon, Woodward argues, is not hypocrisy but an integral element of American politics. The self-justifying pursuit of better politics, at home and abroad, gives licence for the use of various 'extraordinary measures' to keep dangerous populations in check, to allocate precious resources for productive purposes and to guide inexperienced people in the correct behaviour. Nation-building implies destroying whatever came before. Nation-building means forcing people to be free, on American terms.[19]

The victims of nation-building

C. Vann Woodward's *Strange Career* made the case that the experiences of African Americans in the South were not an aberration from American political development, but instead an integral part of it. The enforcement of constitutional democracy and free market capitalism after 1865 contributed to the separate but unequal treatment of former slaves. 'Free Soil, Free Labor, Free Men' did little for those most heavily constrained in the exercise of their newfound freedom. A century later, the Civil Rights Movement used claims to democracy and economic opportunity to challenge segregation, but the movement, by necessity, reaffirmed the basic institutions of governance in the region. African Americans gained greater access to American wealth and governance than ever before, but equality across racial and other groups remained unfulfilled. The nature of nation-building in the South privileged property, law, economic opportunity and political sovereignty over other values, including equal treatment. The nature of nation-building in the South created more expansive governance as it reaffirmed many old exclusions based on race, wealth, gender, education and health. Woodward acknowledged this in later editions of his great work.[20]

The same pattern fits American nation-building in the greater Global South, especially since 1945. The United States has intervened repeatedly in countries as diverse as Haiti, Nicaragua, Cuba, Chile, Indonesia, the Philippines, Egypt, Iran, Iraq, Afghanistan and Syria to overthrow regimes that appeared threatening to American definitions of democracy and capitalism. The perceived threats have come from anti-democratic ideologies, including communism, Islamism and, more frequently, militant nationalism. The perceived threats have also reflected economic preferences that violated free market logics, including import-substitution, state ownership of capital and nationalisation of industry. In all of these cases, and in many others, American economic interests in resource and market access have aligned quite well with assumptions about nation-building. Societies that violate American images of good governance have also challenged American economic interests. That insight provided the foundation for William Appleman Williams's classic argument that the 'open door' – trade and governance on American terms – has driven American foreign policy since the growth of US power in the late nineteenth century.[21]

Historians have examined the many local costs of American interventions in the Global South, as well as the long-term damage to the United States. American leaders have been responsible for hundreds of thousands of deaths. They have disrupted countless local cultures and damaged millions of acres of land. The most modern technology has often produced the least liveable consequences.[22] The abject poverty of a country like Haiti is a testament to the failure of repeated American nation-building efforts, especially on an island so close to the United States.[23]

A high proportion of the victims of American nation-building activities have included men and women of non-white races. That is not a coincidence. Although race has not always driven American decision-making, American citizens have been more willing to accept the suffering of people who look different from themselves, or at least the white-skinned American image of themselves. In their efforts to build democratic and capitalist nations that will secure the American imagining of a peaceful world, American citizens have found it tolerable to discount the suffering of non-white peoples in pursuit of an allegedly higher purpose. When the victims are white – especially in Europe and North America – it has been harder for Americans to discount the suffering. During the 1970s the simultaneous American outpouring of sympathy for East European dissidents and the relative silence of US leaders about apartheid in South Africa captured this prejudice.[24]

The relationship between race and nation-building abroad echoes the relationship at home. In the post-Civil War era, federal and state officials could easily justify rebuilding the damaged Southern parts of the United States on the backs of suffering African Americans – even though the war was fought in large part to free them from slavery. The new investments in industrial farms and factories replaced the plantation economy with modern sources of wealth-creation that required a continuing supply of low-wage labour, often provided by former slaves and their descendants. Federal and local law enforcement also developed new techniques to maintain order through controlled violence that made the South an orderly post-war region, with heavy physical costs for African Americans and other minorities who suffered repeated lynchings and, by the early twenty-first century, one of the highest incarceration rates in the entire world.[25]

Americans turned the backward Confederacy into a modern and prosperous Southern region. That was a great success of nation-building, unparalleled in most other societies after a bloody civil war. Nation-building in the South, however, exploited many non-white citizens as mistreated labour. They were the chief victims of post-Civil War nation-building and their victimhood was distressingly tolerable for most mainstream Americans, at least until a century later. That was a key point of C. Vann Woodward's *Strange Career*. Jim Crow racism made the New South possible, just as international racism made new nations conceivable for American foreign policy.[26]

American state-building carried the same racial baggage abroad as it did at home. It meant democracy and wealth-creation for Americans and their local allies. It meant repression and impoverishment for those who lost access to political power and economic resources as a result of American interventions. These contradictory responses explain how American policies can be judged so differently by diverse groups at the same time. The contradictory perspectives also explain why it is so difficult for Americans to understand the negative responses to their nation-building efforts, especially from citizens with different racial backgrounds.

American nation-building grows out of deeply held domestic beliefs about democracy and capitalism. These beliefs are based on both ideals and interests, and they are firmly rooted in the American historical experience. In their application, at home and abroad, nation-building efforts have empowered some groups and victimised others. American self-righteousness encourages a denial of the costs, the damage and the victims. The evidence of victimisation motivates many observers to question whether the ideals behind American nation-building are serious in the first place. Freedom and liberation for one set of actors connotes repression and imprisonment for another set.

Conclusion: the strange career of nation-building and current policy-making

Both perspectives are, of course, based in fact. American nation-building has spread self-governance and limited it at the same time. It has encouraged wealth-creation and contributed to continued impoverishment. It has ensured peace and instigated war. History is not about simple verdicts, despite the frequent tendency of some historians to offer glib judgements. The record of American nation-building spans more than three centuries and a vast global geography. The impulses behind American efforts and their larger aims have remained consistent, but the consequences are widely diverse. They defy simple categorisation.

In writing the *Strange Career of Jim Crow*, C. Vann Woodward wanted to shake his self-satisfied readers out of the simple categories they used for understanding their own society. He embraced the nobility of the American ambition to spread democracy, order, peace and wealth. He dissected the severe limitations of American racism, ethnocentrism and militarism. Most of all, Woodward counselled for a careful effort to match ideals with circumstances, to make the power of American society serve the hopes of its citizens – all its citizens. This did not mean abandoning the vision of a world with well-functioning governing institutions, but instead renewing activity to build institutions that really served that purpose.

The Civil Rights Movement followed that path in the decade-and-a-half after Woodward published his important book. American foreign policy did not do the same in Vietnam. The overwhelming militarisation of American international activities, the ideological rigidity of American foreign perceptions and the political urge to find quick solutions to international problems have constrained the careful matching of ideals with circumstances, as well as means and ends, that Woodward recommended.[27]

The fundamental problem for American foreign policy is not the nation-building vision so deeply held in the popular conscience. For better and for worse, that is not going to change anytime soon. It is too central to American identity. The contemporary challenge for policy-makers is to apply that intellectual architecture strategically to the problems of the day.

Instead of reacting to threats by launching its power against adversaries and speaking superficially about democratisation, American leaders must have the self-understanding to choose their battles carefully. Where, when and how can the United States encourage productive nation-building? Where, when and how should it refrain and wait? These are the core questions that must underpin a successful policy-making process. These are the core questions that will turn the intellectual assumptions held by Americans into a prudent platform for nurturing a truly better world, at least from the American point of view. The contradictions between ideals and interests will not disappear, but they can be managed to better effect in the United States and abroad.

Notes

1 C. Vann Woodward, *The Strange Career of Jim Crow* (New York: Oxford University Press, 1955), pp. 3–4.
2 See M. D. Lassiter and J. Crespino, *The Myth of Southern Exceptionalism* (New York: Oxford University Press, 2010); J. C. Cobb, *Away Down South: A History of Southern Identity* (New York: Oxford University Press, 2005). Recent scholarship on American political history has extended this examination of the 'strange career' to include the sunbelt southwest. See D. Dochuk, *From Bible Belt to Sunbelt: Plain-Folk Religion, Grassroots Politics, and the Rise of Evangelical Conservatism* (New York: W. W. Norton, 2011); B. Moreton, *To Serve God and Wal-Mart: The Making of Christian Free Enterprise* (Cambridge MA: Harvard University Press, 2009).
3 See F. Gilbert, *To the Farewell Address: Ideas of Early American Foreign Policy* (Princeton: Princeton University Press, 1961); M. H. Hunt, *Ideology and U.S. Foreign Policy* (New Haven: Yale University Press, 1987); W. McDougall, *Promised Land, Crusader State: The American Encounter with the World since 1776* (New York: Houghton Mifflin, 1997); T. J. Knock, *To End All Wars: Woodrow Wilson and the Quest for a New World Order* (Princeton: Princeton University Press, 1992); P. Baker, *Days of Fire: Bush and Cheney in the White House* (New York: Doubleday, 2013).
4 On these points, see J. M. Cooper, Jr., *Woodrow Wilson: A Biography* (New York: Alfred Knopf, 2009); R. Dallek, *Franklin D. Roosevelt and American Foreign Policy, 1932–45* (New York: Oxford University Press, 1979).

5 Remarks by President Barack Obama at the United States Military Academy Commencement Ceremony (28 May 2014), available at: www.whitehouse.gov/the-press-office/2014/05/28/remarks-president-west-point-academy-commencement-ceremony (accessed 7 July 2016).

6 On this point, see Robert Kagan's prominent and widely cited critique of President Obama's foreign policy: 'Superpowers don't get to retire: what our tired country still owes the world', *New Republic* (26 May 2014), available at: www.newrepublic.com/article/117859/allure-normalcy-what-america-still-owes-world (accessed 30 May 2014).

7 See M. Lynch, *The Arab Uprising: The Unfinished Revolutions of the New Middle East* (New York: Public Affairs, 2013).

8 See F. Fukuyama, 'The End of History?', *National Interest*, 16 (Summer 1989), pp. 3–18; F. Fukuyama, *The End of the History and the Last Man* (New York: Free Press, 1992). Henry Kissinger has been one of the most consistent critics of the ahistorical assumptions behind American foreign policy. As a policy-maker he, ironically, replayed many of these assumptions. See J. Suri, *Henry Kissinger and the American Century* (Cambridge MA: Belknap Press of Harvard University Press, 2007), pp. 138–96.

9 On these points, see F. Ninkovich, *Modernity and Power: A History of the Domino Theory in the Twentieth Century* (Chicago: University of Chicago Press, 1994); M. E. Latham, *The Right Kind of Revolution: Modernization, Development, and U.S. Foreign Policy from the Cold War to the Present* (Ithaca: Cornell University Press, 2011); N. Gilman, *Mandarins of the Future: Modernization Theory in Cold War America* (Baltimore: Johns Hopkins University Press, 2007); D. Ekbladh, *The Great American Mission: Modernization and the Construction of an American World Order* (Princeton: Princeton University Press, 2010).

10 This is an argument articulated most clearly in Louis Hartz's famous book *The Liberal Tradition in America* (Orlando: Harcourt, Brace, 1955). See also R. Hofstadter, *The American Political Tradition: And the Men Who Made It* (New York: Alfred Knopf, 1948). For a more recent analysis, see R. Haberski, Jr., *God and War: American Civil Religion since 1945* (New Brunswick: Rutgers University Press, 2012).

11 See D. C. Hendrickson, *Union, Nation, or Empire: The American Debate over International Relations, 1789–1941* (Lawrence: University of Kansas Press, 2009).

12 See D. H. Deudney, *Bounding Power: Republican Security Theory from the Polis to the Global Village* (Princeton: Princeton University Press, 2007).

13 See J. Suri, *Liberty's Surest Guardian: American Nation-Building from the Founders to Obama* (New York: Free Press, 2011).

14 Francis Scott Key wrote the 'Star-Spangled Banner' in September 1814, amidst the British shelling of Fort McHenry in the Chesapeake Bay. It became the official US national anthem, by congressional resolution and presidential signature, in 1931.

15 D. Ross, *The Origins of American Social Science* (New York: Cambridge University Press, 1991).

16 See P. Novick, *That Noble Dream: The 'Objectivity Question' and the American Historical Profession* (New York: Cambridge University Press, 1988); David S. Brown, *Beyond the Frontier: The Midwestern Voice in American Historical Writing* (Chicago: University of Chicago Press, 2009).

17 On the historical and intellectual roots of the contemporary Tea Party in the United States, see J. Lepore, *The Whites of Their Eyes: The Tea Party's Revolution and the Battle Over American History* (Princeton: Princeton University Press, 2010); G. Packer, *The Unwinding: An Inner History of the New America* (New York: Farrar, Straus, and Giroux, 2013).

18 See Suri, *Liberty's Surest Guardian*.

19 For discussions of Kissinger and Obama in this context, see Suri, *Henry Kissinger and the American Century*; D. Remnick, *The Bridge: The Life and Rise of Barack Obama* (New York: Random House, 2010); J. T. Kloppenberg, *Reading Obama: Dreams, Hope, and the American Political Tradition* (Princeton: Princeton University Press, 2011).

20 See the chapters Woodward added and revised on 'The Career Becomes Stranger' and 'Afterword'. Oxford University Press published the final edition of *The Strange Career of Jim Crow* in 2001, two years after Woodward's death. For the classic account of Republican Party ideology – and its limitations – in the Civil War era, see E. Foner, *Free Soil, Free Labor, Free Men: The Ideology of the Republican Party Before the Civil War* (New York: Oxford University Press, 1970).

21 See the classic statement in W. A. Williams, *The Tragedy of American Diplomacy* (New York: W. W. Norton, 1959). See his fuller statement in W. A. Williams, *The Contours of American History* (New York: W. W. Norton, 1988).

22 Among the many important recent books on this topic, see O. A. Westad, *The Global Cold War: Third World Interventions and the Making of Our Times* (New York: Cambridge University Press, 2005); G. Grandin, *Empire's Workshop: Latin America, the United States, and the Rise of the New Imperialism* (New York: Henry Holt, 2006); A. W. McCoy and F. A. Scarano (eds), *Colonial Crucible: Empire in the Making of the Modern American State* (Madison: University of Wisconsin Press, 2009).

23 See M. W. Ghachem, *The Old Regime and the Haitian Revolution* (New York: Cambridge University Press, 2012); M. A. Renda, *Taking Haiti: Military Occupation and the Culture of U.S. Imperialism, 1915–1940* (Chapel Hill: University of North Carolina Press, 2001); L. Dubois, *Haiti: The Aftershocks of History* (New York: Metropolitan Books, 2012).

24 See S. B. Snyder, *Human Rights Activism and the End of the Cold War: A Transnational History of the Helsinki Network* (New York: Cambridge University Press, 2011); T. Borstelmann, *The Cold War and the Color Line: American Race Relations in the Global Arena* (Cambridge MA: Harvard University Press, 2001). On the popular movement against apartheid in the 1970s and 1980s, in opposition to friendly US relations with the Afrikaner regime, see A. Klotz, 'Norms reconstituting interests: global racial equality and U.S. sanctions against South Africa', *International Organization*, 49 (Summer 1995), pp. 451–78.

25 See M. Alexander, *The New Jim Crow: Mass Incarceration in the Age of Colorblindness* (New York: New Press, 2010); B. Useem and A. M. Piehl, *Prison State: The Challenge of Mass Incarceration* (New York: Cambridge University Press, 2008).

26 For recent elaborations on Woodward's pioneering work on these topics, see S. Hahn, *A Nation Under Our Feet: Black Political Struggles in the Rural South from Slavery to the Great Migration* (Cambridge MA: Harvard University Press, 2003); E. L. Ayers, *The Promise of the New South: Life After Reconstruction* (New York: Oxford University Press, 1992).

27 These are criticisms articulated, ironically, by former Secretary of Defense Robert Gates, who served presidents George W. Bush and Barack Obama. See R. M. Gates, *Duty: Memoirs of a Secretary at War* (New York: Alfred Knopf, 2014).

Race, utopia, perpetual peace: Andrew Carnegie's dreamworld

Introduction

What is the intellectual history of American foreign policy? Two methodological issues stand out in thinking through this question. The first concerns the appropriate level of analysis, and thus the range of materials that are suitable for constructing such a history. Must we focus on ideas or conceptual schemes that have directly (or even indirectly) shaped debate and decision-making among the Washington policy elite, or could our analysis also encompass the production and circulation of visions of the United States emanating from multiple institutional sites and intellectual ecologies, from universities and think tanks through to computer games and Hollywood blockbusters? A second issue concerns the conceptual presuppositions involved in writing national histories. Most accounts of the intellectual history of American foreign policy explore how American policy intellectuals envisaged the nature and purpose of the United States. This framing invokes a specific ontology of world politics that privileges the sovereign state. The contours of the tradition are imagined as bounded by the juridical limits of existing state formations, and the state itself is understood as the main (or only) object of reference – the key agent in world politics and thus in the analysis of foreign policy discourse.[1] The intellectual history of American foreign policy is thus construed as a story Americans tell to and about America. While this framing makes sense insofar as much of the intellectual production about American foreign policy assumes exactly this form, it is nevertheless important to remember that there have always been alternative imaginaries of world order, paths not taken.[2]

This chapter analyses an account of world politics that gives ontological priority to 'race' – in this case, the 'Anglo-Saxon' or 'English-speaking' race – and assigns the state a secondary or subordinate function. The vision of politics is woven through the history of Euro-American international thought, gaining prominence at certain moments before retreating to the wings, only to resurface again at a later date. It was at its most prominent as the twentieth century dawned.

The *fin de siècle* was a time of social dreaming on both sides of the Atlantic. New conceptions of politics, of cultural life and of humanity itself circulated widely, (re)shaping political ideologies as well as literary genres.[3] While Bellamy, Morris, Butler and Wells sold in extraordinary quantities, thousands of other novels, short stories and poems likewise sketched a kaleidoscope of future worlds, ranging from the apocalyptically gloomy to the mindlessly sanguine. But it is important not to confine analysis of utopian impulses to speculative literary texts. Indeed I want to argue that we can interpret aspects of the debate over the future of world order – and in particular visions of the 'Angloworld' – as expressions of utopian desire.[4] Both literary fiction and political thought were reacting to a ramifying set of anxieties, and both expressed a desire to confront or defuse those anxieties through the establishment of novel forms of collective life. Both also placed the latest scientific and technological discoveries at the heart of their projects, seeing in them the material and symbolic means through which their grand ambitions could be achieved. Numerous commentators, both American and British, regarded the (re)unification of the British (colonial) Empire and the United States as a harbinger of a better future, one in which the Anglo-Saxon race could dominate the coming century.[5] The most ambitious manifestation of this utopianism resided in the belief that the Angloworld could transform the moral and political configuration of humanity – above all, that it could secure peace, order and justice on a global scale. The consummation of the Anglo-Saxon peoples would bring about the end of history. This represented the divinisation of the political: a theological master narrative infused with ideas about destiny and providence. It was also, and equally, a reflection of the technological fetishism that pervaded the era, the profound belief in the transformative powers of the machine.

Andrew Carnegie was one of one of the leading racial utopians of the age. Or so I will argue. At Skibo, his Scottish castle, he flew a flag with the Union Jack on one side and the Stars and Stripes on the other, a symbolic representation of his own double identity and that of the Angloworld.[6] He saw himself as embodying the transatlantic dream, an Archimedean envoy translating Britain and the United States to each other and the world. Much as Jeremy Bentham had once bombarded the leaders of states with unsolicited constitutional plans, so Carnegie took it upon himself to pepper the White House and Downing Street with advice about how best to deepen harmony. He also sought to convert the intellectual elites of the United States and the British Empire. In Carnegie's writings we glimpse an alternative framing of American intellectual history, one in which a racial formation is both the central category of politics and a vehicle for the creation of a better world. Race, democracy, peace and empire were fused together in a fantasy of liberal white supremacism.

Beyond democracy: racialising perpetual peace

In recent years, many political scientists, philosophers and public policy-makers have fixated on the (dyadic) democratic peace thesis – the proposition that democratic states do not fight one another.[7] Mythopoeic historical genealogies have been elaborated to bolster and legitimate the argument, presenting it as a long-standing line of thought with roots bored deep into the bedrock of Western intellectual history. They typically focus on the late eighteenth century, with Immanuel Kant assigned a starring role. Yet there is something peculiar about the distribution of attention in this historical narrative.[8] It prioritises a moment when democracy was largely absent, a political reality still yet to come, while ignoring the debates about war and popular sovereignty that unfolded across the nineteenth century – the period when democracy was being realised, albeit slowly and unevenly, throughout the Euro-Atlantic world. A rather more complicated picture emerges from those debates. During the first two-thirds of the century many radicals and liberals preached a monadic version of the democratic peace, arguing that democracies would be pacific, or at least more so than the alternatives. This optimism was corroded, though never fully eliminated, following the advent of democratic politics during the second half of the century, chiefly because the vanguard democratic states – notably Britain and the United States – showed few signs of converting swords into ploughshares. Pessimism about the pacific character of democracy intensified as the United States embarked on an imperial war against Spain and the British fought the Boers in South Africa. L. T. Hobhouse's *Democracy and Reaction* indexed the disillusionment. 'Both the friends and enemies of democracy', he commented, once 'inclined to the belief that when the people came into power there would be a time of rapid and radical domestic change combined in all probability with peace abroad – for where was the interest of the masses in any war?'[9] But no longer. 'Aggrandisement, war, compulsory enlistment, lavish expenditure, Protection, arbitrary government, class legislation, follow naturally one upon the other', and 'the conclusion that democracies would not be warlike – if stated as a universal rule – must certainly rank among the shattered illusions' of the age.[10] Even the peace movements in Britain and the United States had shed much of their earlier radicalism: at the dawn of the twentieth century they were dominated by a moderate form of legalism that emphasised the codification of international law and the practice of arbitration.[11] As the British international lawyer John Westlake acknowledged, this signalled a retreat from irenic visions of the future. No longer 'under the spell' of think-ers like Saint Pierre, Bentham or Kant, his contemporaries did not spent time 'sketching imaginary international governments'.[12] Yet the idea of perpetual peace had not disappeared; it was recoded and articulated in different forms. Here I want to outline three types of argument that probed the connections between empire, democracy and war: the 'democratic war thesis', the 'empire peace thesis' and the 'racial peace thesis'.

Democratic war arguments posited a close connection between demo-cratic order and inter-state violence. A strong variant of the argument sug-gested that democracies were intrinsically prone to conflict. In a best-selling book of political prophecy, H. G. Wells argued that the spread of democ-racy was likely to result in spirals of destruction, as democratic politicians needed to 'foster enmity between people and people' in order to retain power. The final development of the democratic system, 'so far as intrinsic forces go', he predicted, 'will be, not the rule of the boss, nor the rule of the trust, nor the rule of the newspaper; no rule, indeed, but international rivalry, international competition, international exasperation and hostility, and at last – irresistible and overwhelming – the definite establishment of the rule of that most stern and educational of all masters – *War*.'[13] The weaker (and more common) variant posited that democratic norms and structures neither amplified nor dampened the violence, instead channelling it in novel 'democratic' forms. Thus William James contended that democratic politics redirected the existing belligerent habits of the people. He singled out the dangerous volatility of 'public opinion', a live issue in the aftermath of the wars in South Africa and the Philippines. 'Our ancestors have bred pugnac-ity into our bone and marrow, and thousands of years won't breed it out of us. The popular imagination fairly fattens on the thought of wars. Let public opinion once reach a certain fighting pitch, and no ruler can withstand it.'[14]

The empire peace thesis, on the other hand, conjectured that war could be diminished, even eliminated, in a world managed by great empires. It also came in two main variants. The generic form claimed that global sta-bility was best secured by a system of imperial administration, in which the dominant powers – democracies and non-democracies alike – main-tained stability by limiting the number of autonomous polities through both formal and informal modalities of rule. As well as being a staple of imperial propaganda, this argument could be found in unexpected places. J. A. Hobson sketched a version in *Imperialism*. Elaborating the benefits of a system of federal empires ruling the 'uncivilised' spaces of the earth, he envisaged a Pan-Anglo-Saxon polity taking its place alongside Pan-Teutonic, Pan-Slavic and Pan-Latin entities, each 'related by ties of com-mon blood, language, and institutions'. 'Inter-imperialism' thus offered 'the best hope of permanent peace'.[15]

The other variant specified that only democratic empires – empires ruled by democratic states – were potential agents of universal peace. Fusing vast economic and military resources with the moral legitimacy bestowed by popular government, they were entitled to govern the world. In one sense this was but the latest iteration of the venerable Western imperial argument about the rights and duties of 'civilised' powers to bring progress to the 'barbarian' places of the earth, but it was inflected with two distinctly *fin de siècle* concerns: physical scale and democratic participation. Franklin Giddings, the most prominent sociologist in the United States, developed one version of the argument.[16] For Giddings, war could only be abolished by drastically reducing the number of independent political units, which necessitated the absorption of smaller states by 'democratic empires', above all the United States and Britain. Drawing on an evolutionary theory of social change, he rejected what he saw as Nietzsche's fetishisation of power and the facile servility of Tolstoy, and argued that '[u]nless the whole course of history is meaningless for the future, there is to be no cessation of war … until vast empires embrace all nations'. But not all imperial forms would suffice, for if they were centralising and despotic – or if they embraced socialism – they would 'end in degeneration'.[17] Democratic empires, on the other hand, upheld the value of individual liberty and tolerated local and ethnic differences. Successfully balancing universalism and particularism, the grateful subject populations would recognise the beneficence of their overlords and social evolution could be channelled in a pacific direction. 'Only when the democratic empire has compassed the uttermost parts of the world', he maintained, 'will there be that perfect understanding among men which is necessary for the growth of moral kinship. Only in the spiritual brotherhood of that secular republic, created by blood and iron not less than by thought and love, will the kingdom of heaven be established on earth.'[18]

A similar argument was defended by the British idealist philosopher D. G. Ritchie. Like Giddings, he believed in both civilisational imperialism and the possibility of perpetual peace – indeed he regarded the former as a necessary condition for the latter. The lesson he drew from Kant had nothing to do with democracy or republicanism, but instead concentrated on political autonomy. 'Kant saw quite clearly', Ritchie maintained, 'that there is only one way in which war between independent nations can be prevented; and that is by the nations ceasing to be independent'. The 'prevention of war within great areas' would thus follow from the absorption of small states by large ones, either through coercion or voluntary union.[19] Again taking his cue from Kant, Ritchie argued that while federation was an important solvent of sovereignty, insofar as it eliminated the anarchic international state of nature, it was radically incomplete, and democratic empires were required to rule the backward populations of the earth. A federation of such polities might encourage 'the diminution, the mitigation, and, possibly, the cessation of wars'.[20]

Finally, the racial peace thesis posited that the (re)unification of the Angloworld could secure global peace. This argument had many advocates, including such notable (and apparently irreconcilable) figures as Wells and Cecil Rhodes.[21] The most widely discussed expression of it flowed from the pen of Andrew Carnegie. In 1893 he predicted that the synthesis of the 'English-speaking peoples' would create a 'new nation' that 'would dominate the world and banish from the earth its greatest stain – the murder of men by men'.[22] A racial utopia beckoned.

Looking ahead

It is unsurprising that Carnegie was a fervent believer in the power of dreams. Born in poverty in Dunfermline, Scotland, his family emigrated to the United States in 1848 and at the age of thirteen he started work in a cotton factory in Pittsburgh. By the time he reached thirty he was a multi-millionaire.[23] After accumulating a vast fortune, he stepped back from the day-to-day running of his business empire and set out to establish himself as a public intellectual, writing widely on the social and political issues of the day. Foremost among his obsessions during the 1880s and 1890s was the reunification of his two homelands.

During the 1880s he invariably yoked Anglo-American reunion to the cause of radical democratic reform in British politics, rendering the creation of the former wholly dependent on the success of the latter. A self-professed radical, Carnegie's most impassioned critique of British politics can be found in *Triumphant Democracy*, published in 1886.[24] Both a love letter to his adopted country and a jeremiad aimed at the land he left behind, it expressed a simple message: to achieve future success Britain needed to mimic its colonial offspring across the Atlantic. The immense potential of the race was being unleashed in a democratic egalitarian polity on one side of the ocean while being hamstrung by lingering feudal traditions on the other. Institutional variation was reflected in contrasting rates of economic growth. Carnegie set out to explain the massive burst in productivity in the United States between 1830 and 1880, and in so doing to demonstrate the intrinsic superiority of republicanism. He delineated three variables: 'the ethnic character of the people, the topographical and climatic conditions under which they developed, and the influence of political institutions founded upon the equality of the citizen'.[25] While all played a significant role, political institutions made the greatest difference. Diagnosing the monarchy as the chief pathology afflicting British socio-economic development, Carnegie called for the abolition of hereditary privilege and a written constitution.

'The Republic', he boasted, 'honors her children at birth with equality; the Monarchy stamps hers with the brand of inferiority.'[26] The reception of *Triumphant Democracy* was largely predictable: while it was lambasted in Britain, it received a much more favourable response in the United States.[27]

This scathing analysis of British government informed Carnegie's early advocacy of racial reunion. In 1887 he called for the British to adopt an American-style constitution, predicting that eventually all of the English-speaking peoples would be governed by republican institutions. Once – and only once – that transformation had occurred could reunion follow.

> How long will it take after that assimilation is perfected before we have a Federal Council that will forever render it impossible that the blood of English-speaking man can be shed by English-speaking man? (*Loud cheers*). Where lies your greatest hopes that your own race, the dominant power of the world, shall coalesce and form a union against which nothing on earth shall stand? (*Loud cheers*). In the assimilation of your institutions. There lies the point.[28]

Three years later he argued that 'there is only one way you can make a step towards the unification and consolidation of the English-speaking race, and that is by bringing this little island into line with the progeny which she has established throughout the world. Monarchy is too small a tail to wag so big a dog as republicanism.' Instituting an elected president, he continued, would be the 'first step' in the 'great mission of the English-speaking race' to enforce disarmament and spread peace. But further ahead, under a distant but perceptible horizon, a still grander apparition could be glimpsed, and he concluded both addresses by invoking the words of Tennyson. 'Beyond this stretches the noble dream of the poet, and I believe it is salutary to dwell upon these dreams – dreams that should become realities ... After the English race become united we have "the Parliament of man, the Federation of the world".'[29] The consummation of the English-speaking peoples would herald the unity of humanity itself.

During the 1890s we can discern a subtle but important shift in Carnegie's argument, as he partially decoupled British political reform from the goal of racial (re)union. He recast domestic change as an inevitable outcome of future development rather than a precondition for initiating a process of racial unity. Time would take care of the matter. This allowed him to short-circuit his previous model of transition, suggesting that the first important steps to reunion could be taken prior to the comprehensive metastasis of republicanism throughout the Anglo-Saxon body politic. Instead, he empha-sised the need to dissolve the British settler empire, calling for independence in Australia, Canada, New Zealand and South Africa. An equally pressing concern was the need to combat the virulent strain of Anglophobia infect-ing American political culture. 'This is all very unfortunate', he warned in

1890, 'but a period cannot be fixed when this feeling against England will cease to affect the Young American.' The main cause, he suggested, was a deformation of collective psychology grounded in intra-familial envy and *ressentiment*.

> The position of affairs between the two branches of the English-speaking race is just this: an eldest son has made a great success since he left his father's roof, and it is difficult for an energetic and pugnacious old gentleman to realize that the son has attained his majority, and has become a man resembling his parent in no quality more than in being determined to make his own way in the world, and work out his destiny after his own fashion, feeling that destiny to be something so grand that the world has never seen the like.[30]

Despite this jealousy, Carnegie was perennially hopeful for the future. Like other proponents of Anglo-American union he had to grapple with the question of how such a radical change in the political order could be instigated. There were two main responses. A minority argued that any change had to be driven from below, emanating from popular shifts in political belief that the governing class could then harness. Others, including Rhodes and Wells, suggested that such change could only be fomented by an enlightened elite, a political avant-garde whose task it was to cajole and direct the ignorant masses. Forming a clerisy, they would act in concert – either openly or in secret – to shape public opinion. Carnegie, the self-declared man of the people, adopted the vanguardist position. 'We must not expect the idea to win its way at first', he confided to his friend, the radical journalist W. T. Stead, 'except with the finest and most intuitive minds: none the less, it is sure to come.'[31]

'A Look Ahead' thus emerged at a propitious moment. The year 1893 saw the appearance of several key prophetic texts. At a lecture in Chicago, Frederick Jackson Turner outlined his 'frontier thesis', warning that the closing of the American West threatened to dissipate the creative dynamism that had shaped the progressive growth of the United States.[32] The Australian radical C. H. Pearson published *National Life and Character*, imagining a future world dominated by bitter geo-racial competition, especially with the Chinese, and concluding that the then current dominant powers may be 'elbowed and hustled and perhaps even thrust aside'.[33] Yin to Carnegie's yang, it was a deeply pessimistic counterblast to the optimism pulsing through utopian visions of Anglo-Saxonism. The leading social gospel theologian Josiah Strong released *The New Era, or, The Coming Kingdom*, its title speaking to the eschatological perfectionism he attributed to the Anglo-Saxons. Unburdened by the anxiety provoking many of his contemporaries into print, Carnegie veered between deterministic historical prediction and strident political advocacy, backing the creation of a 'British American

Union', a polity that he baldly characterised as a 'reunited state'.[34] Turning to history for both guidance and succour, he noted that until the American Revolution 'the English-speaking race dwelt together in unity' and submitted that the future would see this prelapsarian state of affairs recreated as the scattered fragments (re)united in a vast world-transforming whole.[35] The idea, he declared, would be 'hailed with enthusiasm' by citizens, once they understood its manifold benefits.[36] In making his case, Carnegie blended arguments that were to become ubiquitous among unionists with some of his own more distinctive claims.

His geopolitical and economic views were common currency. He warned that Britain faced a stark choice: unify or enter a period of catastrophic decline. If it opted for the latter, it would be demoted to 'comparative insignificance' in a world dominated by the United States, ceding both global power and intra-racial leadership to Washington. If it opted for the former, however, it could retain a pivotal role in shaping the destiny of the world, yoked to the United States in a close embrace. British leaders could thus either fight the tide of history or ride it.[37] In economic terms, meanwhile, Carnegie argued that reunion would benefit all the incorporated polities and help to secure free trade – a somewhat ironic line from a man who had made a fortune behind the steep tariff walls sheltering the US steel market.[38]

A further commonplace – one that shaped much political discourse at the end of the nineteenth century – concerned the role of communications technologies in transforming political possibilities. Arguments about both imperial Greater Britain and Anglo-American union contended that the final quarter of the century was marked by a fundamental transformation in the meaning of time and space. New communications technologies, and in particular the electrical telegraph, radically altered the way in which individuals perceived the physical world and the socio-political possibilities it contained, spawning fantasies about the elimination of geographical distance that prefigure late-twentieth-century narratives about globalisation. This opened up a yawning ontological gap between the past and present, a fundamental change in the order of things. In a symptomatic argument made in the early 1880s J. R. Seeley, the leading British imperial ideologue, hailed the 'unprecedented facility of communication', and suggested that it allowed for (even demanded) the creation of 'new types of state'.[39] Previously viewed as immutable, nature was now open to manipulation, even transcendence. Carnegie's dream was predicated on this cognitive transformation. The oceans of the world, he asserted, 'no longer constitute barriers between nations' and arguments from a distance were thus little more than untimely remnants from a bygone age. The chief agent of change was the electrical telegraph, its wires straddling oceans and continents, its embrace forcing all into close communion. It was 'the most important factor in rendering political union possible, and I venture to say inevitable'. Able to communicate near-instantaneously with one another, people scattered throughout the dispersed zones of the English-speaking world now occupied the same temporal plane. With unprecedented synchronicity, 'the pulse beat of the entire nation can be constantly felt by the government and all the people.'[40] A transoceanic imagined community had been conjured into existence. The coordinates of historical progress was clear. 'All that tends to the brotherhood of man tends to promote it. The tendency of the age is towards consolidation.'[41]

Carnegie also insisted that the English-speaking peoples constituted a single race. Unlike many Anglo-Saxonists, Carnegie was largely free of poisonous racial bigotry. At the height of nativist racism, for example, he praised immigrants and rejected calls for discrimination.[42] Race, though, remained a crucial category in his political thinking. He assumed that race was ontologically prior to political institutions – that kinship and racial solidarity were more fundamental than the institutional architecture of states.[43] Figured as both cause and effect, he viewed it as the main determinant of historical progress and a vital feature of the current distribution of talent and political virtue. He maintained that 'in race – and there is a great deal in race – the American remains three-fourths purely British', and that this fact fundamentally shaped the character of the American polity, rendering it suitable for reunion with the British empire-state.[44] Carnegie's account was heavily indebted to the 'Teutonist' framework that played such a central role in late-nineteenth-century intellectual life in Britain and the United States. I would suggest that he drew inspiration from the British historian Edward Freeman. Teutonism figured the dominant population groups in Britain and the United States as national threads of an overarching Germano-Teutonic race descended from a primitive Aryan ur-race.[45] Thus Carnegie could claim that '[t]he Briton of to-day is himself composed in large measure of the Germanic element, and German, Briton, and American are all of the Teutonic race'.[46] Despite mass immigration and the substantial role played by other European settlers, this Teutonic population shaped American society and politics, giving the country and its people their superior character. 'The amount of blood other than Anglo-Saxon or Germanic which has entered into the American is almost too trifling to deserve notice, and has been absorbed without changing him in any fundamental trait.' The result, he proclaimed, was that '[t]he American remains British'. United in 'language, literature, religion, and law', the two states lacked only a common set of political institutions.[47] Historical evolution would furnish these in due course.

Carnegie also defended some rather more unconventional claims. One concerned the future of the British settler colonies. First, he excluded

Australia and New Zealand from the 'reunited state'. Despite announcing the obsolescence of time and space, he insisted that they were too far away for proper incorporation – and also that they were insufficiently populous or wealthy.[48] Geographic and demographic realities determined the ideal shape of the union. His was to be a North Atlantic racial polity. Second, he proposed that Canada should be absorbed by the United States. Here he adopted an argument common among American thinkers at the time, though one that garnered little support in either Britain or Canada.[49] He thus envisaged a sequence enacted in four distinct steps. Britain would first grant independence to Australia, New Zealand and Canada, before the United States absorbed Canada, whereupon the North American colossus would join with Britain to form 'an indissoluble union of indestructible states'.[50] Finally, the new English-speaking Atlantic polity would divest itself of its imperial possessions throughout the world. The transition to a new world order would be peaceful, for 'such a giant among pigmies would never need to exert its power, but only to intimate its wishes and decisions', and as such, global disarmament would invariably follow, as it 'would be unnecessary for any power to maintain a great standing army or a great navy'.[51] A preponderant power, it would deter other polities from attempting to compete. Perpetual peace would ensue.

Most Anglo-American unionists were imperialists of one stripe or another, envisaging that closer relations between the two powers would result – or even be driven by – a shared interest in governing their respective empires. It was thus quite common to promote both imperial federation and Anglo-American union, the two projects viewed as either complementary (and thus capable of being pursued simultaneously) or as steps in a historical sequence leading to the eventual unification of all the English-speaking peoples as a massive imperial power (in which case it made sense to prioritise one of them). Thus Carnegie's friend W. T. Stead, one of the leading journalists of the age, was both a vociferous imperial federalist and a fierce proponent of Anglo-American union.[52] Carnegie rejected both approaches. An avowed anti-imperialist, he condemned British rule in India, arguing that it was a major economic and moral drain on the home country. Moreover, he regarded attempts to federate the British settler colonies and the 'mother country' as absurd – economically illiterate, politically hopeless and above all a distraction from the more important task of securing Anglo-American union.[53] Here too his views bore a striking resemblance to those of Freeman, who in the early 1890s had called for the immediate dissolution of the British colonial empire, both on grounds of justice – insofar as it was illegitimate for one 'civilised' people to exercise imperial domination over another 'civilised' people – and in order to facilitate closer connections between Britain and the United States.[54] For both of them, dismantling the colonial empire was a precondition for racial concord and deeper Anglo-American relations, though Carnegie went much further in suggesting the need for reunion.

Angloworld unionists largely supported the American war against Spain, viewing the conflict as a great opportunity for constructing an alliance between the two powers. Here too Carnegie was an exception. Appalled by the conflict, he soon emerged as one of the most vocal 'anti-imperialists' in the United States.[55] With war looming, he pointed to the freighted example of the British Empire, which demonstrated the foolhardiness of scrabbling for imperial possessions.

> It has hitherto been the glorious mission of the Republic to establish upon secure foundations Triumphant Democracy, and the world now understands government of the people for the people and by the people. Tires the Republic so soon of its mission that it must, perforce, discard it to undertake the impossible task of establishing Triumphant Despotism, the rule of the foreigner over the people, and must the millions of the Philippines who have been asserting their God-given right to govern themselves, be the first victims of Americans, whose proudest boast is that they conquered independence for themselves?[56]

As the fighting erupted, he counterposed his favoured republican vision of 'Americanism' against a degraded militaristic 'Imperialism' and argued for the immediate independence of Cuba and the Philippines. He offered a variety of reasons for rejecting the war. In military terms, possession of a territorial empire in Asia would expose the United States to grave threats for which it was wholly unprepared.[57] Economically, it offered no commercial benefits and threatened to divert or drain the sources of American wealth.[58] And morally, it exposed the United States to the corrupting dynamics that beset all imperial powers. True republican government, he maintained, was incompatible with empire. 'We are engaged in work which requires suppression of American ideas hitherto held sacred.' The danger of debilitating hypocrisy loomed. 'The American idea of the rights of man and of the right of self-government is not false. It is true. All communities, however low they may be in the scale, have the germ of self-government.'[59] Committed to both a hierarchical vision of global order and a basic universalism, Carnegie suggested that all peoples had a putative right to political independence, though not all of them were yet ready to fully realise it. The war also threatened to poison relations between Britain and the United States, encouraging them to embark on a strategy of cooperative imperialism.

> The author of 'A Look Ahead' … is not likely to be suspected of hostility to the coming together of the English-speaking race. It has been my dream, and it is one of the movements that lie closest to my heart … But I do not favor a formal alliance … On the contrary, I rely upon the 'alliance of hearts', which happily exists to-day. Alliances of fighting power form and dissolve with the

questions which arise from time to time. The patriotism of race lies deeper and is not disturbed by waves upon the surface.[60]

Despite these tribulations, Carnegie's confidence in the dream remained intact. Reflecting on 'A Look Ahead' in 1898, he wrote that 'five years after these words were penned I have nothing to add to or deduct from them, on the contrary, I am as confident as ever of the coming fulfilment of that prediction'.[61]

There were significant limits to Carnegie's professed 'anti-imperialism'. While adamantly opposed to the occupation of Cuba and the Philippines, he nevertheless supported the annexation of Hawaii on the grounds of strategic necessity.[62] Moreover, he was enthusiastic about British settler colonialism, which, in a common nineteenth-century gesture, he distinguished from formal 'imperialism'.[63] While the former was based on avarice and caused endless problems for both the imperial power and those subjected to it, the latter was premised on the grant of self-government to the colonists. Indeed Carnegie assigned colonialism a key role in his evolutionary schema. In settler colonies, he boasted:

> we establish and reproduce our own race. Thus Britain has peopled Canada and Australia with English-speaking people, who have naturally adopted our ideas of self-government. That the world has benefited thereby goes without saying; that Britain has done a great work as the mother of nations is becoming more and more appreciated the more the student learns of worldwide affairs. No nation that ever existed has done so much for the progress of the world as the little islands in the North Sea, known as Britain.[64]

The story of British imperialism therefore encompassed two countervailing trends. One of them, found in India and more recently Africa, was marked by shame and futility, and resulted in the accumulation of worthless – even dangerous – foreign possessions. 'The most grievous burden which Britain has upon her shoulders is that of India, for there it is impossible for our race to grow.'[65] Americans needed to heed the lesson. The other was a story of progressive transformation, the occupation and cultivation of territories that benefited both Britain and the world. He praised the latter as part of the beneficent teleology of evolution, 'the fittest driving out the least fit; the best supplanting the inferior'. This dynamic had been replicated in the violent settling of the American West. The interests of 'civilization rendered the acquisition of the land necessary', and as such it was 'right and proper that the nomadic Indian should give place to the settled husbandman in the prairies of the West; it is also well that the Maori should fade away, and give place to the intelligent, industrious citizen, a member of our race'.[66] Carnegie, in short, was opposed to specific forms of imperialism, chiefly those that involved the occupation and coercive administration of distant territories populated by large numbers of people of a different 'race'. Settler colonialism could be justified as a vehicle of historical progress.

As befits a dream, Carnegie's political vision remained deeply ambiguous. In particular, he was never clear or consistent about the kind of political association that he had in mind. Throughout the 1880s and 1890s he referred to a possible Anglo-American 'federation'.[67] In September 1891, though, he enjoined Stead to see things 'as I do', such that 'each branch must manage its own household, and that there may be an alliance, but not a confederation'.[68] The form of the proposed alliance was left unspecified and when formal transatlantic alliances became a topic of debate during the Spanish–American war, Carnegie firmly rejected the idea.[69] In a 'Look Ahead' he called for a 'common British-American citizenship' – or what would later be called 'isopolity' – which did not require the creation of a new supervenient armature of legal and political institutions; yet his choice of vocabulary often implied something much more institutionally ambitious than transnational citizenship, a defensive alliance, or even confederation, for he referred repeatedly to what he had in mind as a 'reunited state'.[70] But state hardly seems an appropriate designation for a polity in which both constituent elements retained a significant amount of autonomy, such that neither 'the old land or the new binds itself to support the other in all its designs, either at home or abroad'.[71] Indeed in the same text he implied that in the future state sovereignty would be maintained, writing that '[s]ome day … delegates from the three now separated branches will meet in London and readily agree upon and report for approval and ratification a basis for the restoration of an indissoluble union of indestructible states'.[72] Moreover, the exact constitutional relationship between Britain and the United States was left unclear. Indeed, given his belief in the future superiority of the United States, he seems to have meant that this primacy was honorific, Britain playing Greece to America's Rome. The very ambiguity of his pronouncements helped to trigger a debate over the possibilities and pitfalls of reunion.

The dreamer of dreams

The history of Western utopian thinking has been marked by two major conceptual transitions. Classical utopias, from the ancient world to the late eighteenth century, were located in historically contemporaneous yet alien places. 'What was fundamentally missing', Reinhart Koselleck writes, 'was the temporal dimension of utopia as a site of the future.'[73] As the finite world was mapped and conquered by Europeans, so the room for the imaginative projection of alien places was gradually exhausted, although this process was never complete.[74] 'The utopian spaces had been surpassed by experience.'[75] During the long nineteenth century utopia came to be viewed as a possible future state of affairs, a form of society that could be enacted on earth. It was thus 'temporalized', a move that represented 'the metamorphosis of utopia into the philosophy of history'.[76] The second major shift was principally spatial. At the end of the nineteenth century, as industrial capitalism spread across the earth, and as new communications technologies reshaped conceptions of time and space, the geographical scope of utopia was globalised. In a tradition reaching back to Plato, utopias had almost invariably been imagined as circumscribed, bounded spaces – a city, an island, a nation-state.[77] But by the dawn of the twentieth century, such isolated, independent fragments were increasingly supplanted by much more geographically expansive visions.[78] Global utopias – ranging from worldwide socio-political transformations to the Wellsian world state – became far more common. A new era of social prophecy had dawned.

We see in the *fin de siècle* debates over the future of world order – and in Carnegie's political writings – a strain of argument which figured the Anglo-world (and especially Anglo-America) as a utopian space realisable through intentional human action. This utopia had a dualistic structure: life within the Anglo-world was marked by peace and justice, and a level of civilisation higher than any other recorded in human history. It was advancing towards perfection. Meanwhile, the Anglo-world, acting as a single beneficent agent, would help to pacify the non-Anglo spaces of the earth. Through human ingenuity, and above all through the manipulation of new technologies, both communicative and political, it would be possible to create a racial-political order that was capable of riding out the flux of the modern world, and that in doing so promised to bring justice and peace to a violent planet. This extraordinary moment of racial fabulation did not pass unnoticed. In *The Napoleon of Notting Hill*, his witty satire of utopian desire, G. K. Chesterton marvelled at the appearance of 'so many prophets and so many prophecies', and alongside some of the usual suspects – Tolstoy, Edward Carpenter and Wells – he identified W. T. Stead's forecast that 'England would in the twentieth century be united to America'.[79]

Carnegie embraced the visionary character of his beloved project. 'The dream, in which no one perhaps indulges more than the writer, of the union of the English-speaking race, even that entrancing dream must be recognized as only a dream', he wrote.[80] But in a democratic twist to Shelley's boast that poets are the unacknowledged legislators of the world, Carnegie insisted that dreams were both the prerogative and the privilege of the engaged citizen. In the staid career of the 'statesman', marked by cautious incrementalism and pragmatic decision-making, social dreaming was a vice. 'When a statesman has in his keeping the position and interests of his country', he maintained, 'all speculation as to the future fruition of ideas of what should be or what will one day rule the world ... must be resolutely dismissed.' His task was to engage the present, not to speculate about the future.[81] But the private citizen faced no such constraints and was thus ideally placed to scan the horizon.

> It may be all a dream but I am dreamer of dreams. So be it. But if it be true that he who always dreams accomplishes nothing, so also is it none the less true that he who never dreams is equally barren of achievement. And if it be a dream, it is a dream nobler than most realities. If it is never to be realised, none the less it should be realised, and shame to those who come after us if it be not. I believe it will be, for all progress is on its side.[82]

Carnegie's absolute confidence that progress would deliver racial reunion was derived from (or rationalised by) his interpretation of Herbert Spencer's philosophy of history. A man prone to credulous hero-worship, Carnegie placed Spencer, along with Matthew Arnold, in his pantheon of intellectual gods, routinely describing himself as a 'disciple' of the 'master'.[83] His belief in the inviolability of Spencer's system underwrote what his friend John Morley, the liberal historian and politician, once referred to as Carnegie's 'invincible optimism'.[84] Carnegie recalled that after reading Spencer (and Darwin) as a young man, 'light came as in a flood and all was clear. Not only had I got rid of theology and the supernatural, but I had found the truth of evolution.'[85] That Spencerian truth, at least as digested by Carnegie, was that humanity was by nature progressive and perfectible. 'Man', he intoned, 'was not created with an instinct for his own degradation, but from the lower he has risen to the higher forms. Nor is there any conceivable end to his march to perfection.' In good utopian fashion he even speculated that human immortality was a distinct possibility. This Panglossian rendering of Spencer's complex evolutionary social theory was encapsulated in a pithy motto that recurs throughout his writing. 'All is well since all grows better.' Perhaps revealing more than intended, Carnegie concluded that this was his 'true source of comfort'.[86] His account of progressive historical development – a kind of naturalised secular theodicy – sustained his boundless optimism, moralised his rapacious accumulation of capital and guaranteed that his political dreams would be realised. 'Utopian as the dream may seem', he maintained, 'I place on record my belief that it is one day to become a reality.'[87] Incessant travel around the world served only to confirm his sanguine forecast. 'The parts fit into one symmetrical whole', he wrote, 'and you see humanity wherever it is placed working out a destiny tending to one definite end.'[88] Although he never specified in detail what form that end would assume, we can infer that it was a peaceful industrial republican order, led wisely and beneficently by the politically integrated members of the 'English-speaking race'. Carnegie was quick to draw a moral lesson from his sweeping observations on historical destiny. 'Humanity is an organism, inherently rejecting all that is deleterious, that is, wrong, and absorbing after trial what is beneficial, that is, right.'[89] Unwittingly, he thus committed the 'naturalistic fallacy' – the idea that the (moral) good can be derived from (empirical) properties of the world that the philosopher G. E. Moore would soon make famous in his powerful attack on Spencer's ethical naturalism.[90]

Admitting that his dream of reunion might strike others as a hopeless fantasy, Carnegie vacillated between seeing it as either probable or inevitable. In both cases he implicitly distinguished between two modalities of utopian optimism, one that he regarded as admirable, the other as worthy of contempt. The former imagined visions of a perfected future that could be derived from an analysis of the dynamics of social evolution. Anglo-American union was one such utopia. The latter promised something that it could never deliver, conjuring up images of future human organisation that failed to conform to the teleological trajectory of history. Thus in some of his other writings – notably the hugely popular 'Gospel of Wealth' – Carnegie was himself dismissive of what he saw as 'utopian' schemes of social organisation.[91] Dreams thus served a premonitory function, their purpose to delineate the shape of future socio-political orders and identify ways of accelerating (or retarding) their emergence. If done correctly, they were anticipatory interventions into the flow of historical time.

'A Look Ahead' provoked numerous reactions and helped to trigger a debate over Anglo-America that echoed through the early decades of the twentieth century. Many commentators agreed with Carnegie's basic argument about racial kinship, while dissenting from his prescriptions (or what they thought his prescriptions were). Thus A. T. Mahan characterised Carnegie's vision as 'rational but premature', suggesting that close cooperation between the British empire-state and the United States was more plausible than a form of transnational political association.[92] But at least some of the commentators were alive to the utopian dimensions of Carnegie's project. The most perceptive located the unionist argument within the currents of social prophecy circulating at the time. 'It is an inevitable tendency of our age', the military writer G. S. Clarke observed, 'to seek solace in dreams.' The world was undergoing a profound transition, 'the breaking up of old faiths, the oppressive sense of an existence ruled by inexorable law, the increasing subordination of men and matter to mere machinery political or technical', and this had produced a 'mental reaction' that assumed different forms, one of which was unfettered speculation about the future. '[W]hether we linger over an anticipatory retrospect with Mr. Bellamy, indulge in "a look ahead" with Mr. Carnegie, or – far less profitably – attempt to peer across the "Borderland" with Mr. Stead, the same human craving supplies the impulse and explains the fascination.'[93]

Carnegie poured scorn on theological justifications offered for the war against Spain. He mocked the view, widespread at the time, that the United States was God's chosen instrument for bringing about the millennium, for spreading civilisation to the barbarians and for evangelising – and thus saving – a heathen world.[94] The irony, though, was that Carnegie's own dreamworld was not as far removed from the theological vision of racial unity as he liked to imagine. He unwittingly replaced one kind of providentialism with another. Carnegie and the theologians of empire shared a teleological view of history that cast the Anglo-Saxons as agents of progress and regarded human perfectibility (in one form or another) as achievable. While Carnegie denied the role of an omniscient creator in history, he allocated Spencerian evolution an analogous role, as both engine of change and overarching source of moral judgement. Both styles of argument resulted in Panglossian visions of the future, racial theodicies in which suffering was framed in terms of the ultimate triumph of good.

Notes

1 For some more thoughts on the topic, see D. Bell, 'Writing the world: Disciplinary history and beyond', *International Affairs*, 85:1 (2009), pp. 3–22; D. Bell, 'Making and Taking Worlds' in A. Sartori and S. Moyn (eds), *Global Intellectual History* (New York: Columbia University Press, 2012), pp. 254–82.

2 For a sophisticated historical and conceptual argument to this effect, see J. Bartleson, *Visions of World Community* (Cambridge: Cambridge University Press, 2009).

3 M. Beaumont, *Utopia Ltd.: Ideologies of Social Dreaming in England, 1870–1900* (Leiden: Brill, 2005); N. Ruddick, 'The Fantastic Fiction of the Fin de Siècle' in G. Marshall (ed.), *The Cambridge Companion to the Fin de Siècle* (Cambridge: Cambridge University Press, 2007), pp. 189–207.

4 On the 'Angloworld', see J. Belich, *Replenishing the Earth: The Settler Revolution and the Rise of the Angloworld, 1783–1939* (Oxford: Oxford University Press, 2009). For one of the few analyses that discuss utopia and foreign policy, see S. Matrese, *American Foreign Policy and the Utopian Imagination* (Amherst: University of Massachusetts Press, 2001).

5 I explore this discourse in a forthcoming book, *Dreamworlds of Empire*. The material in this chapter is extracted from it.

6 A. Carnegie, 'Americanism versus imperialism', *North American Review*, 168:506 (1899), pp. 5–6; A. Carnegie, 'Speech in Ottawa' (28 April 1906), Library of Congress, Papers of Andrew Carnegie (hereafter AC), Box 252, p. 9; A. Carnegie, notes for a speech at the Presentation of the Freedom of Glasgow (10 September 1909), AC, Box 251, p. 6.

7 P. Ish-Shalom, *Democratic Peace: A Political Biography* (Ann Arbor: University of Michigan Press, 2013).

8 This section draws on D. Bell, 'Before the democratic peace: Racial utopianism, empire, and the abolition of war', *European Journal of International Relations*, 20:3 (2014), pp. 647–70.

9 L. T. Hobhouse, *Democracy and Reaction* (London: Unwin, 1904), pp. 49–50.

10 *Ibid.*, pp. 55, 142.

11 D. Patterson, *Towards a Warless World: The Travail of the American Peace Movement, 1887–1914* (Bloomington: Indiana University Press, 1976); M. Ceadel, *Semi-Detached Idealists: The British Peace Movement and International Relations, 1854–1945* (Oxford: Oxford University Press, 2000); C. Reid, 'Peace and law: Peace activism and international arbitration, 1895–1907', *Peace & Change*, 29:3 (2004), pp. 521–48; S. Wertheim, 'The League of Nations: Retreat from international law?' *Journal of Global History*, 7:2 (2012), pp. 210–32.

12 J. Westlake, 'International arbitration', *International Journal of Ethics*, 7 (1896), pp. 1–20 at p. 2.

13 H. G. Wells, *Anticipations of the Reaction of Mechanical and Scientific Progress upon Human Life and Thought* (Mineola: Dover, 1999 [1902]), p. 95.

14 W. James, 'The Moral Equivalent of War' (1906) in W. James, *Writings, 1902–1910* (New York: Penguin, 1989), p. 1283. James cited Wells repeatedly in this essay.

15 J. A. Hobson, *Imperialism: An Analysis* (London: Macmillan, 1902), p. 332.

16 Giddings was at the time professor of sociology at Columbia. For intellectual and institutional context, see G. Steinmetz (ed.), *Sociology and Empire: The Imperial Entanglements of a Discipline* (Durham NC: Duke University Press, 2013), Chapters 1 and 3.

17 F. Giddings, *Democracy and Empire* (London: Macmillan, 1900), p. 357.

18 *Ibid.*

19 D. G. Ritchie, 'War and peace', *International Journal of Ethics*, 11:2 (1900), pp. 137–58 at p. 157.

20 *Ibid.*, pp. 157–8.

21 Bell, *Dreamworlds of Empire.*

22 A. Carnegie, *The Reunion of Britain and America: A Look Ahead* (Edinburgh: Andrew Elliott, 1893), pp. 12–13. I use this pamphlet edition throughout the chapter.

23 The best account of his life is D. Nasaw, *Andrew Carnegie* (London: Penguin, 2006).

24 A. Carnegie, *Triumphant Democracy, or, Fifty Years' March of the Republic* (New York: Scribner's & Sons, 1886). For a useful analysis, see A. S. Eisenstadt, *Carnegie's Model Republic: Triumphant Democracy and the British-American Relationship* (Albany: State University of New York Press, 2007).

25 Carnegie, *Triumphant Democracy*, p. 11.

26 *Ibid.*, p. 498.

27 Eisenstadt, *Carnegie's Model Republic*, Chapters 5 (on Britain) and 6 (on the United States); Nasaw, *Andrew Carnegie*, pp. 275–6. It sold 17,000 copies in the first few months (Eisenstadt, *Carnegie's Model Republic*, p. 8).

28 A. Carnegie, 'Home Rule in America' (Glasgow, 13 September 1887), AC, Box 250, p. 52.

29 A. Carnegie, 'Some Facts about the American Republic' (*Dundee Advertiser*, 4 September 1890), AC, Box 250, p. 14; Carnegie, 'Home Rule in America', pp. 52–3. The phrase is from Tennyson's 'Locksley Hall' (1842).

30 A. Carnegie *et al.*, 'Do Americans hate England?' *North American Review*, 150:403 (1890), pp. 748–78 at pp. 753, 758.

31 A. Carnegie, Letter to W. T. Stead (11 August 1893), AC, Folder 21.

32 F. J. Turner, 'The Significance of the Frontier in American History' (1893) in *Rereading Frederick Jackson Turner*, ed. J. M. Faragher (London: Yale University Press, 1998). See also K. Klein, *Frontiers of Historical Imagination: Narrating the European Conquest of Native America, 1890–1990* (Berkeley: University of California Press, 1997).

33 C. H. Pearson, *National Life and Character: A Forecast* (London: Macmillan, 1893), p. 85.

34 Carnegie, *The Reunion of Britain and America: A Look Ahead*, p. 32.

35 *Ibid.*, p. 3.

36 *Ibid.*, p. 18.

37 *Ibid.*

38 On the debate over imperial federation, see D. Bell, *The Idea of Greater Britain: Empire and the Future of World Order, 1860–1900* (Princeton: Princeton University Press, 2007).

39 J. R. Seeley, *The Expansion of England: Two Courses of Lectures* (London: Macmillan, 1883), p. 62. See also D. Bell, *Reordering the World: Essays on Liberalism and Empire* (Princeton: Princeton University Press, 2016), Chapters 6 and 8.

40 Carnegie, *The Reunion of Britain and America: A Look Ahead*, p. 11.

41 *Ibid.*, pp. 31–2.

42 Nasaw, *Andrew Carnegie*, p. 662.

43 For my account of how race was typically figured as a 'bio-cultural assemblage', see D. Bell, 'Beyond the sovereign state: Isopolitan citizenship, race, and Anglo-American union', *Political Studies*, 62:2 (2014), pp. 418–34.

44 Carnegie, *The Reunion of Britain and America: A Look Ahead*, p. 9.

45 Key Teutonist texts included H. Maine, *Ancient Law* (London: Dent, 1861) and E. Freeman, *Comparative Politics* (London: Macmillan, 1873). On Teutonist influence on the origins of American politics science, see R. Adcock, *Liberalism and the Emergence of American Political Science* (Oxford: Oxford University Press, 2014), Chapter 5.

46 Carnegie, *The Reunion of Britain and America: A Look Ahead*, p. 11. Freeman is one of the handful of sources cited directly in *A Look Ahead*.

47 Carnegie, *The Reunion of Britain and America: A Look Ahead*, pp. 9–10.

48 *Ibid.*, p. 28.

49 For debates over annexation, see D. C. Bélanger, *Prejudice and Pride: Canadian Intellectuals Confront the United States, 1891–1945* (Toronto: University of Toronto Press, 2011), Chapter 7.

50 Carnegie, *The Reunion of Britain and America: A Look Ahead*, p. 31.

51 *Ibid.*, p. 13.

52 Bell, *Dreamworlds of Empire*.

53 Carnegie, *The Reunion of Britain and America: A Look Ahead*, pp. 23–4; A. Carnegie, 'Imperial federation', *The Nineteenth Century*, 30 (1891), pp. 490–508.

54 E. A. Freeman, *Greater Greece and Greater Britain* (London: Macmillan, 1886). See also D. Bell, 'Alter Orbis: E. A. Freeman on Empire and Racial Destiny' in J. Conlin and A. Bremner (eds), *Making History: Edward Augustus Freeman and Victorian Cultural Politics* (Oxford: Oxford University Press, 2015).

55 On the anti-imperial debate, see M. P. Cullinane, *Liberty and American Anti-Imperialism, 1898–1909* (Basingstoke: Palgrave, 2012).

56 A. Carnegie, 'Distant possessions: The parting of the ways', *North American Review*, 167:501 (1898), pp. 239–48 at pp. 244–5. For further discussion of the negative lesson taught by Britain, see also Carnegie's comments in A. Stevenson *et al.*, 'Bryan or McKinley? The present duty of American citizens', *North American Review*, 171:527 (1900), pp. 433–516 at pp. 496–7.

57 Carnegie, 'Americanism versus imperialism'.

58 A. Carnegie, 'Americanism versus imperialism: II', *North American Review*, 168:508 (1899), pp. 362–72 at p. 362.

59 A. Carnegie, 'The opportunity of the United States', *North American Review*, 174:546 (1902), pp. 606–12 at p. 611.

60 Carnegie, 'Americanism versus Imperialism', pp. 5–6.

61 A. Carnegie, 'Anglo-American Alliance. A Look Today' [hand written: 'And a Look Ahead] (1898), AC, Box 251, p. 1.

62 Carnegie, 'Distant possessions', pp. 242–3.

63 D. Bell, 'Ideologies of Empire' in M. Freeden, L. T. Sargent and M. Stears (eds), *The Oxford Handbook of Political Ideologies* (Oxford: Oxford University Press, 2013), pp. 562–83; J. Tully, 'Lineages of Contemporary Imperialism' in D. Kelly (ed.), *Lineages of Empire: The Historical Roots of British Imperial Thought* (Oxford: Oxford University Press, 2009), pp. 3–31.

64 Carnegie, 'Distant possessions', p. 240.

65 *Ibid.*, p. 240. He was also a critic of the British war in South Africa: A. Carnegie, 'The South African question', *North American Review*, 169:517 (1899), pp. 798–804.

66 A. Carnegie, 'The Venezuelan Question', *North American Review*, 162/471 (1896), pp. 129–44 at p. 133.

67 Carnegie, 'Home Rule in America', p. 52; Carnegie, *The Reunion of Britain and America: A Look Ahead*, p. 27; A. Carnegie, Letter to Stead (11 August 1893), AC, Folder 21.

68 A. Carnegie, Letter to Stead (9 September 1891), AC, Folder 12.

69 Carnegie, 'Americanism versus imperialism', pp. 5–6.

70 Carnegie, *The Reunion of Britain and America: A Look Ahead*, pp. 10, 32. On Anglo-American isopolity, a concept popularised by A. V. Dicey, see Bell, 'Beyond the sovereign state'.

71 *Ibid.*, p. 6.

72 *Ibid.*, p. 31.

73 R. Koselleck, 'The Temporalization of Utopia' in R. Koselleck, *The Practice of Conceptual History: Timing History, Spacing Concepts*, trans. T. S. Presener *et al.* (Stanford: Stanford University Press, 2002), p. 86.

74 On my account, a political project can be considered utopian if, and only if, it invokes or prescribes the radical transformation or elimination of one or more pervasive practices or ordering principles that shape human collective life. These can include, for example, poverty, socio-economic inequality, war, the biochemical composition of the environment or the ontological constitution of human beings, including death itself.

75 Koselleck, 'The Temporalization of Utopia', p. 86. On the meaning of 'experience' in this context, see R. Koselleck, *Futures Past: On the Semantics of Historical Time*, trans. K. Tribe (Cambridge MA: MIT Press, 2004), Chapter 14.

76 Koselleck, 'The Temporalization of Utopia,' p. 86.

77 For the interweaving of the nation and utopia, see P. Wegner, *Imaginary Communities: Utopia, the Nation and the Spatial Histories of Modernity* (Berkeley: University of California Press, 2002).

78 A version of this argument can be found in H. U. Seeber, 'Utopia, Nation-Building, and the Dissolution of the Nation-State Around 1900' in R. Pordzik (ed.), *Futurescapes: Space in Utopian and Science Fiction Discourses* (Amsterdam: Rodopi, 2009), pp. 53–79.

79 G. K. Chesterton, *The Napoleon of Notting Hill* (London: William Clowes, 1904), pp. 14–15.

80 Carnegie, *The Reunion of Britain and America*, p. 8.

81 Carnegie, 'Americanism versus imperialism', p. 8.

82 Carnegie, *The Reunion of Britain and America: A Look Ahead*, p. 31.

83 A. Carnegie, *The Autobiography of Andrew Carnegie* (London: Penguin, 2006 [1920]), Chapters 22 and 25; Nasaw, *Andrew Carnegie*, Chapter 12.

84 J. Morley, *Recollections* (London: Macmillan, 1917), vol. 2, p. 111.

85 Carnegie, *Autobiography*, p. 291. Carnegie rated Spencer more highly as a thinker than Darwin.

86 *Ibid.*; A. Carnegie, Letter to David Jayne Hill (27 August 1906), AC, Folder 132. See J. White, 'Andrew Carnegie and Herbert Spencer: A special relationship', *Journal of American Studies*, 13 (1979), pp. 57–71.

87 Carnegie, *The Reunion of Britain and America: A Look Ahead*, p. 3.

88 Carnegie, *Autobiography*, p. 180.

89 *Ibid.*, p. 291.

90 G. E. Moore, *Principia Ethica* (Cambridge: Cambridge University Press, 1903), p. 58.

91 A. Carnegie, 'The Gospel of Wealth' [1889], reprinted in Carnegie, *Autobiography*, pp. 323–36.

92 A. T. Mahan and C. Beresford, 'Possibilities of an Anglo-American reunion', *North American Review*, 159:456 (1894), pp. 551–73 at p. 555.

93 G. S. Clarke, 'A naval union with Great Britain. A reply to Mr. Andrew Carnegie', *North American Review*, 158:448 (1894), pp. 353–65 at p. 353. Clarke was a senior British military officer and politician. The reference to Stead's 'borderland' concerns his penchant for spiritualism.

94 Carnegie, 'Americanism versus imperialism: II', pp. 364–5. For a valuable survey, see A. Preston, *Sword of the Spirit, Shield of Faith: Religion in American War and Diplomacy* (New York: Random House, 2012), Part 3.

Carl Schmitt and the American century

This chapter offers an exegesis of the US foreign policy narrative nested in the political thought of the German jurist Carl Schmitt (1888–1985). Along with his friend Martin Heidegger (1889–1976), Schmitt is one of the most controversial thinkers of the twentieth century. His career as a legal theorist and public intellectual defies the sort of short, snappy introduction that has come to be expected of academic writers in our contemporary publishing culture. So let me instead begin by stating the obvious.

Unlike most of the other intellectuals discussed in this volume, Schmitt never had any insider's understanding of the US foreign policy-making process. Schmitt experienced US foreign policy at the receiving end. After being arrested and then released by the Red Army in Berlin in April 1945, he was arrested again by the Americans at the end of September and detained in various camps as a potential defendant for participation in a 'conspiracy to wage aggressive war' at the proceedings of the Nuremberg International Military Tribunal. According to one of his political biographers, 'the decision to interrogate him at Nuremberg was largely due to the infamous reputation he had acquired abroad … as the "Crown Jurist" of the Third Reich and the theorist of Nazi expansionism'.[1] Schmitt owed this mythical reputation in part to Frankfurt School intellectuals Franz Neumann, Otto Kirchheimer and Herbert Marcuse, who fled the Nazi regime during the interwar period and found refuge in the United States. During the war, the Research and Analysis Branch of the US Office of Strategic Services (a precursor to the CIA) recruited the three Marxist scholars to help them understand the Nazi state.[2] After the war, Neumann became Chief of Research for Justice Robert H. Jackson, the chief prosecutor for the United States at Nuremberg. He personally made sure that Schmitt was detained, and that he was confronted by his friend and colleague in charge of the interrogations for the Americans, the German-born Jewish American lawyer Robert Kempner.

Being the vain and opportunist scholar that he was, Schmitt made no effort at downplaying the significance that his work had had on German intellectual debates since the 1920s. But he dismissed all suggestions that he had any close direct contact with those within the Nazi executives who planned and conducted the war. As he wrote in his reply to Kempner and his team:

> This is no place to expand upon the general situation of a university professor in a totalitarian system. Enough to say here that it was impossible for a chair in jurisprudence to be regarded as a decisive position or as a basis for exercising a decisive influence at decisive points in Hitler's totalitarian system, given its prevailing conception of science, education and jurisprudence … Theories and ideas do have influence, but this influence is not traceable to 'decisive points'.[3]

Schmitt never stood trial. But although he did indeed have nothing to do with the planning of the war, we know for a fact that the professor's involvement with the Nazis went well beyond the abstractions of academic debates. Schmitt joined the Nazi Party in 1933 and remained a member until the very end. Under the patronage of Herman Göring and Hans Frank, he was appointed to the Prussian State Council and became Director of the Berlin Faculty branch of the National Socialist Lawyers' Association (NSLA), where he also received a professorship. In June 1934 Schmitt was also appointed editor-in-chief of the Nazi news organ for lawyers, the *Deutsche Juristen-Zeitung*. In these different roles he assisted with the drafting of Nazi legislation, contributed to the handling of various legal-administrative questions and defended the extra-judicial executions of Hitler's political rivals within the Nazi movement.[4]

Then when he began to lose influence after his denunciation for lack of ideological convictions by SS fanatics in 1936, Schmitt made a series of pathetic public interventions designed to draw attention to his commitment to anti-Semitism and official Nazi philosophy. His anxieties during this period can be read between the lines of his 1938 *The Leviathan in the State Theory of Thomas Hobbes: Meaning and Failure of a Political Symbol*. After the war Schmitt even claimed that the book was a form of esoteric resistance in which he used the Englishman as a mouthpiece to express his own subdued disappointment with Nazi orthodoxy.[5] There is probably some truth in this. After all, Schmitt's Weimar writings always had more affinities with the fascist tradition exemplified by Maurras, Gentile, Mussolini and Franco than with the racially based totalitarianism of German National Socialism.[6] But this is precisely the point. To the extent that his political and legal theory differed or deviated from official Nazi doctrines, there never was anything in there that could have served as a significant bulwark against a racist, totalitarian Nazi appropriation.[7]

But this does not really go to the bottom of things. For along with the reactionary tirades and revolting anti-Semitic tracts, Schmitt is also the author of some of the most thought-provoking legal and political treatises written in the twentieth century. After being banned from post-war academic life, Schmitt went on to live a secluded life in his native town of Plettenberg. From there, he became a key background figure in the intellectual debates of the Federal German Republic, and he published a number of important studies on various subjects including political theology, asymmetrical warfare and the emerging Cold War order. By far the most significant of these is his *The Nomos of the Earth in the International Law of the Jus Publicum Europaeum*, which he wrote in the early 1940s but was only allowed to publish in 1950.[8] In contemporary discourse, the Greek term *nomos* is usually translated as 'law', 'norm' or 'regulation'. But Schmitt uses it in its original spatial meaning to designate the concrete division and redistribution of the earth that grounds public and international law in any historical period. Although certainly not without its suspicious omissions and analytical shortcomings, Schmitt's *Nomos* is an erudite account of the rise and fall of the modern Eurocentric global order, which concludes with a deeply critical analysis of the prospects for a new world order grounded in American power.

For obvious reasons, Schmitt's *Nomos* was largely ignored in the Anglo-Saxon world during the entire duration of the Cold War. However, the collapse of communism and the subsequent terrorist attacks of 11 September 2001 have breathed new life into his analyses, generating an important new wave of secondary literature and translations of his works into English.[9] Along the way, observers have also identified important affinities between Schmitt's critique of liberalism and the confrontational style of 'friend and enemy' politics pursued by the American Right at home and abroad since the late 1960s. This controversial issue of lineage is to do mainly with the influence exercised by conservative European immigrants and German Jewish refugees such as Joseph Schumpeter, Friedrich von Hayek and Leo Strauss, who in all sorts of complex and mediated ways acted as an intellectual 'transmission belt' between the authoritarian milieu of interwar Europe and neoconservative critiques of the liberal state.[10]

Within the discipline of international relations, intellectual historians have also drawn attention to the important formative influence that Schmitt exercised on the young Hans Morgenthau before the latter sought refuge in America and became the leading figure of the post-war realist tradition.[11] The continuity of Schmitt's subterranean presence in realist circles since the 1970s has been ensured by George D. Schwab, the American foreign policy expert of Latvian-Jewish descent with whom Morgenthau founded the National Committee on American Foreign Policy (NCAFP) in

1974. The NCAFP is a centre-right think tank dedicated to the advancement of American foreign policy interests 'from a nonpartisan perspective within the framework of political realism'.[12] Schwab has been the president since the early 1990s. In his functions as the English-language executor of the Schmitt Estate, he has translated three of Schmitt's most important works, and he published the first overview of his political philosophy in the English-speaking world in 1970.[13] Since the late 1980s Schwab has also been instrumental in the intriguing transformation of Paul Piccone's influential academic journal *Telos* from a New Left vehicle for the dissemination of Frankfurt School Critical Theory in the United States into an outlet for forgotten or repressed critics of mainstream liberalism on both sides of the political spectrum – Schmitt being the most significant of them. Incidentally, the other prominent Schmitt scholar who contributed to this transformation is the leading 'paleoconservative' intellectual historian of American conservatism Paul Gottfried. Gottfried was a close friend of Richard Nixon and a long-time political adviser to Pat Buchanan, and has been a critic of the Republican establishment.

In what follows, I reconstruct Schmitt's interpretation of US foreign policy with an eye to this ambivalence structuring the reception of his legacy in the English-speaking world. The analysis draws particular attention to the philosophical prisms through which Schmitt came to conceptualise the relationship between technology, political violence and universal 'values' during the second half of the twentieth century. Although this is a somewhat more sinuous path to Schmitt's international political thought, it provides us with an understanding of his antagonism towards America that goes beyond the atavistic nostalgia of his own politics, and generates apposite insights into the webs of confused categories concerning war, space and historical time hardwired in the normative fabric of the 'American century'.

Of states, wars and sea monsters

Our main point of entry into Schmitt's reading of American foreign policy is the aforementioned 1938 book on Hobbes. For although America is rarely ever mentioned in it, much of the conceptual framework that Schmitt brings to bear on his analyses of US foreign policy in subsequent studies is laid out here in his discussion of Hobbesian political theory.

As the title suggests, *The Leviathan in the State Theory of Thomas Hobbes: Meaning and Failure of a Political Symbol* is a critical assessment of the achievements and failures of Hobbesian political theory from the 'not so contextual' perspective of the turbulent 1930s. In the first instance, the book presents Hobbes's *Leviathan* as the most creative and influential justification of the absolutist political order that prevailed between the mid-seventeenth century and the nineteenth century – the so-called *Jus Publicum Europaeum*. In ideal typical form, the *Jus Publicum Europaeum* was a reorganisation of European public space into two clearly separated domains: a domain of political authority reserved for the sovereign and governed by the principle of *raison d'état*, and a subordinate domain of apolitical subjects where culture, morality and commerce developed according to their own immanent principles. As a symbolic representation of this European order, Schmitt argues that Hobbes's *Leviathan* 'achieved its highest degree of mythical force' by ensuring the preservation of an external space where sovereign states could affirm their 'force and vitality' against one another, and remind their subjects of the 'reasons' why the state was created in the first place.[14] The absorption of all rationality and legality by the absolutist state meant that those who faced one another as enemies no longer did so as religious foes, but as states and according to the secular dictates of *raison d'état*: 'Wars become pure wars between states.' It follows from this that one could no longer talk of just and unjust wars between states since the juridical categories of the system of international law no longer took their bearing from a transcendent theology, but from the concept of the state and its immanent ethics of *raison d'état*: '*Ordo hoc non includit*. The state has its order in, not outside, itself.'[15]

Schmitt considers this de-moralisation of warfare as one of the great humanising achievements of the age of absolutism. This is because war fighting took place on the basis of a clear distinction between civilians and combatants, and combat was operationalised on the basis of a strict hierarchical chain of command. Wars had to be lawfully declared; and they could be ended with formal peace treaties because their aims were of limited and primarily material character. To be sure, none of this applied in the Americas or anywhere beyond the European continent, where European powers showed little restraint towards non-white civilian populations and in their conflicts with one another. And even within Europe, the ideal of 'bracketed warfare' as a gentlemanly duel was just that – that is, an ideal that was routinely ignored and violated. But what fascinated Schmitt was that this ideal of limited, regulated warfare was upheld in the first place.

And yet, Schmitt argues that it is precisely the absence of a genuinely transcendent political theology in the Hobbesian concept of the state that would eventually lead to the decline of the absolutist order.[16] The crux of the argument is that Hobbes's *Leviathan* owes its demise to the strict separation between morality proper and the self-referential ethics of the state upon which it was erected. Under the doctrine of *raison d'état*, the absolutist state took leave from traditional moral norms and subordinated all religious and rational claims of individual morality to political necessity. But in doing so, it created a foothold for the emergence of a private realm autonomous from the state where a well-financed and intellectually influent civil society would grow and acquire a monopoly on 'morality proper'. Because Hobbes considered freedom from politics to be the ultimate moral good, he could not have conceived that the emergence of a bourgeois civil society could be a potential political threat to the state. Yet it is precisely this moral rejection of politics that established a comfortable critical vantage point from which the immoral substance of the absolutist order would eventually be brought into question by a civil society emancipated from the state of nature. For as the secularising process continued to unfold in the seventeenth, eighteenth and nineteenth centuries, the new bourgeois public sphere progressively turned its attention away from religion and began to exercise its critical spirit on earthly matters. It slowly extended itself into politics through legal criticism enunciated from within the realm of government, until it eventually turned against the state itself.

Schmitt argues that Hobbes's *Leviathan* fell short of serving its ordering function because its mythical element failed to establish a clear political distinction between 'us and them' and 'friend and enemy', which transcends the public–private distinction and cultivates the cultural homogeneity of the political community. Schmitt's suggestion here is that the heterogeneous elements of 'society' could only be maintained as long as the 'civil society versus state' line of enmity existed. When this strict opposition progressively dissolved, enlightenment criticism failed to reconcile its anti-political morality with the amorality of the political realm. As a mode of social integration, moral critique could not succeed without succumbing to the autonomy and primacy of the political: 'The old adversaries, the "indirect" powers of the church and of interest groups, reappeared in that century as modern political parties, trade unions, social organizations, in a phrase, as "forces of society" ... The institutions and concepts of liberalism became weapons and power positions in the hands of the most illiberal forces.'[17]

But that is not all. According to Schmitt, Hobbes's poor 'mythological sense' had led him to choose a sea monster over the terrestrial monster Behemoth to capture the symbolic essence of his treatise on the sovereign territorial state. Hobbes's confused choice of biblical creature reflected his blindness to the political passage from land to sea that had been in the process of transforming England since the Elizabethan era. As Schmitt points out, the Hobbesian ideal of the state realised itself on the Continent, mainly in France and in Prussia, but never in England: 'The English Isle and its world-conquering seafaring needed no absolute monarchy, no standing land army, no state bureaucracy, no legal system of a law state such as became characteristic of continental states ... the English people withdrew from these kinds of closed states and remained "open".'[18] Those who created the British Empire were privateers (individuals who considered maritime violence a private matter), commercial adventurers, immigrants and other social forces associated with the Puritan revolution, and who found in colonial expansion a means to escape from the hierarchical politics of statehood.

According to Schmitt, this would in great part account for the indirect methods, channels and means by which British sovereignty came to be exercised in the world: Freemasonry, liberal constitutionalism, industrialism and other such consequences and by-products of Britain's de-territorialised relationship to machinery and *techne*. As the earth came to be increasingly envisaged from the perspective of the sea, a 'virtual geography' transmuted itself into a genuine 'political reality' completely antithetical to Continental political and juridical institutions. Unlike the Continental order, which rested on closed delimitated spaces, the sea would remain free and open to commercial and war-making activities. It would 'belong to nobody, or everybody, but in reality, it would belong to a single country: England'.[19] And as Schmitt is keen to point out, these basic spatial premises also generated two antithetical conceptions of warfare and enmity:

> [T]he naval wars were based on the idea of the necessity of treating the enemy's trade and economy as one. Hence the enemy was no longer the opponent in arms alone, but every inhabitant of the enemy nation, and ultimately every neutral country that had economic links with the enemy. Land warfare implied a decisive confrontation in the field. While not excluding naval combat, the maritime war, on the other hand, favored such characteristic means as bombardment, the blockade of the enemy shores, and the capture of enemy and neutral merchantmen in virtue of the right to capture.[20]

Schmitt dates the official disintegration of the *Jus Publicum Europaeum* to the great scramble for Africa and the Congo Conference of 1885. The subsequent Hague Peace Conferences of 1899 and 1907 marked the transition from a Eurocentric world order to one rooted in the spacelessness of an abstract, general universalism. By then, the Industrial Revolution had completely 'transformed the children of the sea into machine-builders and servants of machines'.[21] For Schmitt, however, the end of the British hegemony, the First World War, decolonisation and the establishment of the League of Nations did not so much mark the expansion of the European state system to the rest of the world as its superseding by a new *Großräume* order driven by the rise of American power.

America and the *Großräume* order

Schmitt's concept of *Großräume* refers to the geographical delimitation of a state's special 'sphere of interests', or 'zone of security', extending way

beyond its legal territorial borders. The politics of *Großräume* would therefore be a politics of supranational formations, in which the globe would be
divided among a small number of hegemonic powers seeking to guarantee
the integrity and independence of subordinate states on the basis of their
political homogeneity.[22] Schmitt would come to read the Second World War
in this optic as the first war for the organisation of planetary space, the
meaning and significance of which he did not see in the fight against Soviet
Russia but in the struggle against Great Britain and Roosevelt's America.

Like many analysts at the time, Schmitt understands the dissolution of
the colonial empires to be an implicit motive for the United States' late
entry into the war in December 1941. He traces the intellectual origins of
this grand strategy in the writings of the American Admiral Alfred Thayer
Mahan (1840–1914). In July 1894 Mahan published an article in which he
explored the possibility of a reunification between Great Britain and the
United States. Mahan considered racial, linguistic and cultural commonali-
ties to be important sources of motivations. But for him it was geography
and the need for Anglo-Saxon geopolitical security that provided the primary rationale: 'In the evolving modern world, England had grown too
small.'[23] Just as Disraeli had proposed to displace the seat of the declining
Empire from London to Delhi in the 1840s, Mahan now saw America as 'the
larger island, through which the British mastery of the seas would be per-
petuated as an Anglo-American maritime dominion of the world on a larger
scale'.[24] For the Admiral, the old Continental conception of the 'Western
hemisphere' at the heart of the Monroe Doctrine had run its course. The
time had come to move towards the Pacific and submit vast new spaces to
the new 'open door' policy of the United States.

The originality of Schmitt's analysis lies in the metaphysical significance
that he reads into this betrayal of the Monroe Doctrine. In his 1941 book
Völkerrechtliche Großraumordnung (The Regional Order in International
Law), Schmitt controversially argues that '[t]he 1823 Monroe Doctrine was
in the recent history of international law the first and to date most successful example of a regional [*Großraum*] international law. That is the real
precedent for the German Reich.'[25] Originally formulated by John Quincy
Adams (1767–1848), the Monroe Doctrine stipulated that no more colonisation and extension of the European system would be allowed anywhere
in the Western hemisphere. In the guise of reciprocity, the United States
would not interfere with the existing European colonies in the New World
or with the internal affairs of European nations.[26] The Monroe doctrine
thus established the basis of a world based on two geopolitical 'spheres of
influence' transcending existing regimes of state sovereignty. It also affirmed
the Western hemisphere as a US regime of freedom, justice, peace, virtue and
self-determination against the old and morally corrupt order of European

absolutism. According to Schmitt, the goal of this negative identification with the 'old occident' was not to fragment or 'dethrone' the idea of the occident as such, but to take its place as the main 'axis of world history and centre of the world'.[27] Through this expansionist act of geopolitical isolation, the Monroe Doctrine limited European presence in the Western hemisphere and preserved the independence to act unilaterally, conquer and settle the remaining parts of the West.

In light of the parliamentary corruption and degeneracy of European absolutism during the eighteenth century, and given the servile character of the post-Napoleonic reaction and restoration during the nineteenth century, America appeared to stand a real chance of becoming the more authentic representative of the European ideal. As Schmitt points out, after the bourgeois revolutions of 1848, thousands of disillusioned intellectuals and political activists fled the old reactionary Continent and immigrated to America in the hope of finding a more receptive audience for their transformative visions.[28] In concrete geopolitical terms, however, the pronouncement of the Monroe Doctrine in 1823 was of limited significance. For the United States neither had the navy nor the military power to enforce such an ambitious policy pronouncement. It went relatively unnoticed abroad for the best part of the nineteenth century, and was randomly violated by European powers on several occasions. By the time America had acquired the maritime capability to enforce its declared *Großräume* at the beginning of the twentieth century, optimistic beliefs about the novelty, liberty and possibilities of the Western hemisphere had all but completely disappeared.

In line with contemporary Marxist theories, Schmitt argues that the opening of new imperialist horizons towards Asia under Roosevelt was inexorably linked to a domestic contraction of economic opportunities. Schmitt invokes John Dewey's appropriation of Frederick Jackson Turner's famous 'frontier thesis'.[29] The frontier thesis argued that many of the dominant attributes of American culture such as individualism, democracy and civic nationalism had been made possible by and depended on westward expansion across the American continent.[30] The early success and wide appeal of American democracy was predicated on the abundant availability of cheap agricultural land, and on the interpretation of democratic freedom as the freedom to own and accumulate property unimpaired by government. This allowed for a relatively high level of social mobility, which in turn strengthened the belief that individual effort leads to individual achievement. It also helped to account for the perception of a situation of relatively widespread economic equality in the United States compared to Europe during the eighteenth and nineteenth centuries. But this period came to an end with the closing of the Western frontiers in the early 1890s. America's 'living space' was now limited and could no longer rely on this geographical safety valve to guarantee its continued stability and prosperity:

> At this moment, America's *nomos* – that is the foundations of all social and legal relations – changed completely ... More rapidly than anyone could have anticipated, the new Europe was transformed into a vulgar and enlarged image of the old one. The social question, problems of demographics, race, unemployment and political freedoms all presented themselves as in Europe but on a much larger scale and with ten times the intensity.[31]

Although there was relatively little disagreement within the economic and political elites that expansion was necessary, this expansion had to be formulated in ways that did not offend the cultural tradition of liberty, self-determination and progress so central to discourses of American identity. Roosevelt did this by 'exploiting the Monroe Doctrine and using it as a pretext to promote a particularly rude form of liberal capitalist "dollar diplomacy"'.[32] Roosevelt's dollar diplomacy was anchored in a broader foreign policy vision characterised by an unstable mixture of progressive and social-Darwinian concerns over the debilitating consequences of mass consumerism on American society.[33] These tensions found expression in his exaltation of martial virtues and his belief that America had an obligation to use its growing military and industrial capability to develop and modernise the 'wasted spaces' of the earth in the interest of humanity as a whole. As he told a crowd in a famous speech shortly after his inauguration: 'Chronic wrongdoing may in America, as elsewhere, ultimately require intervention by some civilized nation, and in the Western Hemisphere the adherence of the United States to the Monroe Doctrine may force the United States, however reluctantly, in flagrant cases of such wrongdoing or impotence, to the exercise of an international police power'.[34]

According to Schmitt, the 'Roosevelt corollary' to the Monroe Doctrine rested on a dual conflation of practices that had very significant implications for the exercise of American foreign policy in the twentieth century. The first concerns the merging of two sets of political commitments that are both geographically and normatively antithetical to one another. Whereas the Monroe Doctrine is based on an authentic notion of space implying concrete limitations, dollar diplomacy has nothing but contempt for spatial boundaries:

> The sanctified tradition of always being the country of free land is underpinned by a consequent isolationism. Yet the imperial reality of economic ambitions in world commerce calls for unlimited universal intervention. The traditional separation of commerce from politics – as much commerce as possible and as little politics as possible – has lost its inner truth because, in the long run, there cannot be any world commerce without world politics.[35]

What is really important for Schmitt in these developments is the shift in the ethico-political disposition that characterises America's act of self-isolation from the rest of the world. Many other peoples, states and empires have in the past sought to draw defensive geopolitical lines to quarantine themselves from external contaminations. Schmitt draws attention to the Great Wall of China and the Pillars of Hercules flanking the entrance to the Straight of Gibraltar as examples of such symbolic frontiers. What is different with the Roosevelt corollary is that the defensive and spatially demarcated line of self-retrenchment constitutive of the Monroe Doctrine mutates into its opposite – that is a spaceless offensive line of discrimination against the rest of the world that demands integration and adherence to a substantively prescribed normative order.[36]

Wilsonian liberal internationalism, with its encouragement to 'all the peoples of the world' to adopt the right to self-determination, was a logical extension of the Roosevelt corollary. This was followed by the Stimson Doctrine of 1932, which reiterated America's right to deny recognition to any state or government anywhere in the world that did not come to power through 'legitimate' means. It did so, for example, by maintaining the convention of recognising not states but only governments considered 'lawful' according to the United States' own understanding of legality. The Stimson doctrine was pronounced on the juridical basis of the Kellog–Briand Pact of 1928 and the covenant of the League of Nations. In this same discriminatory spirit, the League not only appropriated the universal right to determine which sides of a conflict were 'just and unjust', but also claimed the authority to impose this decision on all neutral parties. The move was facilitated by a discursive rearticulation of interstate conflicts in terms of a series of oppositions between the League's 'pacifying interventions' and the 'crimes' and 'terrorism' of its opponents. And because no one can remain neutral in the face of terror and crime, the League effectively transformed the pacific concept of neutrality into a concept of war.[37]

This is the other main source of Schmitt's resentment against American foreign policy. For the jurist, 'police' refers to the legitimate use of force by the sovereign state to secure domestic order. It must not be conflated with the activity of warfare occurring strictly between sovereigns: 'War in this system of international law is a relationship of one order to another order, and not from order to disorder. This relationship of order to disorder is "civil war".'[38] Schmitt traces the origins of this criminalisation of war to the American entry into the Second World War. In *Nomos*, he quotes specifically from the 31 March 1941 proclamation of Justice Jackson, the then US attorney general, who explicitly confirmed the change from an older understanding of war to a new order where aggression would be punished.[39] Schmitt sees important parallels between these developments and the theological just war tradition that had been abandoned with the emergence of the *Jus Publicum Europaeum*.[40] Yet against the opinion of the American jurist James Brown Scott, he insists that the emergence of this new discriminatory conception of war should be seen as a completely new ideological phenomenon associated with the industrial-technological development of late-modern means of destruction:

> This is not the 'just' war of Middle Ages theologians, of which spoke Vittoria and, under his influence, Grotius and the internationalists of the seventeenth and eighteenth centuries. This attempt at eliminating one's political adversary by portraying him as a criminal and the ultimate obstacle to world peace is radically new because it embraces the whole world ... By claiming not only the right to defend itself against a political adversary, but also the right to disqualify and slander this adversary from the point of view of international law, Washington intends to introduce humanity to a new type of war in international law. For the first time in history, war is a global world war.[41]

Nuremberg and the tragic limits of international law

What should we make of these claims? As various commentators have pointed out, the obvious problem with Schmitt's narrative is that it suggests that it was the United States who unilaterally transgressed and discredited classical doctrines of war, diplomacy and international law by declaring war on Germany in 1941. By emphasising the moralisation of the political at the heart of America's discourse on war, and associating it with changes in technologies of warfare, Schmitt implicitly normalises Hitler's genocidal war in Europe as a classic conflict of 'reason of state' fought between *Großräume*. It is almost as if the war of extermination fought by the Nazis and the *Wehrmacht* had nothing to do with America's appropriation of the just war paradigm as a framework to address these atrocities.[42]

This seriously undermines the analytical credibility and ethical status of Schmitt's critique. Yet it is important that we do not reduce our assessment of Schmitt's enterprise to this apparent normalisation of Nazi atrocities, lest we fail to understand the nuances, ambiguities and continued significance of his analyses despite their dubious motivations and conclusions. Further insights can be gleaned from Schmitt's reflections on the Nuremberg trials.

Here again, Schmitt seems a lot more anxious to debunk the Allies' justifications of the Nuremberg criminalisation of warfare than he is with acknowledging the 'rights' of the victims of Nazi atrocities. Whenever he refers to the participation of the *Wehrmacht* in the mass killings of civilians and the Holocaust, he primarily does it to draw a distinction between the undeniable guilt of the German high command and the much more ambiguous responsibility of 'ordinary Germans' who were only indirectly or passively involved. According to Schmitt, international law could not possibly expect civilians to make their own judgement on 'just' and 'unjust' wars and commit treason against their own country simply by fear of being prosecuted for complicity in war crimes.[43] For those who contemplated treason or resistance against their own state at the time had absolutely no legal reason to expect significant protection from international institutions. Non-resistance to the Nazi leviathan may well have been cowardly, but it was certainly not the same as collaboration and could hardly be treated as an aggressive crime. If Nazi Germany was condemned for walking over the 1907 Hague Convention on the laws of war, then the victors also had to comply with the terms of the said Convention, which they were enforcing.[44]

As Schmitt saw it, the fundamental problem with Nuremberg was that the trials had been instituted so as to exclude the possibility of ascribing responsibility for the causes of the war, and to criminalise the 'aggression' as such. This amounted to a politically motivated depoliticisation of legalism that would have serious debilitating consequences for the future credibility of international law.[45] Although Schmitt denied all legal plausibility to the Allies' accusations concerning Germany's war motivations and responsibility, he agreed unreservedly that Germany had to be punished for the Holocaust and traditional crimes of war. But while traditional war crimes could be dealt with under the existing laws of war, he insisted that the violence of the Holocaust exceeded the scope of existing categories of positive public and international law. Instead, Schmitt argued that the atrocities committed by Hitler's regime were so overwhelmingly extreme that SS and Gestapo high commands had to be brought before a tribunal to be condemned and punished very publicly on a moral rather than a juridical basis: 'There are problems for which Themis has no scale ... The problem at Nuremberg was not to do with law as such, but with the limits of what men have a right to affirm as a right by means of a trial.'[46]

Schmitt sensed Justice Jackson's unease concerning the juridical process over which he presided. For when establishing collective responsibility for such large-scale atrocities, no one can rest satisfied with the fact that the victors simply dictate their laws to the defeated. Schmitt understood the situation as a radical expression of the liminal dilemmas of the German idealist tradition. If it is the case that the victors dictate their laws to the defeated, and if the defeated simply accept this dictate submissively, then relations between victors and the defeated are nothing but meaningless relations of factual material power. On the other hand, if one is serious about the ideals invested in a given conflict, one must submit to the potentially suicidal either/or a priori logic inherent to all ideals, lest one abandons these ideals to a nihilistic, positivistic neutralism. While recognising German guilt, Schmitt constructed this guilt against the tragedy of the human condition.

He saw this tragic sense of life as a characteristic feature of the German self-understanding, and something from which one could derive a certain right to political 'error' that was a lot more human than the self-aggrandising human rights discourse of his accusers:

> Empedocles' death, his heroic descent into the solar fire of the earth, and the releasing of atomic energy (that is to say unconstrained solar energy), these are one and the same thing. This is enlightenment philosophy, or the philosophy of the German spirit. It is in its name that the world conducts against us, we who anticipated this disaster, an idiotic war morally just.[47]

In sum, unlike what Jürgen Habermas has argued in an influential critique of his right-wing compatriot, Schmitt's position is not that there exist no legitimate elements of normative universalism in world politics that can serve as a basis for social and moral criticism.[48] On the contrary, the problem is that there is too much of it. Because no one can 'know' with certainty what these universals are and how they should guide collective action, political communities will consciously or unconsciously mobilise universal moral tropes for their own particular political purposes. Given the legal difficulties associated with the lack of clear definition, sanctions and organisational means of enforcement in international relations, Schmitt believed that the procedural rationalism of the *Jus Publicum Europaeum* constituted a better source of restraint against the tendency of substantive philosophical universalisms to degenerate into parochial irrationalism.

Technology and the Cold War

Schmitt's claim that America's rendition of the just war tradition expresses a new ideological phenomenon attending to the technological development of contemporary means of violence must be read in the context of this distinctively German strain of political realism. Always implicit but never clearly stated in his polemics, the full force of Schmitt's thesis rides on the critique of technology that he developed during and after the First World War, and which spurred an important three-way exchange with his friends Martin Heidegger and Ernst Jünger during the 1920s and 1930s.[49]

Without going into the specific terms of agreement and disagreement of this exchange, the main thesis common to all three authors is that the seemingly neutral and soulless character of *techne* and mechanics is in fact driven by an anthropocentric metaphysics of control, production and distribution/redistribution that is rife with violence and antagonistic potential. This diagnosis hinges on the claim that technology is not only about material artefacts such as transportation, computing and communication 'systems' and 'machineries'. More fundamentally, it is a way of thinking in which humanity itself becomes absorbed as a source of supplies into the technical web of valuation, calculation and exchange that is the world as resource for exploitation, management and manipulation. Jünger gives the definitive statement in his famous interwar essay 'Total Mobilization':

> The era of the well-aimed shot is already behind us. Giving out the night-flight bombing order, the squadron leader no longer sees a difference between combatants and civilians, and the deadly gas cloud hovers like an elementary power over everything that lives. But the possibility of such menace is based neither on a partial nor general, but rather a *total* mobilization. It extends to the child in the cradle, who is threatened like everyone else even more so.

> It suffices simply to consider our daily life, with its inexorability and merciless discipline, its smoking, glowing districts, the physics and metaphysics of its commerce, its motors, airplanes, and burgeoning cities. With a pleasure-tinged horror, we sense that here, not a single atom is not in motion – that we are profoundly inscribed in this raging process. Total Mobilization is far less consummated than it consummates itself; in war and peace, it expresses the secret and inexorable claim to which our life in the age of masses and machines subjects us.[50]

Shortly after the American landing in North Africa in November 1942, Jünger wrote in his diary that the violence and animosity of the Second World War was a lot more intense than what he had experienced in the trenches during the First World War. Whereas the First World War was fought over the metaphysics of the European nation-state, the Second World War felt more like a 'universal civil war' (*Weltbürgerkrieg*).[51] Schmitt had developed the notion of universal civil war a few years earlier.[52] In the conservative literature during the Cold War period, the term universal civil war would often be used to discredit revolutionary hopes and activities, suggesting that the latter could never achieve their unrealistic aims and instead only fomented the prospects of endless violence.[53] But for Schmitt, as for Jünger at the time, what also gave the Second World War the apparent quality of a universal civil war was the fact that it stemmed from conflicts between imperial powers that had been forced by increasing interdependence to preside 'together' in a supranational institution over the dissolving of the Westphalian system of sovereign states into one single post-national normative order. As in civil war, what was at stake in the struggle between the mass ideologies of fascism, Bolshevism and liberalism was the nature of the social bond that would unite this emerging supranational polity. And because in an undivided polity only one party can hold a monopoly on legitimate violence, the defeated party must either be completely subdued or destroyed. This inevitably raised the stakes of the conflict as it implicitly ruled out the possibility of any compromise that might have allowed for the continued coexistence of the warring factions.[54] As Schmitt explains in *Nomos*:

> Civil War has something gruesome about it. It is fraternal war, because it is pursued within a common political unity that includes also the opponent, and within the same legal order, and because both belligerent sides absolutely and simultaneously affirm and negate this common unity. Both consider their opponent to be absolutely and unconditionally wrong. Both reject the right of the opponent, but in the name of the law. Civil war is subject essentially to the jurisdiction of the enemy. Thus, civil war has a narrow, specifically dialectical relation to law. It cannot be anything other than *just* in the sense of being self-righteous, and on this basis becomes the prototype of just and self-righteous war.[55]

Roosevelt's and Churchill's insistence on the 'unconditional surrender' of the Axis Powers at the Casablanca Conference of January 1943 confers a certain plausibly to Schmitt's theses. The most famous early use of the notion of 'unconditional surrender' goes back to the 1862 battle of Fort Donelson in the American Civil War, during which Brigadier General Ulysses S. Grant stated that 'no terms except an unconditional and immediate surrender' of the southern states could be accepted.[56] Like Jünger, Schmitt was perfectly aware of this precedent. What both men would come to realise during the early 1940s is that America's discriminatory war discourse was an ideological offshoot of the totalising way of war developed during the American Civil War of 1861–65. As one historian reminds us, the American Civil War contained practically all of the technological ingredients accounting for the total character of the First and Second World Wars: 'the mobilizations by railroad, the massive armies sent into battle, the automatization of killing resulting from the invention of the machine gun, the ambushes carried out by lurking submarines, the involvement and suffering of the civilian population, above all the fusion of warfare and economic productivity.'[57] Nineteenth-century Europeans were very much aware of these developments. But the significance and implications of this 'New World' phenomenon did not really begin to sink in until the Franco-Prussian War of 1870–71, which effectively ended the strategic culture forged by the Restoration of 1815.[58]

Yet it is important to understand that Schmitt's global civil war discourse is not a claim that geopolitics since the First World War could plausibly be read as a continuous internationalised civil war, as in Ernst Nolte's revisionist history of the twentieth century.[59] Rather, Schmitt mobilises the language of global civil war to highlight the fact that classical conceptual categories of warfare have lost their normative force and explanatory power in the historical period of transition that we have come to associate with 'globalisation'. What Schmitt perceived better than anyone else at the time is that the techno-militarisation woven into the socio-economic and political fabric of American foreign policy was transforming the role of imperial military force. Thanks to the superseding of naval power by air power, force would no longer be deployed to achieve clearly defined expansionist objectives, but for the indefinite objective of policing the globe in the name of abstract ideals and an abstract system of economic exchange that were in the process of stripping humankind of all its concrete ties to the earth:

> My *Nomos of the Earth* is arriving at an appropriate historical juncture. The time is coming (Nietzsche said in 1881–1882) when the struggle for the domination of the earth will be fought; it will be fought in the name of fundamental philosophical doctrines; i.e. an ideological battle for unity. The Kellog Pact is opening a free path; war as a means of rational politics is despised, condemned; war as a means of global domination of the earth is the just war. As Martin Heidegger argues, the world becomes object.[60]

Into the abyss of total devaluation

Schmitt's reference to Nietzsche and Heidegger in the above diary entry from August 1950 announces another important twist that he is about to incorporate into his narrative in the coming decade. This concerns the rhetoric of 'values' that became so central to the ways in which the United States and the USSR articulated their conflict over 'fundamental philosophical doctrines' during the Cold War. The key text here is a relatively unknown treatise that he wrote as a rejoinder to a conference paper given by his friend, the conservative jurist Ernst Forsthoff, on 'Virtue and Value in the Theory of the State' in 1959. Schmitt wrote another version in 1967, which was then reprinted with the original in 1979 as a small book entitled *The Tyranny of Values*.[61] There, Schmitt draws on Heidegger's philosophical critique of values to construct a political critique of values linking back to his earlier discourse on technology and the just war doctrine.

As is widely acknowledged in the specialised literature, the modern language of values began to emerge in the mid-nineteenth century as an attempt to carve a space for freedom and moral responsibility in the face of rapid scientific modernisation. It did this mainly by opposing a realm of ideal valuations based on *Weltanschauungen* (comprehensive worldviews) with an objectivist scientific realm of being in which everything is causally understood.[62] Like most observers during this period, Heidegger reads Nietzsche's revaluation of all values as the definitive hinge between the nineteenth and twentieth centuries in this respect. Although he is in many ways sympathetic to Nietzsche's project, Heidegger argues that Nietzsche's uncritical appropriation of the language of values to confront the European crisis of nihilism had only succeeded in prolonging the agonising decline of the West.[63]

Without going into the fine details of Heidegger's analysis, the main issue is to do with the subjectivism by which values are called into being. Under the sway of modern physics and mathematics, subjectivism conceives of reality as a series of categories that the human subject has deliberately constructed and meaningfully projected onto the world. In doing so, subjectivism 'forgets' that beings always reveal themselves to us as meaningful before we make any value judgements about them: 'In interpreting, we do not, so to speak, throw a "signification" over some naked thing which is present-at-hand, we do not stick a value on it; but when something within-the-world is encountered as such, the thing in question already has an involvement which is disclosed in our understanding of the world, and this involvement is one which gets laid out by the interpretation.'[64]

For Heidegger then, the problem is not to do with whether or not men should prioritise certain normative goods over others (of course they should). Rather, the issue is that by elevating our insight into reality by considering it as 'value-laden', we misconstrue everything that is not human (i.e. nature) in terms of a valueless and static realm of things. In doing so, we deracinate ourselves from Being as a dynamic event of self-emerging presence. As Heidegger explains in his 'Letter on Humanism' (1947), to assign value to something is to rob it of its worth, insofar as 'what is valued is admitted only as an object for man's estimation. But what a thing is in its Being is not exhausted by its being an object, particularly when objectivity takes the form of value. Every valuing, even where it is values positively, is a subjectivising. It does not let beings: be. Rather, valuing lets beings: be valid – solely as the objects of its doing.'[65] And so because the goal of this cognitive process is ultimately to control and use the material universe, subjectivism is not so much the antithesis of scientific objectivism as a more extreme form of nihilistic objectification. It is the very core of a modern scientific worldview in which '[v]alue and what is valuable are turned into a positivistic substitute for the metaphysical.'[66]

Heidegger rarely ever mentions Weber by name in his published writings. But it is obvious that Weber's famous distinction between scientific observation and subjective valuation based on worldviews is one of the main targets of his invectives against value thinking. Schmitt picks up on this in order to read his own provocative Hobbesian narrative into Weber's *Vocation Lectures*. According to Schmitt, Weberian political sociology constitutes the most insightful demonstration of the latent political violence nested in the elusive ontology of values. What Weber made clear for us is that since values are in fact only acts of valuation based on either tradition or charisma, their psychological and socio-cultural significance is nil unless they are accepted by others: 'Value must continuously valuate, that is to say, it must bring its influence to bear: otherwise it dissolves into an empty manifestation.'[67]

For Schmitt then, the issue is not only that values presuppose an endless possibility of self-referential appraising positions: standpoint, viewpoint, vantage point, starting point and so on. More fundamentally, it is that this pluralism is constantly abstracted and reabstracted from the empirically determined position of individuals who, in reality, cannot valuate without simultaneously devaluating in accordance with their own perceived interests: 'Whoever sets a value, takes position against a disvalue by that very action. The boundless tolerance and the neutrality of the standpoints and viewpoints turn themselves very quickly into their opposite, into enmity, as soon as the enforcement is carried out in earnest. The valuation pressure of the value is irresistible.'[68] According to Schmitt, this is why Weber's famous distinction between an ethics of responsibility (in which the political actor is primarily concerned with costs and takes personal responsibility for the 'foreseeable results' of his action) and an ethics of conviction (in which the political actor pursues certain ends or ideals, regardless of the cost) had proven to be completely untenable in the technological context of the twentieth century:

> [T]he absolute value-freedom of scientific positivism is circumvented, and values are set free from it, in the opposite direction, namely, of the subjective world outlook. The genuinely subjective freedom of value-setting leads, however, to an endless struggle of all against all, to an endless *bellum omnium contra omnes*. In such circumstances, the very presuppositions about a ruthless human nature on which Thomas Hobbes' philosophy of the state rests, seem quite idyllic by comparison. The old gods rise from their graves and fight their old battles on and on, but disenchanted and, as we today must add, with new fighting means that are no longer weapons, but rather abominable instruments of annihilation and processes of extermination, horrible products of value-free science and of the technology and industrial production that follow suit.[69]

The reader perhaps sees where this is going. Because values are a form of secularised religious commitments but without the ontological clarity of theology, Schmitt argues that the techno-liberal resurrection of the just war tradition in the guise of values has rendered ideological conflicts 'more ghostlike and the fighters more dogmatic' than they ever were in the past. For if the abstract pluralism of values is inherently prone to degenerate into concrete relations of enmity, just war campaigns are inherently prone to degenerate into relations of total enmity: 'That lies in the nature of the thing itself. All respect for the opponent disappears – well, it turns into a disvalue – whenever the struggle against the opponent is a struggle for the highest value. Disvalue has no rights over value, and there is no price too high to pay in order to force the highest value through.' In this setting, all mediating criteria of both *jus ad bellum* and *jus in bello* fall 'hopelessly victim to this valuelessness. The urge to make values prevail becomes a coercion to enact values directly.'[70]

Schmitt saw post-Second World War America as the main symbol and vehicle of the techno-nihilism of values afflicting Western civilisation. Like Heidegger, he associated the scope, pace and intensity of the Cold War with the spaceless, ahistorical character of American narratives of identity.[71] While insisting on the analogous uses and misuses that the two superpowers made of international legality in the name of humanity as a whole, Schmitt saw that the revolutionary character of American universals differed significantly from the universals of both the French and Bolshevik Revolutions. Whereas the Continental revolutions were driven by a historical *telos* rooted in a pre-existing political order that needed to be transformed, America invented a new order out of itself. The United States certainly possessed a chronicle of past events. But as an order of human and civil rights America had neither history nor ties to any spatial order. It was the ultimate utopia – literally, a 'no place'. Schmitt's point, of course, was that in reality the American utopia was just like any other legal-normative order, underpinned by an original act of land appropriation, division and redistribution. Its projection onto the rest of the world after the Second World War was a reflection of this reality – a continuation of the logic of land and sea appropriation underpinning the Monroe Doctrine in the guise of industrial appropriation:

> If you ask me what is the present *nomos* of the earth, I will answer without hesitation: it is the division and redistribution of the earth into industrially developed regions and underdeveloped regions, knowing that we must ask ourselves who offers development aid to whom and who accepts it from whom … It has its primary official source in article 4 of the Truman Doctrine expounded on 20 January 1949, which explicitly institutes this division while solemnly proclaiming that the industrial development of the earth is the plan and the goal of the United States.[72]

As for Soviet Russia, Schmitt believed that the alleged internationalism of the Eastern Bloc had never been anything else than a schizophrenic form of Soviet nationalism. On the one hand, this nationalism could only legitimise itself at home and abroad by virtue of its professed revolutionary enmity towards the liberal bourgeois values of the West. On the other hand, concrete differentials of power meant that Soviet foreign policy was factually driven by anxious efforts to find grounds for accommodation with the United States. The aim was to share the governance of this emerging liberal international order through the principle of 'spheres of influence'. This was not exactly the *Entente Cordiale*. But it was enough to prompt Stalin to intervene to prevent the success of communist revolutions in Greece and in Spain, and to sign a treaty of friendship with the anti-communist regime of Chiang Kai-shek. The Tito–Stalin and Sino-Soviet splits, as well as the indecisive character and outcome of the Berlin Crisis and the Korean War, were all manifestations of this pseudo-universalism. Although the genuine risk of a global revolutionary civil war had all but completely disappeared, the ideal could still serve as a pressure point in negotiations with the West.[73]

Thus, unlike many other realist analysts of the Cold War at the time, Schmitt did not associate the danger of nuclear annihilation with the security dilemma attending to the anarchical structure of the international state system. As we have seen, Schmitt believed that the legal-conceptual categories presupposed by such reified accounts of international anarchy had become a thing of the past. For him, what had become truly decisive since 1945 was the 'abyss of total devaluation' latent in the cultural fabric of globalising liberal modernity, which along with the disorientation of the theatres of war risked exceeding the rational limitations of the 'belligerent peace' cultivated by superpowers and supranational institutions. The danger here did not reside strictly in the disunity and devaluation intrinsic to the unification sought by the superpowers. It also stemmed from the fact that there would always exist terse powers and elements of resistance beyond the false East–West alternative. Schmitt saw that it was in the very nature of values and the horizontal mode of network governance through which they were instantiated and policed that they would bring back precisely what they purported to transcend: hierarchy, locality and identity. Resistance in this setting would take the form of the 'partisan' defined by his ties to soil, land and indigenous population, and, most of all, by his irregularity and intensity: 'The modern partisan expects neither law nor mercy from the enemy. He has moved away from the conventional enmity of controlled and bracketed war, and into the realm of another, real enmity, which intensifies through terror and counter-terror until it ends in extermination.'[74] As modern relationships of protection and obedience dissolved in the face of new technologies of aerial and nuclear warfare, police action against such 'criminals' and 'pests' would have to be intensified, and so would the justification of the methods used:

> Thus, the ultimate danger exists not even in the present weapons of mass destruction and in a premeditated evil of men, but rather in the inescapability of a moral compulsion. Men who use these weapons against other men feel compelled morally to destroy these other men, i.e., as offerings and objects. They must declare their opponents to be totally criminal and inhuman, to be a total non-value. Otherwise, they are nothing more than criminals and brutes. The logic of value and non-value reaches its full destructive consequence, and creates ever newer, ever deeper discriminations, criminalizations, and devaluations, until all non-valuable life has been destroyed.[75]

Conclusion: Schmitt and the contemporary American right

We do not have to agree with Schmitt's nostalgic assessment of the *Jus Publicum Europaeum* to appreciate the foresight and conceptual fecundity of his analyses. When he wrote his treatises on values and partisan warfare in the late 1950s/early 1960s, the Algerian War, the Vietnam War and the Portuguese Colonial War were in full swing, and the cultural revolutions were just about to kick off. In the United States this would lead to the collapse of the Cold War liberal consensus, and to the emergence of a whole new breed of 'value conservatism' that would forever change the face of mainstream American politics.[76]

As *The Economist* reported on the eve of the re-election of George W. Bush in 2004, it is in great part due to the steady rise of this so-called 'neo-conservatism' that America has become so exceptional in the extent to which its politics tend to be determined by questions of religious and moral values rather than economics and traditional class politics. To be sure, the American political elites and political system tend to exaggerate the real extent to which these conflicts over values actually divide the polity. Political pundits, journalists and party activists – all share an interest in narratives of division rather than unity: 'The rise in partisanship has gone along with the decline of political competition, as gerrymandered safe seats proliferate and a tiny group of party activists gains growing leverage over the political system.' Yet the reason why this is the case is that those who feel strongly about cultural values are increasingly the only ones motivated enough to play a sustained proactive role in the political arena.[77] And this, of course, was precisely Schmitt's point. For what is much less clear in all this is the ontological and epistemological status of the high moral ground from which neoconservatives condemn the liberal elites that they hold responsible for this unravelling of the American social compact. As Paul Gottfried pointed out, neoconservatives are 'for "values" and against "relativism" while keeping their options open as to which values need defending'.[78]

And yet, if we put the rhetoric of 'values' aside for a moment, there are genuine affinities between our contemporary neoconservative politics and Schmitt's own Weimar critique of liberal democracy. For as in Schmitt, the ultimate aim of this cultural politics is to keep state and society as differentiated as possible so as to prevent issues of socio-economic exclusions and pluralism of interests to enter the realm of democratic politics. Over the past few decades, this has taken the form of various campaigns against multiculturalism, feminism, 'cultural Marxism', cosmopolitanism and other post-national ideologies perceived to be weakening state authority, empowering minorities and undermining the hegemony of the majority culture.

That these politico-cultural reactions exhibit strong tendencies to feed into belligerent foreign policy programmes should not surprise us. The sublimation of domestic challenges through military expeditions and foreign policy grand strategising has been one of the most constant themes in the history of international relations. But what reading Schmitt in this context also highlights for us is the important linkage between these domestic culture wars and the American Right's hostility towards international law. Beyond traditional realist concerns over the inexpediency of multilateral diplomacy and the lack of viable enforcement mechanisms, the Right has a vested interest in opposing the constitutionalisation of the global liberal order simply because the pluralist procedural ethics that underpins the latter reduces the scope for a moralisation of politics outside of positive law. In doing so, international law mines the authority of the ethnocentric universals that are so central to the hegemonic discourse of the majority culture and deprives the Right of its favourite terrain. As we have seen since from around the 1990s, the scope of these sovereigntist discourses go way beyond the alleged 'internationalisation of the domestic legal order' by human rights regime and environmental protocols. It also extends to a whole range of issues concerning the use of force, from the Mine Ban Treaty and Anti-Ballistic Missile Treaty to the authority of the Security Council, the Geneva Conventions and the Convention on Torture to fight terrorism.[79] Apart from their one-sided nature, what is peculiar about these sovereigntist discourses is the fact that their protagonists understand them to be perfectly in line with America's historical role as the main purveyor of universal values to the rest of the world. As Robert Kagan so candidly explained in the aftermath of the American invasion of Iraq: 'By nature, tradition, and ideology, the United States has generally favored the promotion of American liberal principles over the niceties of Westphalian diplomacy. Despite its role in helping to create the UN and draft the UN Charter, the United States has never fully accepted the organisation's legitimacy or the charter's doctrine of sovereign equality.'[80]

It is this disregard for 'European-style' procedural diplomacy that constitutes the main difference between Schmittian internationalism and neoconservative internationalism. Neoconservative discourses link American sovereignty with the self-realisation of a historical community of 'values' by affirming the ethnocentric universals of the majority culture over the formal processes of legality and interests mediation that endow international norms with a minimum of universal validity. As we have seen in the context of the war on terror, this tends to generate a particularly aggressive and totalising form of internationalism that is radically anti-pluralist both inside and outside the state and leaves no possibility for dissent to find any legitimate form of expression. This is a crusading form of conservatism that thrives on the cultivation of otherness and enmity while at the same time seeking to overcome all estrangement from the 'other' by putting enemies beyond the realm of humanity and cultivating contempt for dissenting friends and allies who challenge unmediated expressions of 'American values'.

Barack Obama's use of the defence of the just war tradition when announcing the escalation of the war in Afghanistan in his Nobel peace prize acceptance speech in December 2009 also highlights the continued relevance of Schmitt's analyses beyond the Bush presidencies. To be sure, Schmitt's geopolitical distinction between land and sea has long dissolved into an a-spatial globalisation, in which drones controlled by computer geeks sitting in an Oklahoma basement are used for manhunts in the same mountainous caves that witnessed the Great Game a hundred years before. Civilians in these new conflicts are no longer just suffering wars, but are also fighting them. One could also add that 'partisan' resistance to imperial universals in this globalised order can no longer be understood in terms of its ties to the land and locality. For the transnational network governance structure of most prominent terrorist and 'irregular' organisations these days simply mirror the political order that they seek to negate. Yet none of this seems to have diminished the relevance of the main provocation underlying Schmitt's US foreign policy narrative. And that is the possibility that the barbarian fury of organisations such as Al Qaeda and the Islamic State of Iraq and Syria (ISIS) is not the extrinsic other of the liberal peace forged during the American century, but a constitutive expression of its own nihilistic *telos*.

Notes

1 J. W. Bendersky, 'Carl Schmitt at Nuremberg', *Telos*, 72 (1987), pp. 91–6 at p. 91.
2 F. Neumann, H. Marcuse and O. Kirchheimer, *Secret Reports on Nazi Germany: The Frankfurt School's Contribution to the War Effort*, ed. R. Laudani (Princeton: Princeton University Press, 2013). See also M. Salter, 'Neo-fascist legal theory on trial: An interpretation of Carl Schmitt's defence at Nuremberg from the perspective of Franz Neumann's critical theory of law', *Res Publica*, 5 (1999), pp. 161–93.
3 C. Schmitt, 'Interrogation of Carl Schmitt by Robert Kempner', *Telos*, 72 (1987), pp. 97–129 at p. 128.
4 See J. W. Bendersky, *Carl Schmitt: Theorist for the Reich* (Princeton: Princeton University Press, 2014) and R. Mehring, *Carl Schmitt: A Biography* (Cambridge: Polity Press, 2014).
5 See G. Schwab, 'Introduction' in C. Schmitt, *The Leviathan in the State Theory of Thomas Hobbes: Meaning and Failure of a Political Symbol*, trans. G. Schwab and E. Hilfstein (Westport: Greenwood, 1996 [1938]).
6 For a key statement see C. Schmitt, 'Strong State, Free Economy' in R. Cristi, *Carl Schmitt and Authoritarian Liberalism* (Cardiff: University of Wales, 1998), pp. 212–32.

7 On this see J. McCormick, 'Fear, technology, and the state: Carl Schmitt, Leo Strauss, and the revival of Hobbes in Weimar and National Socialist Germany', *Political Theory*, 22:4 (1994), pp. 619–52; E. Balibar, 'Le Hobbes de Schmitt, le Schmitt de Hobbes', 'Introduction' in C. Schmitt, *Le Léviathan dans la doctrine de l'état de Thomas Hobbes* (Paris: Seuil, 2002).

8 C. Schmitt, *The Nomos of the Earth in the International Law of the Jus Publicum Europaeum*, trans. G. L. Ulmen (New York: Telos Press, 2006 [1950]).

9 For an important early engagement see G. Ulmen, 'American imperialism and international law: Carl Schmitt on the US in world affairs', *Telos*, 72 (1987), pp. 43–71. For an overview of the rapidly expanding literature in English see L. Odysseos and F. Pettio (eds), *The International Political Thought of Carl Schmitt: Terror, Liberal War and the Crisis of Global Order* (London: Routledge, 2007). For a rigorous Marxist critique see B. Teschke, 'Fatal attraction: a critique of Carl Schmitt's international political and legal theory', *International Theory*, 3:2 (2011), pp. 179–227.

10 W. Scheuerman, *Carl Schmitt: The End of Law* (New York: Rowman & Littlefield, 1999), pp. 183–208, 209–24; H. Meier, *Carl Schmitt and Leo Strauss: The Hidden Dialogue* (Chicago: Chicago University Press, 1995); J. F. Drolet, *American Neoconservatism: The Politics and Culture of a Reactionary Idealism* (New York: Columbia University Press, 2011).

11 H. J. Morgenthau, *The Concept of the Political*, eds H. Behr and F. Rosch (London: Palgrave, 2012); C. Frei, *Hans J. Morgenthau, An Intellectual Biography* (Baton Rouge: Louisiana University Press, 2001); M. Koskenniemi, *The Gentle Civilizer of Nations* (Cambridge: Cambridge University Press, 2010), pp. 413–509; Scheuerman, *Carl Schmitt: The End of Law*, pp. 225–52.

12 See www.ncafp.org/about-us/our-mission/ (accessed 7 April 2014).

13 G. Schwab, *The Challenge of the Exception: An Introduction to the Political Ideas of Carl Schmitt 1921–1936* (New York: Praeger, 1989 [1970]).

14 Schmitt, *The Leviathan in the State Theory of Thomas Hobbes*, pp. 48–9.

15 *Ibid.*, pp. 47–8.

16 *Ibid.*, pp. 33–4.

17 *Ibid.*, pp. 73–4.

18 *Ibid.*, p. 80.

19 C. Schmitt, *Land and Sea*, trans. S. Draghici (Washington DC: Plutarch Press, 1997 [1942]), p. 46.

20 *Ibid.*, pp. 47–8.

21 *Ibid.*, p. 54.

22 C. Schmitt, 'Großraum gegen Universalismus' (1939), in *Positionen und Begriffe im Kampf mit Weimar-Genf-Versailles, 1923–1939* (Berlin: Duncker & Humblot, 1994 [1940]), pp. 335–43. See also C. Schmitt, 'The *Großraum* Order of International Law with a Ban on Intervention for Spatially Foreign Powers: A Contribution to the Concept of *Reich* in International Law (1939–1941), in *Writings on War*, trans. T. Numan (Cambridge: Polity Press, 2011).

23 Schmitt, *Land and Sea*, p. 56.

24 *Ibid.*, p. 55.

25 C. Schmitt, *Völkerrechtliche Großraumordnung* (Berlin: Deutscher Rechtsverlag, 1941), p. 13. My translation.

26 B. Perkins, *The Creation of a Republican Empire: 1776–1865* (Cambridge: Cambridge University Press, 1993), pp. 147–69.

27 C. Schmitt, 'Changement de structure du droit international' in *La Guerre Civile Mondiale. Essais (1943–1978)*, trans. C. Jouin (Alfortville: Ere, 2006 [1943]), p. 39. This is a conference paper that Schmitt gave in Spanish at the Instituto de Estudios Políticos in Madrid on 1 June 1943.

28 *Ibid.*, p. 40.

29 *Ibid.*, p. 41.

30 F. J. Turner, 'The Significance of the Frontier in American History' (1893), reprinted in *The Frontier in American History* (New York: Holt, 1921), pp. 30–52.

31 Schmitt, 'Changement de structure du droit international', p. 41. My translation.

32 Schmitt, 'Großraum gegen Universalismus', p. 336.

33 See F. Ninkovich, 'Theodore Roosevelt: Civilization as ideology', *Diplomatic History*, 10:3 (1986), pp. 222–30.

34 'Transcript of Theodore Roosevelt's Corrolary to the Monroe Doctrine' (1905), available at: www.ourdocuments.gov/doc.php?doc=56&page=transcript (accessed 22 April 2015).

35 C. Schmitt, 'Beschleuniger wider Willen oder: Problematik der Westlichen Hemisphäre' in *Staat, Großraum, Nomos, Arbeiten aus den Jahren 1916–1969* (Berlin: Duncker & Humblot, 1995), pp. 431–7. This text originally appeared in the Nazi Party weekly *Das Reich* on 19 April 1942. My translation.

36 Schmitt, 'Changement de structure du droit international', pp. 41–2.

37 C. Schmitt, 'The Turn to the Discriminating Concept of War' in *Writings on War*, pp. 30–71.

38 Schmitt, 'The *Großraum* Order of International Law', p. 105.

39 Schmitt, *The Nomos of the Earth*, pp. 297–8.

40 Schmitt, 'Changement de structure du droit international', p. 43.

41 *Ibid.* My translation.

42 P. U. Hohendahl, 'Reflections on war and peace after 1940: Ernst Jünger and Carl Schmitt', *Cultural Critique*, 69 (2008), pp. 22–51; C. Brown, 'From Humanised War to Humanitarian Intervention: Carl Schmitt's Critique of the Just War Tradition' in Odysseos and Pettio, *The International Political Thought of Carl Schmitt*, pp. 56–70; B. Teschke, 'Carl Schmitt's Concept of War: A Categorical Failure' in J. Meierheinrich and O. Simmons (eds), *The Oxford Handbook of Carl Schmitt* (Oxford: Oxford University Press, 2015).

43 G. Ulmen, 'Just wars or just enemies', *Telos*, 109 (1996), pp. 99–112 at p. 111.

44 C. Schmitt, *Das internationalrechtliche Verbrechen des Angriffskrieges und der Grundsatz 'Nullen crimen, nulla poene sine lege'*, ed. H. Quaritsch (Berlin: Duncker & Humblot, 1994 [1945]), pp. 76–8. See also C. Jouin, 'Carl Schmitt à Nuremberg. Une théorie en accusation', *Genèse*, 74 (2009), pp. 46–73.

45 C. Schmitt, *Glossarium: Aufzeichnungen der Jahre 1947–51* (Berlin: Duncker & Humblot, 1991), 17 July 1949, p. 258.

46 *Ibid*. See also Schmitt, *Das internationalrechtliche Verbrechen*, p. 16; C. Jouin, *Le retour de la guerre juste: Droit international, épistémologie et idéologie chez Carl Schmitt* (Paris: Vrin, 2013), pp. 291–5.

47 Schmitt, *Glossarium*, 30 June 1949, p. 251.

48 J. Habermas, *The Past as Future*, trans. M. Pensky (Lincoln: University of Nebraska Press, 1994), pp. 9–10, 21–2.

49 See C. Schmitt, *Theodor Däublers, 'Nordlicht': Drei Studien über die Elemente, den Geist und die Aktualität des Werkes* (Berlin: Duncker & Humblot, 1989 [1916]), and 'The Age of Neutralizations and Politicizations' (1929), reprinted in C. Schmitt, *The Concept of the Political*, trans. T. Strong (Chicago: Chicago University Press, 2007 [1927]), pp. 80–97. See also J. McCormick, *Carl Schmitt's Critique of Liberalism: Against Politics as Technology* (Cambridge: Cambridge University Press, 1997).

50 E. Jünger, 'Total Mobilization', reprinted in R. Wolin, *The Heidegger Controversy: A Critical Reader* (Cambridge MA: MIT Press, 1993 [1930]), p. 128 (original emphasis).

51 E. Jünger, *Tagebücher* in E. Jünger, *Werke*, vol. 2 (Stuttgart: Klett, 1962), p. 433.

52 Schmitt uses the term 'international civil war' for the first time in 1938 in *The Leviathan in the State Theory of Thomas Hobbes*, p. 59. He starts using the term 'universal civil war' a year later in 'Neutralität und Neutralisierungen' in *Positionen unde Begriffe im Kampf mit Weimar-Genf-Versailles, 1923–1939* (Berlin: Duncker & Humblot, 1994 [1940]), p. 325.

53 See, for instance, E. Jünger, *The Peace* (Hinsdale: Henry Regnery Company, 1948 [1947]); R. Koselleck, *Critique and Crisis: Enlightenment and the Pathogenesis of Modern Society* (Cambridge MA: MIT Press, 1988 [1959]); E. Nolte, 'Weltbürgerkrieg 1917–1989' in E. Jesse (ed.), *Totalitarismus im 20. Jahrhundert: Eine Bilanz der internationalen Forschung* (Baden-Baden: Nomos, 1996), pp. 357–69. On the history of the concept see H. Kesting, *Geschichtsphilosophie und Weltbürgerkrieg: Deutungen der Geschichte von der Französischen Revolution bis zum Ost-West-Konflikt* (Heidelberg: Winter, 1959).

54 Jouin, *Le retour de la guerre juste*, pp. 269–72; N. Grangé, 'Carl Schmitt, Ernst Jünger et le spectre de la guerre civile. L'individu, le "soldat", l'état' in N. Grangé (ed.), *Carl Schmitt: Nomos, droit et conflit dans les relations internationales* (Rennes: Presses Universitaires de Rennes, 2013), pp. 39–60.

55 Schmitt, *The Nomos of the Earth*, pp. 56–7 (original emphasis).

56 See M. Balfour, 'Another look at unconditional surrender', *International Affairs*, 46:4 (1970), pp. 719–36.

57 D. Diner, *Cataclysms: A History of the Twentieth Century from Europe's Edge* (Madison: University of Wisconsin Press, 2008), p. 17.

58 *Ibid*.

59 E. Nolte, *Der Europäische Bürgerkrieg 1917–1945: Nationalsozialismus und Bolschewismus* (Berlin: Propylän Verlag, 1987); E. Nolte, 'Weltbürgerkrieg 1917–1989'.

60 Schmitt, *Glossarium*, 29 August 1950, p. 255.

61 C. Schmitt, *The Tyranny of Values*, trans. S. Draghici (Washington DC: Plutarch Press, 1996). All citations are from a non-paginated online version of this

out-of-print and very rare English translation: www.counter-currents.com/2014/07/the-tyranny-of-values-1959/ (accessed 8 August 2014).

62 C. G. Shaw, 'The theory of value and its place in the history of ethics', *International Journal of Ethics*, 11:3 (1901), pp. 306–20; H. Schnädelbach, *Philosophy in Germany, 1831–1933* (Cambridge: Cambridge University Press, 1984), pp. 161–91.

63 M. Heidegger, 'Nietzsche's Word: "God is Dead" ' in J. Young and K. Haynes (eds), *Off the Beaten Track* (Cambridge: Cambridge University Press, 2002 [1943]), pp. 157–99.

64 M. Heidegger, *Being and Time*, trans. J. Macquarrie and E. Robinson (New York: Harper and Row, 1962 [1927]), pp. 190–1.

65 M. Heidegger, 'Letter on Humanism' in D. F. Krell (ed.), *Basic Writings* (London: Routledge, 2002 [1947]), p. 251.

66 Heidegger, 'Nietzsche's Word', p. 170.

67 Schmitt, *The Tyranny of Values*.

68 *Ibid.*

69 *Ibid.*

70 *Ibid.*

71 On Heidegger and America see J. W. Ceaser, *Reconstructing America: The Symbol of America in Modern Thought* (New Haven: Yale University Press, 1997), pp. 187–213.

72 C. Schmitt, 'L'ordre du monde après la Deuxième Guerre mondiale' in *La Guerre Civile Mondiale*, p. 81. My translation. This is a transcript from a conference that Schmitt gave in Spanish at the Instituto de Estudios Políticos in Madrid in 1962. As Céline Jouin points out in her editorial notes, Schmitt confuses the actual pronouncement of the Truman Doctrine before Congress on 12 March 1947 with the fourth point of Truman's 1949 inauguration speech. Note 9, p. 173.

73 C. Jouin, 'Introduction' to Schmitt, *La Guerre Civile Mondiale*, p. 18.

74 C. Schmitt, *Theory of the Partisan* (New York: Telos, 2004 [1963]), p. 11.

75 *Ibid.*, p.94.

76 P. Steinfels, *The Neoconservatives: The Men Who Are Changing America's Politics* (New York: Simon and Schuster, 1979); S. Diamond, *Roads to Dominion: Right-Wing Movements and Political Power in the United States* (New York: Guilford Press, 1995); Drolet, *American Neoconservatism*.

77 'The Politics of Values', *The Economist* (7 October 2004), available at: www.economist.com/node/3258082 (accessed 12 August 2014).

78 P. E. Gottfried, *Conservatism in America: Making Sense of the American Right* (New York: Palgrave Macmillan, 2007), p. 53.

79 For an overview see American Enterprise Institute Conference, 'Trends in global governance: Do they threaten American sovereignty?', *Chicago Journal of International Law*, 1:2 (2000). For a more substantive analysis see J. F. Drolet, 'Containing the Kantian revolutions: A theoretical analysis of the neoconservative critique of global liberal governance', *Review of International Studies*, 26:3 (2010), pp. 533–60.

80 R. Kagan, 'America's crisis of legitimacy', *Foreign Affairs*, 83:2 (2004), pp. 65–82 at p. 79.

Realist exceptionalism: philosophy, politics and foreign policy in America's 'second modernity'

Introduction

Exceptionalism is a dominant theme in intellectual histories of American foreign policy. The idea that the United States is somehow special, that it possesses unique qualities or a special character that sets it apart from other nations, has long been established as the principal framework for thinking about the country and its place in the world.[1] Indeed, the idea of exceptionalism is so dominant that it has even come to define alternatives, many of which spend most of their time trying to debunk it directly by showing that America is really just like every other state (or worse), or demonstrating the baleful and ultimately self-defeating consequences to which the belief in exceptionalism leads.[2]

Given this prevalence, there might seem little value in yet another excursion down the well-travelled paths of American exceptionalism. Such a view is misleading. Exceptionalism remains crucial – not only because of its continuing prominence in political debate, but also for its potential as a window onto the intellectual history of American foreign policy and important, but generally ignored or overlooked, trajectories within it. This chapter seeks to sketch that potential by arguing that there are actually two forms of American exceptionalism. The first, which comes in a number of different versions, is what we usually think of as exceptionalism: a narrative of new beginnings and historical transcendence tied to Americas 'first modernity' – its independence, founding and westward expansion – and to a vision of the United States in a world historical role as salvation or saviour. Capable of supporting either moralistic isolationism or messianic globalism, this is the exceptionalism with which we are all familiar and which post-war realists, as well as many other critics, spend much of their time attempting to debunk or restrain.

However, there is a second form of American exceptionalism. Much less well recognised, and often obscured or misunderstood, its origins lie not in seventeenth-century Puritan visions of a City Upon a Hill, or in nineteenth-century claims of a Manifest Destiny, but in responses to a series of political crises arising in the first half of the twentieth century. In this later form, the most exceptional thing about the United States was the ability of its pluralist democracy to cope with the radical demands and novel challenges posed by modern society and politics. In this 'second modernity' the rise of mass society, and the processes of individualisation, social differentiation and secularisation that accompanied it, placed enormous strains and radical demands on democratic polities, throwing into stark relief (and often violent challenge) their ability to found, integrate, legitimate and govern themselves.[3] In the eyes of some observers, however, the American polity demonstrated an exceptional ability to avoid the collapse of liberalism witnessed in European states throughout the 1930s and 1940s. As Ira Katznelson has influentially characterised the situation, for political analysts across the analytic and ideological spectrum, the collapse of Europe's pluralist democracies was compounded by the realisation that 'just across the Atlantic, the United States – stable, liberal, enlightened – offered, or seemed to offer, the most inviting of alternatives ... the United States stood tall as the great historical counterfactual, thus soliciting close scrutiny of its political tradition, fresh accounts of its liberal regime, and focused inquiry about the singular personality of its liberal state.'[4]

Analyses of this exceptionalism focused first and foremost on the domestic institutions of the American polity and, as Katznelson shows, spanned an intellectual and ideological spectrum that ran from Karl Polanyi and Hannah Arendt, to Robert Dahl, Richard Hofstadter, and beyond. Yet these themes can also be found in assessments of American foreign policy and the nascent field of international relations.[5] Indeed, some of the most severe and profound critics of traditional American exceptionalism were themselves exceptionalists in this second sense – and paradoxically, some of the most important and sophisticated of these thinkers were called realists.

This is not the standard story in intellectual histories of American foreign policy. Realists are not generally considered exceptionalists.[6] Indeed, if there is one thing that most people would probably identify with realist visions of US foreign policy, it would be an implacable hostility to American exceptionalism. There are obviously good grounds for this. For thinkers such as George Kennan, opposition to exceptionalism was the hallmark of realist politics, and it is nearly impossible to find a realist past or present with a good word to say about what they perceive as the most destructive and misguided of all intellectual traditions in US foreign policy.

Yet realism actually has a much more complex and important relationship to exceptionalism than this stark opposition allows. In fact, the rise of a distinctively 'American realism' was part of a wider exceptionalist moment in the middle of the twentieth century, a moment that was concerned with both the exceptionality of the United States as a form of political order and the implications of this specific kind of exceptionality for its foreign relations. If liberal democracy was to have a future both at home and abroad in the post-war world, America would require political knowledge about the exceptional foundations of its political order as well as geopolitical muscle; moreover, to play that geopolitical role effectively and responsibly meant overcoming the seductions of traditional visions of American exceptionalism. Each was crucial to the success of the other. Scathing as many post-war realists were of this traditional vision of America and its place in the world, they were convinced that America *was* in some sense exceptional. In fact, they argued, understanding the true nature of American exceptionalism was essential for a properly realist politics: one that was ethically and politically responsible, and that was capable of developing a viable rhetorical strategy that could effectively battle the moralistic and messianic seductions of prevailing visions of exceptionalism.

Understanding the nature of this realist exceptionalism properly requires rethinking the ideas and intellectual legacy of figures like Hans Morgenthau, Reinhold Niebuhr and Arthur Schlesinger Jr. It also means rethinking the relationship between realism and liberalism – entertaining (and perhaps even embracing) the possibility that realism was not simply an implacable opponent of liberalism and exceptionalism, or a completely 'foreign' mode of thought standing outside American intellectual lineages and traditions, but that it was instead (at least in part) an embedded critic of the American liberal tradition that sought to realise its potential in both domestic and foreign policy. This is not the conventional tale of realists' admiration for the Founders of the Republic, the sobriety of the Federalist Papers or the prudence of the American constitution. It is the story of realism's – and liberalism's – engagement with the high modernity of the twentieth century – the liberalism of America's second modernity.

This chapter develops this argument in two phases. First, its sketches the landscape of traditional exceptionalist thinking and its ties to America's first modernity by briefly surveying the three most prominent visions of American uniqueness and their bases in factors ranging from geopolitical conditions and religious values, to political or constitutional foundations. The argument then turns to the second form of exceptionalism that is its core concern: developing a notion of post-war realism as a distinctively American realism by embedding its formation and concerns within America's second modernity, and the novel demands this placed on the plurality and yet unity of the United States as a liberal democratic order. This means examining the nature of realist scholarship in the period itself; it also means addressing the deep and generally overlooked

ties between their realist scholars' own concerns with political pluralism, civic identity and public political culture and those of contemporary
pragmatists, progressives and conservatives. The early Cold War period
laid down an intellectual, political and social landscape whose contours
still mark much of American political thought and politics. As such, it
remains understudied,[7] and perhaps no more so than in its – exceptional –
cross-ideological debates over how to constitute and secure a truly plural
and yet integrative political order, and a responsive and yet responsible
foreign policy.

Exceptionalism(s) and the American beginning

Unsurprisingly – and for good reasons – US foreign policy remains a
topic largely framed within the imaginary of America as somehow 'exceptional': of intellectual persuasions, moral qualities or institutional designs
somehow unique to the American polity and expressed in the way it relates
to the world. Further – and again for good reasons – almost all attempts to
come to grips with that uniqueness share the Tocquevillian fixation with
origins and his claim that the very DNA of America may be traced to the
first pioneers to set foot on its shores. Endorsing or despairing, debates over
whether or not America really is different – and if so, how – almost all take
their point of departure in a claim about the centrality of origins or beginnings – of the early period of discovery, colonisation and independence – as
the one and single key to unpacking America today. As is well known to
anyone familiar with debates over American foreign policy, the overwhelming nature of the nuances, detail or sheer quantity of this literature make it
impossible to do any real justice to it here. Three overall (different, if obviously interconnected) strands stand out, however, and before proceeding to
suggest a very different moment in the history of American exceptionalism,
it is helpful briefly to rehearse their claims. For not only do the narratives
and imaginaries of this 'first modernity' in the development of the American
polity provide an obvious discursive background echoed in the later version
that is the real interest of this chapter, but the narrative landscape of the
early republic's exceptional nature, and the purpose, cohesion and integration of American politics in this era that this reveals, also throws into relief
the challenges of a decidedly more divisive and secularised public sphere,
combined with the increased need for public support and political legitimation that comes with mature mass politics, and that characterises the second
moment of American exceptionalism.

For a long time perhaps the most prominent narrative of American
exceptionalism was that of its unique geopolitical conditions and the character traits that such conditions had purportedly nurtured in the American

polity and people. This is the exceptionalism of a virgin America, protected by oceans, gifted with plentiful lands, and hence uniquely free(d) from being sucked into the 'entangling alliances' and corrupting cynicism of European power politics. It is also the exceptionalism of a pioneer America, whose settler experience has equipped it with a very different set of qualities than those expressed by 'Old' Europe: practical and problem-solving – not abstract and cunning; industrious and innovative – not hesitant or conformist. It is the frontier America – the New World – of Thomas Paine's *Common Sense*, John Quincy Adams's famous farewell address, Frederick Jackson Turner's frontier thesis and Henry Luce's *American Century*:[8] blessed with a unique location of isolation and security and shaped by the experience of expansion and settlement, an America of impartiality, ingenuity and flexibility, always in search of challenge and transformation.

Equally powerful, and of renewed interest in recent scholarship on the sources of American foreign policy,[9] is the narrative of an America built on (perhaps even preordained by) a unique set of religious values. This is the narrative of the Redeemer Nation, of John Winthrop's Puritan America, exemplary America, *City Upon a Hill* America.[10] It is also the story of John O'Sullivan's manifest destiny America, whether in the unabashedly nationalist and millennial version of an America willed and planned by God to overtake the American continent, or the more complex versions of an America granted religious permission for westward expansion because of the natural rights of those (Christians) capable and willing to reap the gifts of the earth, and hence to multiply the talents conferred on man by his ultimate Creator.[11] As such it is the narrative of an America defined by its concern with faith, virtue and values, whether truly righteous or desperately and balefully wrong; a soul-searching America, different from other nations because of its relentless concern with policies that put principle over power.[12]

Finally, and in terms of academic scholarship certainly the most complex and overwhelming, there is the narrative of an America exceptional because of its unique political or constitutional foundations. This is the narrative of a republican rather than imperial America, endorsed by the Founders themselves and perpetually reformulated in the century of expansion that followed the American constitution. It is the narrative of exceptionalism that has led – and continues to lead – American protagonists to speak of US interventionism as 'different', driven not by nationalist desires of conquest, but by political virtue and liberal ideals of emancipation.[13] In terms of its political manifestation, this is the narrative of an America superior because of its checks and balances – driven by political design and identity to act in a more enlightened, more restrained or more rational manner on the world stage. In terms of its intellectual lineage, it is the exceptionalism originally defined by Hartz[14] as singularly 'Lockean', 'liberal' and hence uniquely (and, in Hartz's view, balefully) 'blinded by birth' in its rationalist optimism; or, in response to Hartz, since reinterpreted in a new set of exceptionalist clothes: not Lockean, but Burkean and Machiavellian, not Liberal but Republican,[15] not optimist but sceptical Calvinist,[16] and for all those reasons, uniquely prudent, moderate and balanced in origin and operation.

The differences and overlaps, tensions and trade-offs between all of these versions of why the American polity is or is not different remain topics of complex and heated debate. Yet for all the diversity – and all the deep political and normative divisions – of much of this debate, it also revolves around a strange consensus: that it is in the early phase of the American polity that its most defining traits were established, and hence also in its early phase that the most important intellectual traditions of American foreign policy may be found. Whether endorsing or critiquing the idea of American exceptionalism, analyses have tended to return either to the founding of the late eighteenth century or the early westward expansion of the nineteenth century. For both these positions and their critics, however, the defining problem was how to found or expand the American polity. For critics and proponents of an American exceptionalism alike, this results in a tendency to see only singularity: the American approach to the world was laid down by, and is now guided or blinded (depending on one's political colours) by, its origins in a geopolitical/religious/constitutional uniqueness. It tends, in other words, to tie the study of American foreign policy to the same conclusion that so traumatised Louis Hartz – that America had only one political tradition, only one place from which to view the world, only one colossal, uniform and all-encompassing box from which to conduct its relations with the world.[17]

In many ways, much of the critical scholarship on American exceptionalism and imperial foreign policy that has followed in the wake of the linguistic turn has only further increased this tendency. As one deconstructive analysis after the other has hammered away at the preponderance of the pioneer arrogance, the messianic impulse or the liberal rationalism in American formulation of identity and interest, the possibilities of imagining room for manoeuvre or reflexivity in American foreign policy has shrunk to near vanishing. Even 'critical' international relations scholarship in other words, has largely operated within the boundaries of the Hartzian thesis: that America (in Tocqueville's famous phrase) was 'born free without having to become so', that this lack of ideological pluralism explains the discursive uniformity of US relations with the world, and that American diplomacy – tragically – has no easy exit from the conundrum, precisely because its shallow historical experience leaves it no vantage point from which to deconstruct or historicise its own assumptions of 'special' providence, privilege or power.

Realism and exceptionalism: a second American modernity?

As an intellectual lineage in US foreign policy, realism is generally portrayed as the great refusal of exceptionalist seductions and liberal, rationalist illusions. These claims no doubt capture important aspects of realism in America, but they are only part of the story – and the part they miss is the story of the second history of exceptionalism in American foreign policy. For while realists were constant critics of exceptionalist excesses, significant parts of post-war realism were explicitly concerned with the question of American exceptionalism that preoccupied many of their contemporaries across political studies. Rejecting its universalising or messianic forms, these realists sought to articulate a new way of thinking about the historical uniqueness and potential of the United States as a polity, and its potential for fostering a robust and yet reasonable and restrained – that is in their eyes, realist – foreign policy.

At the centre of this endeavour was liberal pluralism. Realism is almost as regularly defined by its opposition to liberal pluralism as by its hostility to exceptionalism, and in fact its emergence in the 1930s and 1940s has often been linked to its critique of American social and political science dominated by simplistic naïve liberal pluralism and intellectual rationalism, and thus incapable of even comprehending the challenges it faced, let alone of mastering them.[18] To be clear, realists were certainly hostile to the facile forms of pluralism and liberal theory (and their practical expressions) that they believed were at work in Europe in the 1930s, and which they held at least partly to blame for the collapse of the Weimar Republic and the rise of fascism. Their mission, as they saw it, was to rid naïve Americans of their liberal and pluralist illusions as quickly as possible. Over time and in different ways, however, this position changed. Although never retreating from their critique of liberal rationalism, realists began to suspect that their critique of liberal pluralism might be less universal and all-embracing than they had believed.

The source of these doubts was America itself, which seemed to demonstrate that the defining crisis of the Weimar Republic and the travails of European liberalism were not the inevitable outcome of pluralist politics in the modern age. For far from succumbing to the malaise predicted by many realists (and others), the United States emerged from the Second World War with its pluralist institutions relatively intact and its geopolitical position greatly enhanced. This situation posed a puzzle for post-war realists, and they were not alone. The nature and significance of American pluralism, the *exceptional* nature of the United States as a liberal, pluralist – and yet cohesive, adaptive and decisive – society with a form of government capable of meeting the challenges of contemporary capitalism, mass politics and modern geopolitics, became the crucial question for post-war political science. If that pluralist order was to continue to succeed, it was essential to understand its foundations and strengths, as well as its existing and potential weaknesses. If liberal polities were able to overcome the fragility in domestic politics and the inertia and weakness in foreign policy that realists saw as their fate, the question was how, and how would they be able to continue to do so?[19] If liberal pluralism was to be revived in places where it had been extinguished, and perhaps even exported to places where it had never existed, could the American experience provide clues about the conditions for success or failure?[20] And finally – and of particular importance in foreign policy – if correctly grasped, might this form of exceptionalism provide a counter to the destructive seductions of competing forms of exceptionalism – an alternative that could command public and political support, that is, an alternative with *power*? Telling the American public and political leadership that the United States was not exceptional, or that believing it was so would always end in disaster, was not enough. The first had limited appeal in the face of long-standing exceptionalist attitudes; the second could always be contested in terms of purported past successes (Manifest Destiny) or the promise of future glory. Negative realism was not realistic enough. What was needed was an alternative grounded in a different exceptionalism – an alternative with real, mobilisable roots in American intellectual and political traditions, with the capacity to tap into popular beliefs and political discourses, and in line with current and emerging social structures and forces. This might provide foundations for successfully combatting the crusading universalism or righteous isolationism that were its twin opponents.

American realism

These themes could be traced across the intellectual landscape of post-war American foreign policy debates. Renowned figures such as Reinhold Niebuhr, Arthur Schlesinger Jr. and Hans Morgenthau each explored different aspects of this second vision of American exceptionalism and its connections to liberal democratic politics. The remainder of this chapter traces these concerns in the thinking of the most influential scholar of international politics and foreign policy in the period, Hans J. Morgenthau. Morgenthau's hostility toward exceptionalism seems paradigmatic. Yet it is for exactly this reason that his extensive engagement with a second vision exceptionalism, and with its significance in and for America's second modernity, is so significant. To begin to trace these generally overlooked facets of American foreign policy's intellectual history requires a shift of focus. In fact, it demands that we reconsider realism's relationship to two seemingly unlikely interlocutors: American law and American political theory. At first glance, each seems surprising. After all, law is seen as the *bête noir* of realism – and the realist tradition is often seen as synonymous with an assault on the grip of legalism on American thinking about international affairs. Similarly, realism is often defined as drawing a clear distinction between the concerns of political theory with the 'good life' within the state and the conflictual domain of 'survival' between them, as a bracing (if sometimes disillusioning and potentially dangerous) dose of European sophistication administered to America's sunny, simple-minded optimism. Yet a closer look reveals that both American law and the country's traditions of political thinking provided key resources that post-war realists drew upon in their attempt to construct an alternative American exceptionalism. Although the connection and issues involved can only be hinted at in this context, they hopefully provide at least prima facie evidence for their importance and the value of tracing them – and their implications – in fuller detail in the future.

Early on, Morgenthau clearly viewed American pluralist politics, liberal philosophy, and political science with the same combination of derision, despair, and foreboding shared by a range of *émigré* thinkers such as Leo Strauss, Eric Vogelin and others – including, it is important to note, some now generally forgotten but then-influential Americans such as William Yandell Elliott.[21] It is fair to say that like many others then and since, Morgenthau initially held a vision of American politics and intellectual traditions as being marked by 'an obsessive and unconscious commitment to a liberal faith that prevents it from asking profound questions. Incapable of envisaging alternatives, American political thought is said to be mired in the legacy of John Locke and a mindless optimism … our petty intellectual squabbles are mere shadow-boxing compared to the *real* thing, the kind of ideological combat that feudalism and class war generated in Europe.'[22]

These views permeate Morgenthau's early writings, and come together powerfully in *Scientific Man Versus Power Politics*.[23] Some years after his arrival in the United States, however, his views began to change significantly. His respect for some of the Founders, particularly Madison, is perhaps hardly surprising – it followed fairly well-worn themes and was shared by many conservatively inclined thinkers, including realists like Kennan. More intriguing is his engagement with two other figures: Abraham Lincoln and Oliver Wendell Holmes. In both cases his writings began to evince a different and deeper appreciation of American intellectual traditions.

Holmes (as the understandably least well-recognised of the two in foreign policy terms) is worthy of first attention, since this draws attention to the complex, important and yet under-examined relationship between American pragmatist philosophy, legal realism in the nation's jurisprudence and political realism in international affairs and foreign policy.[24] Of the many and varied jurists whom Morgenthau addresses throughout his writings, Holmes is an object of his enduring interest. Indeed, despite Morgenthau's well-known turn away from the international legal focus of his early career, Holmes continues to resurface in some of his most interesting political reflections on US politics. What is it that this famously anti-legalistic political analyst found in one of America's greatest and most controversial Justices of the Supreme Court? More than anything, we might suggest, it was the way that Holmes drew on pragmatist philosophy to develop a pluralist understanding of law and society that was deeply congenial to Morgenthau's own views. Holmes's vision of law was based less (in the eyes of his critics, if at all)[25] on natural or abstract rights, and more on maintaining a pluralist polity by balancing social forces and using law to that end. This was, as Holmes well knew, a tricky endeavour, and Morgenthau often quoted with scepticism from the Justice's most (in) famously blunt statements of his legal realism – that ultimately, 'I have no practical criticism [with regard to the laws] except what the crowd wants'.[26] Morgenthau immediately points out that this dictum contains the dangerous 'potential for extreme relativism and subjectivism inherent in American conformity, a potential that … has been realized in our time', and that he identifies with some of the most destructive tendencies in modern American society and politics. Yet having identified its dangerous, he immediately turns to note the strengths of such a pragmatic and realist theory of law, and the virtues of Holmes as its proponent. He continues:

> Yet the very permissiveness of the American consensus in terms of content requires the commitment to a definite modus operandi. That modus operandi is but the reflection of the American purpose in the unorganized social sphere. Equality in freedom here becomes freedom of competition for social approval. Here again Mr. Justice Holmes is the authentic voice of the American spirit: 'the best test of truth is the power of the thought to get itself accepted in the competition of the market.' Today's truth, then, becomes tomorrow's error, once it has lost out in that competition. The only permanent commitment of the American consensus is to the freedom to compete on equal terms of opportunity to determine the content of that consensus.[27]

Holmes's jurisprudence suggested to Morgenthau how putting power at the centre of political order did not have to mean surrendering to power. It showed how legal thought and action could support a pluralist polity without falling prey to legalistic fallacies, or a naïve belief in a natural harmony of interests. This intellectual legacy connected Morgenthau directly to long-standing American controversies surrounding pragmatism and its political consequences, controversies that stretched all the way back to the Civil War and forward to the 1930s.[28] US intellectual traditions no longer looked like an arid desert of liberal optimism: they instead resembled in key ways many of the philosophical and political questions that Morgenthau grappled with in the Weimar Republic, and they held the promise of showing how liberal pluralism and realist politics could be combined to positive effect.

Law itself, of course, could never be sufficient. Like realists such as Neibuhr, Morgenthau held that law – even a 'realist' jurisprudence like that of Holmes – needed to be embedded in and aligned with wider social norms and mores if it was to be effective. The solution to the puzzle of American liberal pluralism thus could not lie in law alone, but also in its relationship to the wider political culture and institutions of American life. Here, Morgenthau was spurred toward a deeper enquiry into the specificity of the American polity. In works such as *The Purpose of American Politics* he joined thinkers such as Hannah Arendt in a quest to find the transcendent, but not transcendental, principles of American liberal democracy. This was a search for an exceptional America quite different from that of Manifest Destiny. It involved an exploration of the American spirit and its complex role in creating a political culture, a People and set of institutions that were dynamic and yet self-limiting, realistic and yet not cynical – a vibrant pluralism capable of avoiding both liberal entropy and messianic crusading.

To a degree, Morgenthau believed that this spirit could be identified and its political genius, as well as its pitfalls, discerned.[29] However, as a political realist he was convinced that principles alone were insufficient, and he worried that the processes of modernisation were fundamentally undermining the viability of the very political culture he felt it was vital to retain. These concerns explain his attraction to the politics of leadership, something he shared with the other significant realists of the time. In readings of classical realism that locate it wholly within European lineages, individual greatness and leadership almost inevitably call two names to mind: Nietzsche and Weber. These lineages were beyond doubt essential in Morgenthau's political vision, but to see them as the limits of that vision is blinding. For it is possible to see that Morgenthau also found in America a different vision of leadership, one indebted to Emerson and to Lincoln, rather than to Nietzsche, Weber and Schmitt, and one that provided at least the promise of a liberal and democratic path. This vision of greatness has been evocatively sketched by Shklar, who argues that Emerson's attempt to wrest the idea of 'great men' away from the hero-worship of romantics in general, and Carlyle in particular, marked an attempt to 'remember those who were truly great and tried to integrate them into a democratic faith. *Representative Men* was Emerson's answer to Carlyle's hero worship. The term *representative* was deliberately political. Great men could not be great unless they were able to move, and be moved by, their public. Greatness was a transaction in which we all had a part. Aristocracy was tamed.'[30] Morgenthau sought to use historical greatness to the same end. Lincoln could provide a means of revivifying the crucial democratic elements in American culture that were most vital and now most endangered. And he could provide a representative model for contemporary leaders to follow.[31]

While Morgenthau declared the uniqueness and historical importance of the American republic and its guiding purpose of 'equality in freedom', he held that the promise of American politics also held dangers and contained deep injustices. The abstract nature of 'freedom' at the heart of that purpose was a source of great strength, an impulse toward renewal and reform. But it was also a cause of continual crises, as the ability to live up to these ideals both at home and abroad – to give, in other words, concrete content to abstract principles – caused continual problems and forced an engagement with power and domination. In seeking to create freedom, the republic often ended up exercising a 'brutal domination' that justified itself in terms of ideals, while in systematic bad faith it denied the reality of its actions,[32] and in the process risked either rejecting its purpose by retreating into isolationism or denying that purpose through imperial domination or an aggressive moral universalism.[33] When confronted with such a dilemma, the tendency of American egalitarianism is, as Tocqueville asserted long ago, to elevate conformism, and to cast dissent as treason. As a result, the role of power as domination (both inside and outside the state) was either denied or moralised: neither option, Morgenthau averred, was realistic; and both were dangerous and potentially self-defeating – and were ever more so under the conditions of mass politics and social dislocation that characterised America's second modernity. The experience of the Weimar Republic, where the crisis of liberalism gave rise to a radically anti liberal politics, hovers in the background of many of his writings on both domestic politics and foreign policy. His worry was not only that an uncritical liberalism might become too weak to sustain a vibrant democracy – he was equally (and often even more) concerned that a reaction against these dilemmas, especially in a situation exacerbated by high levels of insecurity or international tensions, would lead liberal democracies to overreactions that posed at least as great a threat to their principles and liberties. Appeals to leadership and a principled patriotism could easily contribute to a political culture prone to an imprudent and crusading foreign policy. Similarly, while calling for a need to recognise the attractions of 'national greatness' as an antidote to some of modernity's most corrosive dynamics, he refused to regard these ideals as adequately realised within the United States itself, and was fearful that engaging in foreign adventures would prove a tempting if ultimately illusory response to deep domestic difficulties.[34]

A keen awareness, and stinging critique, of these domestic failings was yet another area where Morgenthau's extensive engagement with the dilemmas of mass politics shines through clearly. Concerns with decadence and hedonism, with the ascendance of private interests and the decline of the public sphere, are part of Morgenthau's early thinking that he never left behind. He remained concerned that the (Weberian) bureaucratisation, political majoritarianism, and rule by opinion poles and media manipulation had become a threat to the principle of equality and to the future of democracy in America itself. In terms of equality, these dynamics have led to ever greater domination of the state by powerful private interests and to the effective political disenfranchisement of the weakest and the poorest.[35] At the same time, effective public policy was undermined not only by these structures of political domination, but also by the entropy of interest-group pluralism.[36] Inequality, the loss of a public sphere of vibrant political participation and contestation, along with a capacity for the state to act effectively in support of those broad social purposes, were amongst his greatest concerns. He was, accordingly, deeply critical of economic and racial inequalities, and of concentrations of political and economic power. Far from lionising American exceptionalism as an abstract rhetoric, he calls on the nation to examine itself critically, and to live up to its principles. 'The restoration of national purpose', he argued, 'requires a reorientation of the national outlook, a change in our national style.'[37]

In sum, Morgenthau was consistently concerned that declarations of exceptionality could readily become barriers to criticism, a powerful weapon with which to attack critics at home for being insufficiently virtuous, decadently weak and lacking heroic zeal and fortitude, or even as harbouring a suspiciously weak commitment to the American ideal itself. Far from securing democracy, he feared, such ideas could easily become a means for stifling the vibrant debate that is both the lifeblood of democratic politics and a vital contribution to successful policy.[38]

The appropriate response, however, was neither despair nor conservative elitism. It lay instead in the attempt to revitalise precisely those social and historical resources that made America exceptional in Realist eyes. An oft-ignored and puzzling aspect of parts of post-war American realism is its insistence on the importance of 'the people' for the revival of American politics and the redirection of American foreign policy.[39] Morgenthau's *In Defense of the National Interest*,[40] for instance, underscored the extent to which the shortcomings of American foreign policy were not the result of American leaders' failure to 'realistically' ignore public opinion or to manipulate it effectively. Rather, they reflected 'a profound misunderstanding of the nature of public opinion and of the intelligence and moral character of the American people'.[41] These themes were not idiosyncratic: Reinhold Niebuhr's political writings similarly and consistently defend a particular form of mobilised public contestation. Seducing 'the people' into conformity and consent was part of the problem; a public sphere mobilised to vital contestation was part of the solution.[42] The very title of Schlesinger's *The Vital Center*[43] reflected the same conviction.

Naturally, the shades and shapes of this response varied greatly, often taking its colours from thinkers on the outside, or at the margins, of the realist intellectual environment. John Dewey's hugely influential work on publicity, democracy and civic mobilisation, as well as the long-standing pragmatist interest in fostering an organic and participatory public, was (despite the animosity between realism and pragmatism) of a kindred spirit to the realist endeavour.[44] So too was Walter Lippmann's extensive engagement with the relationship between foreign policy and public opinion. But while Lippmann's questions and concerns made an impact on the realists, they ultimately rejected his despair about the potential for responsible collective action in the age of the 'phantom public' and his turn toward elitism. Autocracy was not the solution. Only an approach that worked with the reality of pluralism, turning resigned fragmentation into creative conflict, held promise.

In response, realist exceptionalism engaged the American founding as a moment of what George Kateb aptly terms 'grand politics' – a pulling back of the political order to its unifying principles and sense of common order and purpose.[45] Approaching the constitution and the republican political tradition that grew from it as examples of how to (re)institute responsible political power, the realists deemed America living proof of an idea Weber had considered but quickly given up: that of collective rather than personal charisma. This meant tying the body politic together through collective purpose rather than the radiance of a single leader or a defining enemy. As Morgenthau explained in *The Purpose of American Politics*, 'America' – owing 'its creation and continuing existence as a nation not to geographic proximity, ethnic identity, monarchical legitimacy, or a long historic tradition, but to an act of will repeated over and over again by successive waves of immigrants' – had a looseness in its social fabric that made it uniquely dependent on solving the problem of constituent power, of articulating unity, identity, we-ness. Although acutely aware of the potential pathologies generated by this lack of unity and identity (and the temptation to create it via what we might today call 'othering'), the realists believed that this same looseness potentially equipped America with the vibrancy needed to energise *and* restrain national will through the balancing function of competition. Awakening this potential meant renewing the republic's sceptical, transformative and self-limiting language of purpose, and adopting a very particular kind of leadership capable of stirring and shaping vibrant and contestative political debate.

Read in this context, it is clear that post-war realists adopted a political understanding strikingly akin to Hannah Arendt's conception of the republican tradition in America. They sought repeatedly to reinstitute and remobilise the American national 'we', to activate and restrain its vitality, by delivering a language of political leadership capable of generating substantial and appealing political visions and – through the counterviews ignited by such visions – of submitting political leaders to continuous public scrutiny and critique. Of course, realists acknowledged that opposition and dissent alone cannot be the foundation of effective foreign policy. Eventually, a consensus must be reached. But this is healthy only once it results from a real and genuinely antagonistic struggle. Constitutional divisions of power are crucial, but the cultivation of cohesive political contestation means more for realist politics. Here, realism sought a strategy of simultaneous mobilisation and restraint: mobilisation through political leadership; restraint through a transcendent note to such narratives, always instilling a chastening self-doubt into the public vocabulary. In this fashion, responsible leaders might inject into the public realm a renewed dose of the 'Calvinist iron' that realist exceptionalism found so central to the American founding, which could turn back the tide, renewing national will behind grand strategy while combining this with a deeper sense of limits, restraint and critique. Lincoln stood perhaps as *the* prime example of such 'heroic' leadership. Heir to the darker, sceptical vein in the Calvinist trajectory, and open to the idea that self-limitation and public contestation must be a central part of democratic politics, Lincoln still believed that politics, even war, could be a medium in the struggle for justice, however compromised by human fallibility.[46]

Conclusion

The notion that US foreign policy debates in the Cold War context were largely framed as a realist critique of the New World's (liberal) delusions of exceptionality and virtue is a well-rehearsed truism. This reading casts post-war realists as fierce opponents to the US conviction that it had something distinctive to bring to global politics in the modern age. At a more foundational level, it portrays the realist persuasion as basically at odds with twentieth-century America – anti-modern, anti-democratic, anti-pluralist – implicitly purporting that the most productive lines of controversy in Cold War American foreign policy debates ran along the liberal/anti-liberal divide.[47]

This chapter has tried to suggest a very different and potentially more productive account. One strand in the works of post-war realists was indeed the critique of what notions of exceptionality do to a nation's outlook on (and ability to get along with) the world. But their overall concerns were congruent with the extensive mid-twentieth-century American debates over how to govern (with) pluralism. America was different. Not different because of special geographical origins, transcendental purposes or inherent political virtues. Different because of a series of historical and above all modern experiences and coincidences that had set the United States on a different course to Europe in response to the radical pluralism which defined the age of mass politics and the novel demands which that pluralism placed on the exercise and legitimation of democratic governance. Structured around the notion of the late nineteenth and early twentieth century as defined by a 'second' or 'high modernity', the overall purpose of this chapter has been to suggest that what we normally recognise as realist anti-exceptionalism was in fact engagement with a set of deep discussions over America's distinctiveness – and that these discussions, as they played themselves out in the period running from roughly 1930 to 1960, were in many ways remarkably, and by today's standards certainly exceptionally, cross-ideological. It was not pragmatist liberalism versus elitist or conservative realism: it was pluralism at work, a moment in American intellectual life defined by a rare consensus not around what to answer, but what to ask. The people, the public sphere and all of the questions attached to it – reason, affect, unity, diversity, consensus and critique – created for a brief while, a unitary platform upon which to design, deconstruct and disagree over the nature and future of the American polity. The ideas laid down in American political culture by the founding generations of its institutional, social and religious framework might have some part to play in why the US response to that second modernity ultimately was different from that of Europe. But most of all, the exceptionality of America's response to the problems and promise of pluralism was tied to developments integral to, and distinctive of, the post-Civil War republic.

If admittedly complex, this rewriting of the history of post-war realism as both critic and proponent of US exceptionalism is also rewarding. Not only does the claim that post-war realism was distinctive open up a whole range of avenues for understanding the mid-twentieth-century context. It also puts the history of international relations disciplinary debates (back) into context and contact with wider currents in intellectual history, and enquiries into political thought and science in the post-war American context. It also provides a map of an intellectual landscape whose history few now remember, but whose language communities, intellectual borderlines and ideological controversies still serve as the arena in which contemporary American politics play themselves out, even if often unaware of their own historical moorings. In fact, we would contend that there is no way of understanding the politics of a President Obama or his relentless Republican and neoconservative opponents without understanding this historical backdrop. Finally, and related to this, it directs attention to a period which put the question of crowds, publics and persuasion at centre stage – a topic which, in the midst of new public formations, economic challenges, popular uprisings and civic discontent across the Arab, European and American world, has once again gained importance. Not much in contemporary literature enables us to understand these phenomena not simply as isolated issues of 'affect' or 'emotion' for academic theorisation, but as integral features to the study of democratic politics.[48] A revived intellectual history of American exceptionalism might paradoxically, and perhaps even ironically, be one means of pointing toward new and important forms of historical and contemporary engagement with American foreign policy.

Notes

1 Almost all discussions over why and when the United States truly entered the global stage are constructed around the concept of exceptionalism and the United States' reinterpretation of its implications somewhere around the beginning of the twentieth century: from exemplar to empire, see H. W. Brands, 'Exemplary America versus Interventionist America' in R. Hutchings, *At the End of the American Century: America's Role in the Post-Cold War World* (Washington DC: The Woodrow Wilson Center, 1998); J. B. Litke, 'American Exceptionalism: From Exemplar to Empire' (PhD thesis, Georgetown University, 2010); from promised land to crusader state, see W. McDougall, *Promised Land, Crusader State* (Boston MA: Houghton Mifflin, 1997); J. Ceaser, 'The origins and character of American exceptionalism', *American Political Thought: Journal of Ideas, Institutions and Culture*, I (2012), pp. 1–26. The list goes on and on.

2 Here, too, the list is close to endless; see A. Bacevich, *The Limits of Power: The End of American Exceptionalism* (London: MacMillan, 2008); S. Martin Lipset, *American Exceptionalism: A Double-Edged Sword* (New York: Norton, 1996); A. Stephanson, *Manifest Destiny: American Expansion and the Empire of Right* (New York: Hill and Wang, 1995).

3 F. M. N. Giglioli, *Legitimacy and Revolution in a Society of Masses* (New York: Transaction, 2013); J. W. Muller, *Contesting Democracy* (New Haven: Yale University Press, 2011).

4 I. Katznelson, *Desolation and Enlightenment* (New York: Columbia University Press, 2003), p. 106. According to John Gunnell, concerns with the exceptionalism of American pluralism can be found in American political science at least as early as the 1930s, when it was also seen 'necessary to probe and grasp the character of the American political system. This was almost the exact syndrome that would reappear in the 1950s. The greatest impetus behind the idea of a science of politics was, first, to find democracy, and second, to gain the cognitive and practical purchase necessary to sustain and enhance it.' J. Gunnell, *Imagining the American Polity: Political Science and the Discourse of Democracy* (University Park: The Pennsylvania State University Press, 2004), p. 177. Nor, it is important to note, is Katznelson's view simply celebratory – as he details in a later work, these positive aspects were complexly connected to some of the most oppressive parts of American politics, particularly its racial order; see I. Katznelson, *Fear Itself: The New Deal and the Origins of Our Time* (New York: Liveright, 2014).

5 For a fuller account, see M. C. Williams, 'In the beginning: The IR enlightenment and the ends of IR theory', *European Journal of International Relations*, 19:3 (2013), pp. 647–65.

6 J. Rosenthal's *Righteous Realists: Political Realism, Responsible Power, and American Culture in the Nuclear Age* (Baton Rouge: Louisiana State University Press, 1991) approaches the formation and purpose of a 'post-war Realism' in terms most akin those considered here.

7 For a recent statement on the need to investigate the many meanings, histories and legacies of the Cold War, see D. Bell and J. Isaac, *Uncertain Empire: American History and the Idea of the Cold War* (Oxford: Oxford University Press, 2012).

8 H. Luce, 'The American Century', *Life Magazine* (17 February 1941).

9 A. Preston, *Sword of the Spirit, Shield of Faith: Religion in American War and Diplomacy* (New York: Anchor Books, 2012).

10 The classics here of course are P. Miller, *Errand into the Wilderness* (Cambridge: Cambridge University Press, 1958) and S. Bercovitch, *The American Jeremiad* (Madison: University of Wisconsin Press, 1975); D. W. Howe, *What Hath God Wrought: The Transformation of America, 1815–1845* (Oxford: Oxford University Press, 2007).

11 Stephanson, *Manifest Destiny*; T. R. Hietala, *Manifest Design: American Exceptionalism and Empire* (Ithaca: Cornell University Press, 2003).

12 See again, Preston, *Sword of the Spirit, Shield of Faith*.

13 All three of these exceptionalisms remain present at the subtler discursive levels in American foreign policy-making today. At the most explicit rhetorical level, the narrative of an America more liberal than other nations remains a powerful one across the political spectrum, running the gamut from the mildly commending (American liberal internationalism has in general been morally superior to many forms of European expansionary nationalism), to the wildly, unabashedly celebratory (American interventionism is superior full stop and needs no qualifications, let alone limits). Indeed, the political narrative of American exceptionalism – and hence also of an American exemptionalism from the regulations of international law – found passionate and unreserved support in the neoconservative writings on American foreign policy of the twenty-first century.

14 L. Hartz, *The Liberal Tradition in America* (New York: Harcourt, Brace & World, 1955).

15 G. Wood, *The Creation of the American Republic: 1776–1789* (Chapel Hill: University of North Carolina Press, 1969) and G. Wood, *The Idea of America: Reflections on the Birth of the United States* (New York: Penguin, 2011); J. G. A. Pocock, *The Machiavellian Moment: Florentine Political Thought and the Atlantic Republican Tradition* (Princeton: Princeton University Press, 1975); A. Kalyvas and I. Katznelson, *Liberal Beginnings* (Cambridge: Cambridge University Press, 2008).

16 For a wider context, see J. P. Diggins, *The Promise of Pragmatism: Modernism and the Crisis of Knowledge and Authority* (Chicago: Chicago University Press, 1994), and J. P. Diggins, 'From pragmatism to natural law: Walter Lippmann's quest for the foundations of legitimacy', *Political Theory*, 19:4 (1991), pp. 519–38.

17 Hartz, *The Liberal Tradition in America*, p. 287.
18 William Scheuerman was amongst the most important initiators of this important theme; for an overview, see W. Sheuerman, *Morgenthau* (Cambridge: Polity Press, 2009). See particularly, N. Guilhot, 'The realist gambit: Postwar American political science and the birth of IR theory', *International Political Sociology*, 2:4 (2008), pp. 281–304; and N. Guilhot, 'American Katechon: When political theology became international relations theory', *Constellations*, 17:2 (2010), pp. 224–53.
19 This dilemma also provided one of the prime and generally hidden dimensions of the move from realism to neorealism in the American study of international relations, primarily under the guidance of Kenneth Waltz. For analyses, see M. C. Williams, 'Waltz, Realism, and Democracy', *International Relations*, 23:3 (2009), pp. 328–40; and D. Bessner and N. Guilhot, 'How realism Waltzed off: Liberalism and decisionmaking in Kenneth Waltz's Neorealism', *International Security*, 40:2 (2015), pp. 87–118.
20 The roots of comparative political science are of course found in the American experience – as does the ambivalent and often highly critical attitude of many realists toward modernisation theory.
21 See particularly W. Y. Elliott, *The Pragmatic Revolt in Politics: Syndicalism, Fascism, and the Constitutional State* (New York: Macmillan, 1928), and the revealing reconstruction in Gunnell, *Imagining the American Polity*, pp. 150–75 especially.
22 J. Shklar, *Redeeming American Political Thought* (Chicago: University of Chicago Press, 1998), p. 91 (original emphasis).
23 Hans J. Morgenthau, *Scientific Man Versus Power Politics*. (Chicago: University of Chicago Press, 1946).
24 For examinations, although not in the directions pursued here, see M. Koskenniemi, *The Gentle Civilizer of Nations* (Cambridge: Cambridge University Press, 2001) pp. 474–94; and O. Jutersonke, *Morgenthau, Law, and Realism* (Cambridge: Cambridge University Press, 2010), pp. 106–18 especially.
25 A highly critical view of Holmes is presented by A. Alschuler, *Law Without Values: The Life, Work and Legacy of Justice Holmes* (Chicago: University of Chicago Press, 2000).
26 Quoted in H. Morgenthau, *The Purpose of American Politics* (New York: Knopf, 1960), p. 62.
27 *Ibid.*, pp. 62–3.
28 Louis Menand's *The Metaphysical Club: A Story of Ideas in America* (New York: Farrar, Strauss and Giroux, 2001) provides an engaging survey of this movement.
29 America was not one-sidedly exceptional in the negative sense; this negativity was one expression of its positive side. The key in this nearly dialectical vision was to accentuate the latter and restrain the former.
30 Shklar, *Redeeming American Political Thought*, p. 91, original emphasis.
31 H. J. Morgenthau and D. Hein, *Essays on Lincoln's Faith and Politics* (Lanham: University Press of America, 1983).
32 Morgenthau, *The Purpose of American Politics*, p. 112.

33 See, among many possible examples, H. J. Morgenthau, *Politics in the Twentieth Century, Vol. 1: The Decline of Democratic Politics* (Chicago: University of Chicago Press, 1962), pp. 316–26.
34 See particularly Morgenthau, *The Purpose of American Politics*.
35 H. J. Morgenthau, *Truth and Power: Essays of a Decade* (New York: Knopf, 1970), pp. 5–9.
36 Morgenthau, *The Purpose of American Politics*.
37 *Ibid.*, p. 322.
38 Worries most clearly expressed in Morgenthau, *Truth and Power*, pp. 53–4; and Morgenthau, *Politics in the Twentieth Century*, pp. 328–35; and strikingly in relation to international relations theory in 'The Commitments of a Theory of International Politics' in *Politics in the Twentieth Century*, pp. 60–1.
39 These themes are developed at greater length in V. S. Tjalve and M. C. Williams, 'Recovering the rhetoric of realism', *Security Studies*, 24:1 (2015), pp. 37–60, and in V. S. Tjalve and M. C. Williams, 'Rethinking the logic of security: Liberal realism and the recovery of American political thought', *Telos*, 170 (2015), pp. 1–22, elements of which are drawn on here.
40 H. J. Morgenthau, *In Defense of the National Interest* (New York: Knopf, 1951).
41 *Ibid.*, p. 231.
42 R. Niebuhr, *The Children of Light and the Children of Darkness: A Vindication of Democracy and a Critique of its Traditional Defense* (New York: Charles Schribner's Sons, 1944), p. 133.
43 Arthur Schlesinger Jr., *The Vital Center: The Politics of Freedom.* (New York: Houghton Mifflin Co, 1949).
44 Indeed, the realist endeavour had numerous connections to pragmatism, as Niebuhr's biography shows. Sidney Hook in particular provides an example of how closely the pragmatist and realist tempers could be tied; for a closer examination see V. S. Tjalve, 'Realism, pragmatism and the public sphere: Restraining foreign policy in an age of mass politics', *International Politics*, 50:6 (2013), pp. 784–97.
45 G. Kateb, *Hannah Arendt: Politics, Conscience, Evil* (Totowa: Rowman & Alianheld, 1983), p. 18.
46 Garry Wills, *Lincoln at Gettysburg: The Words that Remade America* (New York: Simon & Schuster, 1992), Chapter 3; Hans J. Morgenthau and David Hein, *Essays on Lincoln's Faith and Politics* (ed. Kenneth W. Thompson), Volume IV. (Lanham: University Press of America, 1983).
47 I. Hall, 'The triumph of anti-liberalism? Reconciling radicalism to realism in international relations theory', *Political Studies Review*, 9:1 (2011), pp. 42–52.
48 There is a new and exciting literature here – see for instance G. E. Marcus, *The Sentimental Citizen: Emotion in Democratic Politics* (University Park: Pennsylvania State University Press, 2002); J. Green, *The Eyes of the People: Democracy in an Age of Spectatorship* (Oxford: Oxford University Press, 2009); A. Kalyvas, *Democracy and the Politics of the Extraordinary: Max Weber, Carl Schmitt and Hannah Arendt* (Cambridge: Cambridge University Press, 2009); M. Wenman, *Agonistic Democracy: Constituent Power in the Era of Globalization* (Cambridge: Cambridge University Press, 2013).

The social and political construction of the Cold War

It may be difficult for us to believe but it still may be true that Stalin and Molotov considered at Yalta that by our willingness to accept a general wording of the declaration on Poland and liberated Europe, by our own recognition of the need for the Red Army for security behind its lines and of the predominant interest of Russia and Poland as a friendly neighbor and as a corridor to Germany, we understood and were ready to accept Soviet policies already known to us.

(Averell Harriman as Ambassador to the USSR to Secretary of State James F. Byrnes, 6 April 1946)

The story I want to tell covers more ground than I can possibly deal with in the space allotted – or indeed in something less than a book. Nonetheless, as I want to argue that a myriad of different types of factors came together, to some degree by accident, to result in the Cold War, I need to at least sketch out the factors that are essential to the understanding of what results as the Cold War. The matter is much more complex than the simple United States/USSR opposition (which was itself more complex). Much, though not all, of the information below is known. What is generally not known is how the various pieces interact with each other.

In broad strokes, there are several schools of thought over the origins of the Cold War (and I leave aside for the moment those who suggested before the end of the Second World War that the US army should not stop at Berlin but move on to Moscow). A still standard view sees an aggressive expansionist USSR that needed to be contained. I shall argue that while this appeared to be the message of the Kennan telegram, that telegram was not the sole cause of this view. The second, revisionist, school (e.g. Gar Alperovitz)[1] more or less places the blame on a bullying United States that frightened the USSR into its Cold War stance. A third (e.g. J. L. Gaddis)[2] suggests that the rise of the USA to a position of global dominance produced ambiguities that intensified an inevitable clash of interests between the USA and the USSR.

More recently, a final group (e.g. Alexander Dallin, Gail Lapidus) lays most of the blame on Stalin himself.

I perhaps share the most with the third group, but I think the matter even more complicated both politically and conceptually than this group does. The factors leading to and shaping the Cold War are, it seems to me, the following: (1) a wide range of developments, often ignored, in US domestic politics; (2) a set of bureaucratic dynamics both in the United States and the USSR; (3) internationally, a set of understandable perceptions of the other; and (4) a set of historical contingencies. Each factor is both political and conceptual.

The first issue, generally ignored, has to do with the changing status of the political left in American domestic politics during the 1930s and early to mid-1940s. An initial thing to remember is that during the 1930s and even early 1940s the available political spectrum was far wider than was the case in the United States after the Cold War. While this is anecdotal, I once asked my missionary father, a man of very progressive political views, about the political situation in China (where he had been living in the late 1930s and where later I was born), only to have him answer – as if the answer had been foregone to him at the time – 'You had to choose. You could be a fascist, a nationalist or a communist.' Most relevant here is the fact that in the United States popular sympathies were increasingly supportive of trade unions. The impact of the Wagner Act of 1935 was a rapid growth in unionisation. And much of it, particularly in the trade unions (Congress of Industrial Organizations, CIO) as opposed to the craft unions (American Federation of Labor, AFL), was sympathetic to the left and far left – it is estimated that by 1936 approximately a third of the leadership of the CIO (which had about three million members) were or had been members of the Communist Party USA (CPUSA) or were sympathetic to it – fellow travellers.[3] The existence of a wide range of front groups further softened the boundaries (Eleanor Roosevelt was a member of the American Youth Congress and endorsed 'Six Songs for Democracy', the recording coming out of the experience of the Lincoln Brigade in the Spanish Civil War). If you were actively favourable to racial justice in the 1930s, you were highly likely to have interacted with some front group.[4] More importantly, people moved in and out of the CPUSA or its front groups, in particular during the mid-1930s. One of the reasons that Robert Oppenheimer got into trouble is that it was not unusual to have had friends who were party members or fellow travellers. Frank Coe, Secretary of the International Monetary Fund and a principle architect of Bretton Woods, lost his job because of political sympathies and the probability that his brother was a party member. He ended up in China as a top advisor on international trade and finance.

This growth of the overall left is coupled with an important change in the CPUSA. Earl Browder becomes the General Secretary in 1930, in part because he had not been identified with any of the internecine factions (having been in China for the previous two years). He starts by abolishing the emblems by which the CPUSA had separated itself off from the rest of the labour movement (e.g. CPUSA shop newspapers) and begins to be concerned with success in American politics, rather than simple participation in a worldwide revolutionary movement. In 1935 the slogan 'Towards a Soviet America' is replaced by 'Communism is Twentieth Century Americanism'. By 1936 half the membership is native born (and 'party names' were generally white-bread Anglo-Saxon – Isok Granich becomes Mike Gold).

By the end of the 1930s, Browder comes to think that there is nothing inherently revolutionary in the American working class experience. During presidential campaigns there are parades in places like Des Moines, Iowa, with posters showing Marx, Engels, Washington and Lincoln. Browder offers to run as Norman Thomas's Vice President in 1936. The CPUSA slogan in 1936 is 'Defeat Landon at all costs' – hardly designed to elect Browder. The CPUSA runs no candidate for president in 1944. They are important participants in the founding and development of the CIO in 1935 (John L. Lewis of the United Mine Workers knowingly uses CPUSA organisers). One might note the victory of the CIO (44-day sit-down strike) over General Motors in 1937.[5]

There was some success and possible future to these developments. In 1943 Moscow dissolves the Communist International.[6] Also in 1943, Browder dissolves the CPUSA and replaces it with the Communist Political Association (CPA), which defines itself as 'a non-party organization of Americans which, basing itself on the working class, carries forth the tradition of Washington, Jefferson, Paine, Jackson and Lincoln. It upholds the Declaration of Independence, the Constitution, the Bill of Rights and the achievements of American Democracy against all enemies of popular liberties.'[7] Browder says: 'Roosevelt is the one political figure in our country whose election next November would constitute a guarantee that the policy of Teheran will guide our country for the ensuing four years.'[8] People move in and out of membership: by 1943 there are at least 100,000 card-carrying members with another 10,000 in the armed forces.

Browder was referring to the agreements reached by the Big Three in Teheran in which it appeared – more on this later – that the world and especially Europe was to be divided up into spheres of peaceful coexistence with dominant powers in each. In 1944 Churchill famously had sketched out a loose balance (Yugoslavia and Hungary were 50/50; Romania 90/10; Greece 10/90; Bulgaria 75/25).[9] Roosevelt, Churchill notes, 'did not protest'. (It must be said that there was subsequent dispute over these figures and it is not clear exactly when they mean, except for the fact that in one or another country the dominant influence was to be a given power.)

All of this affects the status of the left in America. The February 1945 Yalta agreements were less than clear about the partition of Europe; it was agreed that USSR would enter war against Japan two to three months after the defeat of Germany; Germany would be de-industrialised and divided into zones (Morgenthau Plan); the United Nations would be established. Stalin was apprised ambiguously of what he already knew – that the United States has developed a new weapon. There was in particular no real resolution of the Poland question. At Yalta, however, the West agreed to recognise the Lublin (pro-Communist) Poles, apparently agreeing with the Soviets as to the seating of three members of the pro-West 'London' Poles and five of the Lublin group, as well as to free elections as soon as possible thereafter.[10] Poland was moved westward to the distress of the British; Outer Mongolia remained under USSR influence. Nothing was said about elections in the Baltics.

At this point, one might still say that if you were a progressive in politics, it looked like a period of coexistence, if not cooperation, might be possible between the United States and the USSR. However, in April 1945 Jacques Duclos published an article 'On the Dissolution of the Communist Party of the USA' in the French Communist journal *Cahiers du communisme*. Probably written by Malenkov, who advocated the strengthening of the USSR and opposed coexistence – and in any case certainly approved by Moscow – the article attacked the Teheran thesis of peaceful coexistence. It (1) said that a seizure of power was prerequisite; (2) accused Browder of transforming a diplomatic settlement into a political programme at home; (3) accused Browder of American exceptionalism; (4) suggested that postwar polarisation of the United States and the USSR was inevitable; and (5) foresaw that, due to end-of-war spending, an economic crisis would bring the working class to power. It is worth noting that there was at this time a split in the Soviet party between those advocating peaceful coexistence (Zhdanov and Litvinov) and those wishing to strengthen the USSR against an inevitable conflict.[11] It is not clear if (a) Stalin's stance had changed from Yalta; or (b) if he had lied at Yalta; or (c) if he had been trying to use the CPUSA to warn Truman; or (d) if Malenkov simply won a bureaucratic turf fight and presented the results to Stalin. It is clear that Stalin was worried about the separatist tendencies of China and Yugoslavia – and thus also of the important US party.

The CPUSA Central Committee (CC) met three times to discuss this (and the Federal Bureau of Investigation (FBI) recorded this from its wire-tap).[12] On 16 May 1945 it is all unclear – they draft a letter to Duclos saying he was right but they (i.e. Browder) are too; on 22 May W. Z. Foster (an old enemy of Browder's) says Browder has to accept Duclos (as Moscow had clearly spoken). Browder says he has no intention of being a zombie. Foster asks what is a zombie and Browder says: 'A zombie is a modern myth about a dead person who has been raised by some magical process and walks about under the control of another mind'. The CC meets again and the entire leadership somersaults one after the other. On 24 May the Duclos article is published in the Communist Party paper, the *Daily Worker*. On 4 June the CC proposes a resolution that Duclos was right. Browder is the only one to vote against it. Browder sticks to his guns on Teheran – the question he poses to the group is, as the FBI took it down: 'is it possible for such a country as the US to find a way of peaceful coexistence and collaboration with the USSR within a single framework of nations which they jointly sustain?' Browder is expelled from the party. I have a document he wrote but never published 'On the Question of Revisionism'.[13]

The first point here is that as the Second World War is ending, the movement of an extended left spectrum towards a participation in regular American politics (from the left) cuts itself off, especially domestically (internationally this had always been complicated by the changes in the line). The USSR, worried no doubt about its centrality, enhances this distancing. (Party members would refer to Moscow as 'Rome' – the seat of correct doctrine.) International events and party structure combine to keep it from expanding what I might call the 'republican tradition'.

The second major element: the struggle in the New Deal

The 1920s had given rise to an America in which the central government was feared (there was, for instance, almost no national data); there was a strong association of private power with independence; a mass market had developed; there were some efforts at benevolent corporate paternalism; unions were weak (less than 10 per cent of non-agricultural workforces are union members while in Western Europe 25 to 40 per cent are); unemployment remains below 5 per cent and often half of that. The 1929 Depression presented the left with an opportunity rectify this as well as a target. The target was this: by 1932, the two hundred largest corporations controlled 56 per cent of output while real gross domestic product (GDP) had fallen by at least 25 per cent. One could no longer claim that prosperity was around the corner, nor that the market was self-correcting.[14] Corporate efforts at paternalism (e.g. Edward Filene and Credit Unions; Gerald Swope and profit-sharing at General Electric) had collapsed; by 1932 manufacturing output was at 54 per cent of the 1929 level. Unemployment was now about 25 per cent of the labour force,[15] with at least 30 per cent in New York City and close to 50 per cent in Philadelphia.

Roosevelt's election had led to the various Acts and policies of what one might call the 'First' New Deal: the Wagner Act; the National Labor Relations Act; the National Industrial Recovery Act (the promulgation of industrial codes of fair competition, guaranteed trade union rights, the regulation of working standards and of the price of certain refined petroleum products and their transportation); the Tennessee Valley Authority; the repealing of poll tax; and the extension of unions to the south.[16]

All of this generated a counter New Deal, mainly through the overturning by the Supreme Court of various New Deal policies as unconstitutional.[17] Roosevelt's court-packing attempt to change the composition of the Court backfires. But Roosevelt is re-elected by an enormous margin in 1936; the CIO makes gains; the left thinks further planning has to come. The Supreme Court bows reluctantly to pressure and reverses some of the earlier decisions with *West Coast Hotel* v. *Parrish* as Justice Roberts switches his position on economic regulation ('a switch in time saves nine'); a new Agricultural Administration Act is passed in 1938; by 1939, 30 per cent of non-agricultural workers are in trade unions.

The domestic end game can be understood by focusing on the figure of Henry Wallace. Wallace had been Secretary of Agriculture in the 1930s and by Roosevelt's insistence was Vice President in 1940. (The Democratic Party bosses had initially refused to nominate him. Roosevelt simply said that in that case he would not accept the presidential nomination. The bosses caved.) Wallace saw the need for an international aspect to the New Deal and was explicitly concerned with America's place in the coming new international order, thinking that democracy at home would require a worldwide New Deal. Colonialism was going, but the colonial powers had little or no regard for their colonies. It was therefore important to help the poor Third World countries so that they could buy the surplus production of the West, as the post-war situation would dramatically cut down domestic spending unless it could be compensated for. He was not naïve about the often unsavoury qualities of the new Third World countries: to combine domestic planning at home and the development of markets abroad would require policies of anti-imperialism and anti-colonialism, as well as anti-fascism. He supported the development of international development banks. So at home the issues became planning and relations to the USSR. And by 1940 traditional elites were already very suspicious of Roosevelt on these matters.

It was also clear to both the progressive and conservative sides that a consequence of the war was the vastly increasing power of Washington and the federal government, and that this would persist. The question became what to do.

Two answers were proposed. Henry Luce famously wrote a long editorial in *Life* magazine, which he titled 'The American Century'. His message was basically that when the United States won the war, it would have the whole world to itself. The United States would be the dominant power in the world and could and should act accordingly. To this Wallace responded with a speech that came to be known as 'The People's Century'. He advocated the policies laid out above and was explicitly aware of the fact that many would use anti-Soviet feelings to oppose those policies.[18]

These issues – domestic democratic planning and relations with the USSR – are the major ones that confront the United States as the war comes to an end. There are important ancillary factors. Domestic politics see a new scope to union power. There had been a no-strike pledge during the war (overly enthusiastically supported by the CPUSA after 1941). An effect of this was that there is not much practical experience with what exactly collective bargaining will entail. There is a set of major strikes in 1945 (the CPUSA helps to organise them). In November 1945 labour and business leaders meet. Labour leaders refuse to list *any* functions that belong exclusively to management. Among the demands at the United Auto Workers strike at General Motors are a 30 per cent rise in wages with no rise in prices and co-management of all the decisions involving production, product development and distribution. Charles E. Wilson, head of General Motors and later Secretary of Defense under Eisenhower, says that this is 'an idea from east of the Rhine'.

At stake before the war was the question whether the CIO (the most left-wing labour group) might join with a major party.[19] This would have important implications. For instance, in September 1945 the Senate had approved a version of what had been Roosevelt's 1944 Full Employment bill – a 'Second Bill of Rights'[20] – by a vote of 71 to 10. It was strongly opposed by much of the House and by business as being paternalistic, socialistic and communistic – and because it would cut into profits. With the Chamber of Commerce the House rewrote the bill to advocate tax cuts rather than planning, and reduced the emphasis on government spending. It took out the claim in the original bill that employment was a right; it replaced 'full employment' with 'maximum employment'; specific public works proposals were replaced by urging the use of 'all practical means'.

All of this is up in the air when Roosevelt comes up for re-election in 1944. The state of his health is the obvious concern and the major matter is thus who will be vice president. Labour and the Old New Deal want Wallace. Southern Democrats and the old machines want someone else. Racial questions are also centrally important.[21] The machines worry that Wallace's support for racial equality would lead to a split-off of the Southern Democrats and that this would in turn weaken the machines and possibly defeat Roosevelt. The CPUSA, astonishingly, is silent, even saying that 'a less controversial candidate might help unify the country'. Roosevelt is publicly silent and this is taken as lack of support for Wallace. He writes a letter that is leaked, indicating that he would accept Truman or Douglas.

After 1942 the New Deal sympathetic Democrats had a bare majority in the House and a majority of ten in the Senate. The Southern Democrats had eliminated the Farm Security Administration and the Civilian Conservation Corps in 1942–43. In addition to re-election fears, Roosevelt probably was mindful of the need of the support of the Southern Democrats for the coming United Nations proposal.

Wallace nominates Roosevelt at the convention – an uncompromising social and economic justice speech. He is almost swept in by acclamation.[22] The Wallace forces know this is their one chance. Edwin Pauley, treasurer of the Democratic National Committee and the head of the anti-Wallace Democrats, actually orders the power leads to the organ to be cut with an axe so as to stop the over-25-minute demonstration. The initial vote is 429.5 to 319.5 in favour of Wallace. This lacks 159.5 votes for a majority, those going to favourite sons. Pauley (with the help of Clark Clifford, a top Truman aide) calls for an adjournment and gavels it in, despite a manifest lack of support from the floor, just seconds before a motion is to be made to nominate Wallace by acclamation. The Truman forces regroup. The next vote is 475.5 to 473, still for Wallace, but then the realignments and shifts are announced and Truman wins 1,031 to 105. Wallace is made Secretary of Commerce and the Congress promptly removes the Reconstruction Finance Corporation[23] from his control. War plants are sold off to private industry. Roosevelt dies on 12 April 1945. Had he died the previous December, Wallace would have been president.

The preceding two sections sketch out the domestic factors that shape the context in which the Cold War is to develop. I need now to turn to the interplay of these factors with the international situation.

The third element: the international situation

During the Second World War the United States, Britain, and Russia – the three major Allies – had agreed on joint three-power military occupation of all the conquered territories. While there were multiple non-observances of agreements, the United States was the first to break the agreement during the war by allowing Russia no role whatever in the military occupation of Italy. Despite this serious breach of agreement, Stalin generally displayed his consistent preference for the conservative interests of the Russian nation-state over cleaving to revolutionary ideology – in particular by repeatedly betraying or curbing indigenous communist movements.

Apparently in order to preserve peaceful relations between Russia and the West, Stalin consistently tried to hold back the success of certain communist movements. He was successful in France and Italy, where communist partisan groups profiting from the legitimacy of a major role in the Resistance might have tried to seize power in the wake of the German military retreat; Stalin ordered them not to do so, and instead persuaded them to join coalition regimes headed by anti-communist parties. In both countries the communists were soon ousted from the coalition. In Greece, where the communist partisans almost did seize power, Stalin irretrievably weakened them by abandoning them and urging them to turn over power to newly invading British troops.

In other countries, particularly ones where communist partisan groups were strong, the communists flatly refused Stalin's requests. In Yugoslavia, the victorious Tito refused Stalin's demand that Tito subordinate himself to the anti-communist Mihailovich in a governing coalition; and Mao refused a similar Stalin demand that he subordinate himself to Chiang Kai-shek. Lu Ding Yi, the head of the Central Propaganda Department of the Chinese Communist Party (CCP) in Yen'an and a top Central Committee figure, told me in 1980 that the CCP received no military support from the USSR and, with a smile, noted that at key times when the CCP were making decisions of import, the radio contact between Moscow and Yen'an would mysteriously go bad. He was still angry at the Soviets.

There is no doubt that these rejections were the beginning of the later, extraordinarily important schisms within the world communist movement. Truman's openly expressed and widely shared attitude, however, was that all Communist Party countries took their orders from Moscow. (There has always been an unanswerable question as to what could have been done in those times between the USA and Yugoslavia, China, Vietnam – places with successful indigenous communist movements.)

Russia, therefore, governed Eastern Europe as a military occupier after winning a war launched against it through those countries. Russia's initial primary goal was probably not to communise Eastern Europe on the back of the Soviet Army, but to gain assurances that Eastern Europe would not be the broad highway for another future assault on Russia, as it had been three times in a century and a half – the last time in a war in which over twenty million Russians had been slaughtered. It is worth noting that the Soviets were suspicious that the West had worked out an agreement with the Germans such that Western forces would occupy most of Germany. Resistance in the East to the advancing Soviet troops was surprisingly much stronger than it was in the West to the Western Allies, as Stalin pointed out in a letter to Roosevelt on 7 April 1945.[24] (On the other hand, the Germans may have simply been more receptive to the Western allies than to the Russians.)

It is also the case, as the war was coming to an end, that some elements in the USSR leadership seemed open to some kind of relations with the United States. In 1945 Molotov indicated to Harriman that the USSR was willing to order US$6 million of American goods when the war ended. He explained that with the end of war production the United States would need new markets (sounding remarkably like Wallace). In August 1945 an article in a party paper (*Bolshevik*) indicated that 'war was not irreversible under present conditions': Stalin endorsed this view the following month (and apparently the US Joint Chiefs of Staff shared this position). I leave aside here the importance and constraint of the now generally recognised facts of the devastation of the USSR and of a Soviet military demobilisation parallel to that of the United States. Importantly, however, in 1946 the Soviet Air Force was elevated to the status of the other armed forces.[25] None of this implies close friendship or even trust: it does make the situation potentially quite fluid, however.

In the meantime there was a great deal of debate in the press (especially in Great Britain) about Soviet intentions. The British were especially strong on pushing the claim that the USSR had wide ambitions. This became the general theme of Churchill's famous 5 March 1946, Fulton, Missouri speech, which drew headlines in the United States as 'A Lesson for America'.[26]

Thus, in the immediate aftermath of the war, opinion in the United States is divided. To some degree, the left had tended to insulate itself, or was insulated from the rest of the political spectrum. The situation in Europe is not clear. The USSR is busy installing pro-Soviet governments in Romania and Bulgaria, as per Teheran; they betray the Greek communists who were supported by Tito, as they do the Iranian communists. Charles Bohlen notes that George Kennan in fact suggested foregoing setting up the United Nations and simply accepting the division of Europe into spheres of influence.[27] The USSR is very anxious about remaining the Rome for the movement. Mao comes to Moscow, and after an initial meeting or two is kept waiting six weeks for any kind of agreement.[28]

At this point there are coalition governments in Hungary and Czechoslovakia and elections are indeed held in which the communists get less than 20 per cent of the ballots. Poland is a particular question in that the pre-war government had fled to London (the so-called London Poles), while the Soviets had backed a resistance group centred around Lublin.[29] This is where the test happens. As Stalin noted in a 7 April telegram to Roosevelt: 'The Polish question has indeed reached an impasse.'[30] Stanisław Mikołajczyk – the leader of the London Poles – returns to Poland. In a 1946 referendum less than a third of voters support policies of land reforms and nationalisation of industry. Mikołajczyk insists on continuing to organise a political group outside the Lublin party. Great conflicts arise, including the arrest and terrorising of members of Mikołajczyk's People's Party. We are still in late 1945 or 1946. But in the January 1947 elections the official result gives 80 per cent to the communist-led Democratic Bloc (BD, comprising the Polish Workers Party, PPR, i.e. communist; the Polish Socialist Party; the People's Party, SL; the Democratic Party, SD; and various unaligned groups). There is strong evidence, however, that the pressure and violence imposed by the occupying Soviet forces (along with a good deal of fraud) is instrumental in producing this result. It is reported to Stalin that at most 50 per cent voted for the BD. Mikołajczyk got 10 per cent (28 seats to the BD's 394). These results effectively imposed a one-party state. (Interestingly, in 1948 Gomulka will be imprisoned as harbouring a 'nationalist tendency' contra Stalin.) Mikołajczyk flees to England and then the USA.

What to make of this? How is one to make something of all this? We are now in the realm of contingencies. Here I must ask you to put yourself in the position of an Assistant or Deputy Assistant Secretary of State for East European Affairs in the American government at this time (or indeed in the British equivalent). An agreement has been reached with the Soviets at Teheran and Yalta. Elections have been held in the westernmost of the East European countries. There was a lot of pressure and indeed violence from the Soviets, in particular in Poland. It is known that Truman is much more hostile to the Soviets than Roosevelt had been.[31] Wallace is not president. There is a split in the Democratic Party. Additionally, Secretary Stimson had proposed in the Truman cabinet in September 1945 that America should share its knowledge about atomic weapons with the Soviets, otherwise there would be an arms race. He had written twice to Truman saying that unless the United States approached the USSR and 'invite[d] them into a partnership', there would be an arms race. He predicted that in any case the USSR would develop an atomic bomb within four to twenty years. On 21 September 1945 the proposal to share US knowledge of atomic weapons with the USSR is placed before the Cabinet. Wallace, Stimson, Acheson, Fortas and Ickes all vote for it; nine others vote against it. Forrestal subsequently leaks a story that Wallace wants to give the atomic bomb to the Russians.

All this is known to you as a Deputy Assistant Secretary of State. What does the world look like to you? The Soviets appear to have kept their promise in Greece; it is hard to care about what they were doing to their portion of Germany (indeed, the United States was doing much the same to the Western occupied zones: this was the Morgenthau plan, not officially abandoned until September 1946). The US elite is divided. Western Europe is economically unstable. Communists get over 25 per cent of the vote in France and are in the government. They receive close to the same vote percentage in Italy in 1946. Colonial empires are collapsing. The progress of the Red Army appears increasingly unstoppable in China, although Stalin urges Mao to not go south of the Yangtze. (When the Kuomintang moves its capital one last time to Guangdong in August 1949, the only power that goes with them is the USSR). The United States is demobilising rapidly. I present these facts chaotically on purpose in order to emphasise that the situation was chaotic. (The question of whether or not the USSR was also confused I leave aside for the minute.)

Put yourself into the American foreign policy bureaucracy. Your boss comes to you and asks something like 'what am I going to tell the President?' You ask for time to figure it out. It is at this point (22 February 1946) that Kennan sends the 8,000-word Long Telegram from Moscow. It identifies what Kennan calls the 'Kremlin's neurotic view of world affairs' and the 'traditional and instinctive Russian sense of insecurity'. For Kennan, Marxism was a 'fig-leaf' that led the Kremlin to view the outside world as hostile. He also refers to their 'disrespect for objective truth – indeed their disbelief in its existence'. They will want to 'disrupt the internal harmony' of American society, destroy its 'traditional way of life', break the 'international authority of our state'. In the *Foreign Policy* 1947 'Mr X' article, but not explicitly in the Long Telegram as best I can determine, Kennan advocates explicitly a policy of containment ('long-term, patient but firm and vigilant' that could take place by the 'adroit and vigilant application of a counterforce at a series of constantly shifting geographical and political points').

There is some debate about how much military force Kennan was willing to countenance; the message, though, was clear – the United States can outlast the Soviets if it just keeps them contained (thus in the Long Telegram he differentiated the USSR from Hitler, who worked 'by fixed plans'). Most of those in authority on either side did not think that a war was inevitable.

The telegram must have been a godsend to officials in the various departments.[32] It made sense of everything that was going on. And it also – I do not mean to be flippant – allowed you to have something to say to your boss that made sense (*a* sense) of everything.

It also had consequences: Kennan did not stop with 'containment' but also spoke of 'an overwhelming threat to our way of life': the American government was instructed to educate the American people. It was easy to point at the subversion of government employees; of the left-wing tendencies of trade unions and political reform organisations as key Soviet tactics. And these mechanisms come slowly into place. The issue was not facts: military intelligence reports from this period indicate that the Soviets were weak and potentially reasonable. But a process is started.

My point is that Kennan's telegram was a godsend to the bureaucrats – it makes sense of the whole confusing and confused situation and gives a direction and a plan, even if, as Kennan later held, that as it was carried out, it was not always done so in a manner completely consonant with Kennan's intentions.

The above developments are tied in with another set of occurrences. During the war the Army Air Force (which became a separate force only in 1947) had developed plans for a system of bases, without knowing about the atom bomb. Yalta comes and goes, resulting in the division of Europe. Stalin knew of the programme to develop the bomb. Roosevelt died in April 1945: many scientists were unclear what to do about the bomb, especially after the surrender of Germany. Truman, as we know, had no such doubts. With the end of the war, however, the military budget is frozen at US$13 billion. The Air Force (still under the Army) is worried about its future role. It realises that its future is assured if American foreign policy focuses on containing the Soviets. The cheapest way to do this is with atomic weapons, for atom bombs are much cheaper than divisions. Only an air force can deliver atomic weapons, however. Bureaucratic survival coincides with the developing policy of containment.

There is an inter-service rivalry for funds. The Air Force, however, has a global strategy (which it could justify with Kennan) and wants three hundred A-bombs to implement it (Curtis Lemay is the important figure here). Given the range of delivery airplanes, the United States also needed to construct bases close enough to the USSR for a containment strategy to be viable. (There does develop an inter-service rivalry for the development of missiles.[33]) *Time* magazine of 4 November 1962 notes that the United States *necessarily* maintains many military installations overseas – 2,230 of them, according to a Pentagon count.[34] Chalmers Johnson in *Sorrows of Empire* notes that the United States at that time still had eight hundred bases.[35] (The French apparently still had five bases in their former colonies in Africa at that time). The Novikov telegram to Stalin of 27 September 1946[36] is a response to Kennan and goes to some length to detail the number of bases planned in 1946 by the United States and their distance from the Soviet mainland.[37]

The timing of the first use of the bomb had been very distressing to the USSR. At Yalta, the *quid pro quo* for post-war agreements was that the USSR would enter the war against Japan a few months after the defeat of Germany. After 6 August 1945, Stalin says: 'Hiroshima has shaken the whole world. The balance has been broken. Build the Bomb – it will remove the great danger from us.'[38] Khrushchev later recalled: 'What if Japan capitulated before we entered the war? The Americans might say, we don't owe you anything.'[39] David Holloway sees this as evidence that Stalin feared that the United States and Great Britain would 'renege on Yalta. Furthermore the bomb demonstrated that the US had the capacity to attack the USSR.'[40] Stalin – who seems persuaded by Malenkov and on-the-ground realities – appears to have hoped for a kind of return to isolationism by the USA.

It was thus important to the USSR that the ring of US bases at least be kept as far away as possible, hence the need for dependable buffers. And that is how the world now seemed to them. The Novikov cable (probably heavily drafted and certainly annotated by Molotov) says that 'The US has abandoned its post-war tradition of isolationism and is now driven by the desire for world domination'.[41] At the Cominform conference of September 1946 in Poland, the Soviets strengthen their control over East European communist parties and impose by 1948 a set of bilateral treaties on East European countries (except for Yugoslavia).[42] Their worry appears to have been an American-sponsored German resurgence.[43]

The pieces are in place

In July 1946 Wallace (as Secretary of Commerce) sends a memo to Truman questioning the Kennan telegram: 'How do American actions appear to the USSR?' In early September he gives a talk, 'Peace – and How to Get Peace', raising the same question to a large audience in Madison Square Garden. He says that 'a large segment of our press is propagandizing our people for war in hope of scaring Russia' and calls this 'criminal foolishness'. Secretary of State Jimmy Byrnes has just given a hard-line speech known as the 'Restatement of Policy' on Germany in Stuttgart, in which he makes it US policy to repudiate the Morgenthau Plan. He states that the US intention is to keep troops in Europe indefinitely and expresses American approval of the territorial annexation of 29 per cent of pre-war Germany, but does not condone further claims. Truman will not stand for the public controversy and fires Wallace.

The Cold War has been launched internationally. The elections of 1946 give the first Republican-controlled House and Senate for thirty years. What does this Congress give the country?

It transforms the relation of the government to the citizenry in manifold ways. Space does not allow a detailed analysis, but one must note the following:

- A searching out of possible spies in government and other groups.
- The establishment of a Loyalty Board in April 1947. Its role is to inquire into political beliefs of all employees. Seth Richardson (head of the Board) says: 'Government is entitled to discharge any employees for any reason that seems reasonable with no hearing. Any suspicion may suffice.' FBI documents cite 'Confidential informants stated to be reliable', and this is enough to indict or dismiss. *Life* Magazine publishes a list and pictures of '50 dupes and fellow travelers' on 4 April 1949.[44]
- A peacetime draft – the Elston Act – is instituted in 1948.

- The Taft Hartley Act of 1947 forbids any union that does not certify that none of its leadership at any level has communist affiliations or sympathies for engaging in collective bargaining. A substantial proportion of the CIO leadership falls into the Taft Hartley category. The CIO caves in, thereby reducing the pressure from the labour movement and leading eventually to its amalgamation with the AFL, always a more conservative movement.
- In April 1948 Wallace starts to run for president with the newly founded Progressive Party on the 'Peace Plan' platform and meets with little success – indeed, several times he is stoned; in July 1948, just before the Progressive Party convention, the FBI, using in part the bugged transcripts described above, arrests the top leadership of the CPUSA under the Smith Act. Wallace (one of *Life* Magazine's dupes, of course) gets 2.6 per cent of the votes (40 per cent of which was in New York City).

There are also consequences internationally, as American foreign policy now supports these positions:

- The Central Intelligence Agency (CIA) pours money into France and Italy in order to undercut the 1946 electoral successes of the communists in those countries.
- The Truman Doctrine uses the Kennan Telegram to assert, in March 1947, the right of United States to 'support free peoples who are resisting takeovers from armed minorities or outside pressure'. I have already noted what happens to the Greece communists.
- In July 1947 Truman scraps Joint Chiefs of Staff policy report (JCS) 1067, which had decreed that one 'take no steps looking toward the economic rehabilitation of Germany [or] designed to maintain or strengthen the German economy' (part of the Morgenthau Plan), and supplants it with JCS 1779, which decrees that 'an orderly and prosperous Europe requires the economic contributions of a stable and productive Germany'.

The Marshall Plan is put into place from early 1947 on. The USSR refuses to participate as anticipated (although Maurice Thorez, head of the French Communist Party, was initially in favour of it). The policy is to rebuild Europe on capitalist lines, and rearm and rebuild West Germany (the USSR had wanted a united neutral Germany). (Ambassador Novikov refers with distress to the 'Monopolistic associations of German industrialists on which German fascism depended'.[45]) In partial response, the USSR clamps down in Hungary, Czechoslovakia and East Berlin. In February 1948 the Soviets advise Western powers that they have learned that the West intends to call a three-power meeting in London to consider policies in the Western zones. The note asserts that given the absence of the (uninvited) USSR, this constitutes a violation of the Potsdam Agreement.[46] The West goes ahead with the meeting. On 20 March 1948 Marshall Sokolovsky, the head of the Soviet Military Administration in Germany, walks out of the Allied Control Council in protest. In June the West engages in currency reform in the West: upon being officially informed of this the USSR closes access to East Berlin.

This leads to the Berlin crisis of 1948–49. To some degree in response, the North Atlantic Treaty Organization (NATO) is established with a nuclear guarantee – Novikov had worried about an official military alliance between the United States and Great Britain in his telegram of 1946.

- The defence budget is US$9billion in 1948; it rises to US$53billion in 1953. It remains in the high 40s for the next several years, rising eventually to and staying well over US$100 billion during the Vietnam War and after.[47]
- The Soviets explode an atomic weapon in 1949.
- The communists triumph in China in the same year, resulting in the completion of the ongoing purge in the State Department of any officer with China expertise.[48]

And with all this, and the effect of the Kennan Telegram, it is unsurprising that in 1949 the United States formulates the principles of its foreign policy in National Security Council Report (NSC) 68, mainly authored by Paul Nitze.[49] The document becomes the basis for American Foreign Policy for the next several decades and, contrary to the many-pronged approach advocated by Kennan, is much more militarily focused. It argues that: (1) the American free society is confronted by a threat to basic values; (2) the integrity of that system will not be jeopardised by anything that the United States does against the USSR; and (3) it calls for a tripling of the defence budget. With the start of the Korean War,[50] the military budget goes from US$13 billion to US$48 billion (one sees the military uses of Keynesianism) and remains high permanently (see above). It thus legitimates as national policy all of the domestic and international elements listed above.

Conclusion

When seeking to understand a historical event, we must not only recognize that there may be multiple causes, but we must also leave open space for accident and contingency. I have tried to sketch here the factors that went into the development of the Cold War. They are domestic; they are international; they are bureaucratic; they are technical; they are matters of historical accident. It is not at all clear to me that the Cold War was inevitable, though it was perhaps in the end over-determined, to use a structuralist term. What is clear is that the period from 1940 until sometime in 1946 is a period in which the dynamics in American society were complex and varied enough to have made possible other outcomes. What is also clear is that whatever made apparently reasonable sense of a very confusing concatenation of events was likely to determine the course the policy would take. In this sense, Kennan made a Cold War possible, although he did not cause it.

Dedicated to the memory of Charles Nathanson.

Notes

1 See G. Alperovitz, *Atomic Diplomacy: Hiroshima and Potsdam* (New York: Simon and Schuster, 1965) and G. Alperovitz, *The Decision to Use the Atomic Bomb and the Architecture of an American Myth* (New York: Knopf, 1995). See also the materials collected at www.doug-long.com/ga1.htm (accessed 11 December 2015).

2 J. L. Gaddis, *The Cold War: A New History* (New York: The Penguin Press, 2005) and inter alia J. L. Gaddis, *The United States and the Origins of the Cold War, 1941–1947* (New York: Columbia University Press, 2000 [1972]).

3 See e.g. M. Isserman, *Which Side Were You On? The American Communist Party during the Second World War* (Urbana: University of Illinois Press, 1993). The 'right-wing' version is given in several books by Harvey Klehr.

4 See e.g. M. Naison, *Communists in Harlem during the Depression* (Urbana: University of Illinois Press, 2005).

5 See the essay on the Flint strike by M. Walzer in his *Obligations: Essays on Disobedience, War and Citizenship* (Cambridge MA: Harvard University Press), Chapter 4.

6 The text, signed by a multinational range of leaders, can be found at www.marxists.org/history/international/comintern/dissolution.htm.

7 The citation is from the opening of the CPA constitution.

8 Isserman, *Which Side Were You On?*, p. 188.

9 W. Churchill, *Triumph and Tragedy (The Second World War)* (New York: Mariner Books, 1986), pp. 227–8.

10 Stalin complains to Roosevelt on 7 April 1945 that this ratio has not been observed: 'At the Crimea Conference the three of us held that five people should be invited for consultation from Poland and three from London, not more. But the U.S. and British Ambassadors have abandoned that position and insist that each member of the Moscow Commission be entitled to invite an unlimited number from Poland and from London.' See www.revolutionarydemocracy.org/Stalin/corrv2_1945.htm (accessed 10 December 2015).

11 *Pravda* even published divergent opinions by the two sides in the same issue of 8 February 1946: see C. Kennedy-Pipe, *Stalin's Cold War: Soviet Strategies in Europe, 1943 to 1956* (Manchester: Manchester University Press, 1995), pp. 95 ff.

12 I have in my possession a copy of the FBI brief to the Justice Department for the Dennis prosecution obtained through a Freedom of Information Act request; it contains verbatim although censored bugged transcripts of the discussions of this letter at CPUSA headquarters.

13 Though he did publish *In Defense of Communism: against W. Z. Foster's 'New Route to Socialism'* in 1949.

14 There is a wonderful book by Galbraith on the denial of the continuing reality of the Great Depression. See J. K. Galbraith, *The Great Crash, 1929* (New York: Mariner Books, 2009 [1955]).

15 This probably significantly underestimates the actual percentage. See A. Keyssar, *Out of Work: The First Century of Unemployment in Massachusetts* (Cambridge: Cambridge University Press, 1986).

16 See the recent book by I. Katznelson, *Fear Itself: The New Deal and the Origins of Our Time* (New York: Liveright, 2013).

17 The best study of these cases is P. Irons, *The New Deal Lawyers* (Princeton: Princeton University Press, 1982). The National Industrial Recovery Act was overturned in *Schechter Poultry v. United States* (1935); the Agricultural Adjustment Act was overturned in 1936 in *United States v. Butler*, which declared the Act unconstitutional for levying this tax on the processors only to have it paid back to the farmers, and declared the regulation of agriculture to be a state and not a federal power. The Tennessee Valley Authority was narrowly upheld however in 1936 (*Ashwander v. Tennessee Valley Authority*).

18 On Wallace see inter alia N. D. Markowitz, *The Rise and Fall of the People's Century: Henry A. Wallace and American Liberalism* (New York: Free Press, 1973).

19 The Republicans thought it had in effect taken over the Democratic Party. In about 1944 Robert McCormick, publisher of the *Chicago Tribune*, wrote: 'They call it the Democratic national convention but obviously it is the CIO convention. Franklin D. Roosevelt is the candidate of the CIO and the Communists because they know if elected, he will continue to put the government of the United States at their service, at home and abroad ... The CIO is in the saddle and the Democrat donkey, under whip and spur, is meekly taking the road to communism and atheism ... Everybody knows that Roosevelt is the Communist candidate, but even the Communists cannot be sure where their place will be if he wins. His purpose is to overthrow the Republic for his own selfish ambitions [but] it is the duty of every American to oppose The Great Deceiver [Roosevelt]'. Cited in D. M. Jordan, *FDR, Dewey, and the Election of 1944* (Bloomington: University of Indiana Press, 2011), p. 201.

20 Included in Roosevelt's 1944 State of the Union message were these rights: to a useful and remunerative job in the nation's mines, industries, farms, and shops; to earn enough to provide adequate food, clothing, and recreation; of every farmer to raise and sell his products at a return that will give him and his family a decent living; of every businessman, large and small, to trade in an atmosphere of freedom from unfair competition and domination by monopolies at home or abroad; of every family to a decent home, to adequate medical care and the

opportunity to achieve and enjoy good health; to adequate protection from the economic fears of old age, sickness, accident, and unemployment; to a good education.

21 See again Katznelson, *Fear Itself.*

22 See R. H. Ferrell, *Choosing Truman: The Democratic Convention of 1944* (Missouri: University of Missouri Press, 2000).

23 Its powers had been expanded during the Second World War and it had merged with the Federal Deposit Insurance Corporation. During the war it established eight new corporations and purchased an existing one.

24 Stalin writes inter alia: 'It is hard to agree that the absence of German resistance on the Western Front is due solely to the fact that they have been beaten. The Germans have 147 divisions on the Eastern Front. They could safely withdraw from 15 to 20 divisions from the Eastern Front to aid their forces on the Western Front. Yet they have not done so, nor are they doing so. They are fighting desperately against the Russians for Zemlenice, an obscure station in Czechoslovakia, which they need just as much as a dead man needs a poultice, but they surrender without any resistance such important towns in the heart of Germany as Osnabrück, Mannheim and Kassel. You will admit that this behavior on the part of the Germans is more than strange and unaccountable.' See www.revolutionarydemocracy.org/Stalin/corrv2_1945.htm (accessed 10 December 2015).

25 See Kennedy-Pipe, *Stalin's Cold War*, pp. 84–6.

26 Churchill said among other things: 'The United States stands at this time at the pinnacle of world power. It is a solemn moment for the American Democracy. For with primacy in power is also joined an awe-inspiring accountability to the future ... Opportunity is here now, clear and shining for both our countries. To reject it or ignore it or fritter it away will bring upon us all the long reproaches of the after-time ... Before we cast away the solid assurances of national armaments for self-preservation we must be certain that our temple is built, not upon shifting sands or quagmires, but upon the rock.' He goes on to say that the dangers are war and tyranny. The sole possession by the United States of atomic weapons makes war unlikely and this would not be the case if the USSR also had them. To deal with tyranny he calls for a 'fraternal association of the English-speaking peoples' explicitly to be military, without which the 'dark ages may return, the Stone Age may return on the gleaming wings of science'. He argues: '[I]t is my duty however, for I am sure you would wish me to state the facts as I see them to you, to place before you certain facts about the present position in Europe. From Stettin in the Baltic to Trieste in the Adriatic, an iron curtain has descended across the Continent ... I do not believe that Soviet Russia desires war. What they desire is the fruits of war and the indefinite expansion of their power and doctrines.' The full text can be found in several places on line.

27 C. E. Bohlen, *Witness to History, 1929–1969* (New York: Norton, 1973), p. 176 (thanks to Kennedy-Pipe).

28 See the discussion in D. Halberstam, *The Coldest Winter: America and the Korean War* (New York: Hyperion, 2007), pp. 352–4. See the text of Mao's telegrams to

the Central Committee of the Chinese Communist Party at http://astro.temple.
edu/~rimmerma/Mao%27s_Moscow_visit.htm (accessed 11 December 2015).

29 See D. Curp, *A Clean Sweep? The Politics of Ethnic Cleansing in Western Poland* (Rochester NY: University of Rochester Press, 2006).

30 See www.marxists.org/reference/archive/stalin/works/correspondence/01/45.htm (accessed 11 December 2015), Document 418.

31 See http://academic.brooklyn.cuny.edu/history/johnson/novikov.htm (accessed 10 December 2015) for the Ambassador Novikov telegram of 27 September 1946 that refers to him as 'politically unstable … with certain conservative tendencies' and sees in the appointment of Byrnes a 'strengthening of the … most reactionary circles of the Democratic Party'. This telegram is in part a reaction to the Kennan telegram discussed below.

32 See in particular H. Mehan, C. E. Nathanson and J. M. Skelly, 'Nuclear discourse in the 1980s: The unravelling conventions of the Cold War', *Discourse and Society*, 1:2 (1990), pp. 133–65.

33 See J. Neufeld, *The Development of Ballistic Missiles in the United States Air Force, 1945–1960* (Washington DC: Office of Air Force History, United States Air Force, 1989). The Redstone missile project is assigned to the US Army Ordnance Corps in 1948. The USSR successfully tests an intercontinental ballistic missile (the R-7) in August 1957; the United States has success with the Atlas in November 1958.

34 These are already of concern in Novikov's 1946 telegram, where he notes that as some of the bases are '10000–12000 km distant from the US there is no doubt as to their aggressive intent'.

35 C. Johnson, *The Sorrows of Empire: Militarism, Secrecy and the End of the Republic* (New York: Metropolitan Books, 2005), Chapter 6.

36 See note 31.

37 In 1949 the United States had 258 bases in Europe, Canada and the North Atlantic. By 1957 it had 566, and 673 in 1967; in the Pacific and South East Asia it had 235 in 1949, and 256 by 1957. See J. R. Blaker, *United States Overseas Basing* (New York: Praeger, 1990), Table 1.2.

38 D. Holloway, 'Entering the nuclear arms race: The Soviet decision to build the atomic bomb, 1939–1945', *Social Studies of Science*, 11:2 (1981), pp. 159–97.

39 W. Taubman, *Khrushchev: The Man and His Era* (New York: Norton, 2004).

40 D. Holloway, 'Nuclear Weapons and the Escalation of the Cold War, 1946–1962', in O. A. Westad and M. Leffer, eds., *The Cambridge History of the Cold War*, vol. I (Cambridge: Cambridge University Press, 2010), 376–97.

41 Novikov Telegram; see also G. K. Zhukov, *The Memoirs of Marshal Zhukov* (London: Cape, 1971), p. 102.

42 The USSR pressure on Tito to come back in line with Moscow failed. See W. O. McCagg Jr, 'Domestic politics and Soviet foreign policy at the Cominform Conference in 1947', *Slavic and Soviet Series*, 2:1 (Spring, 1977), pp. 3–31.

43 See Kennedy-Pipe, *Stalin's Cold War*, pp. 121–2.

44 The list can be found at http://astronauticsnow.com/history/dupes/index.html (accessed 10 November 2015).

45 Novikov Telegram.

46 H. Adomeit, *Soviet Risk-Taking and Crisis Behavior* (London: Allen and Unwin, 1982), pp. 80 ff. I owe this reference to Kennedy-Pipe.

47 See http://federal-budget.insidegov.com (accessed 10 November 2015). These are adjusted figures.

48 See E. J. Kahn, *The China Hands: America's Foreign Service Officers and What Befell Them* (New York: Penguin, 1976). Prominent among the purged were Oliver Edmund Clubb, John Paton Davies Jr., Everett F. Drumright, Fulton Freeman, Raymond P. Ludden, James K. Penfield, Edward E. Rice, Arthur R. Ringwalt, John Stewart Service, Phillip P. Sprouse, John Carter Vincent.

49 See N. Thompson, *The Hawk and the Dove: Paul Nitze, George Kennan, and the History of the Cold War* (New York: Henry Holt, 2009). Text of NSC 68 is available at http://fas.org/irp/offdocs/nsc-hst/nsc-68.htm (accessed 11 November 2015).

50 The history of the origins of the Korean War is complex. It does appear, however, that after some resistance Stalin and later Mao gave into the demands of North Korean President Kim to invade the South on the latter's belief that the United States would not seriously defend the South. (Secretary Acheson had given a speech that appeared to leave South Korea outside the US defence perimeter.) US forces were in fact so unprepared that the initial push of the North Korean Army made it almost to the south coast. See B. Cummings, *Origins of the Korean War* (Princeton: Princeton University Press, 1981) and Halberstam, *The Coldest Winter*.

Chaotic epic: Samuel Huntington's *The Clash of Civilizations and the Remaking of World Order* revisited

I believe the United States and the West should attempt to promote human rights and democracy in other societies, but I do not think it desirable to do this by military force and I do believe it is essential to recognise the difficulties of promoting democracy in poor societies with cultures very different from that of the West.[1]

At a 1997 Harvard conference, scholars reported that the elites of countries comprising at least two-thirds of the world's people – Chinese, Russians, Indians, Arabs, Muslims and Africans – see the United States as the single greatest threat to their societies. They do not regard America as a military threat but as a menace to their integrity, autonomy, prosperity, and freedom of action ... Such actions are to be expected. American leaders believe that the world's business is their business. Other countries believe that what happens in their part of the world is their business, not America's.[2]

The case for revisiting Samuel Huntington's *The Clash of Civilizations and the Remaking of the World Order*, published as an article in 1993 and as a much expanded book in 1996, can readily be made on the grounds of elucidating an infamously fluid and inconsistent text, or on those of reviewing the intellectual and policy environment of the immediate post-Cold War years. What is not, however, required is any effort to rescue the argument from some supposed marginality or obscurity.

The article was translated into twenty-six languages, and the book (which is the version that will almost exclusively concern us here) has never gone out of print in English; in 2015 the 2002 edition stood at number 3 in Amazon's ranking of defence and strategy titles. In March 2015, seven years after Huntington's death, a commentator on the escalating economic crisis in Greece noted, without any evident need to elaborate his increasingly salient argument, that the country did not belong to the 'West', but formed part of an Orthodox Christian civilisation alongside Russia and Serbia.[3] Although Huntington's reputation would be substantially tarnished by his final book *Who Are We? America's Great Debate* (2004),[4] and that volume would likewise generate extensive controversy, it was in many senses presaged by *Clash of Civilizations* and never displaced it as the central contribution by an academic who had for several decades enjoyed the status of public intellectual, foreign policy adviser and international affairs pundit. Both mainstream and maverick, Huntington would certainly qualify as a member of Perry Anderson's category of 'ecstatic hybrid' intellectuals in US foreign policy circles.[5] Godfrey Hodgson's obituary for the *Guardian* was quite representative of those published elsewhere in the international press: 'A cold war liberal with a conservative cast of mind, he tossed highly personal ideas around like confetti. Some were wild and, for many, pernicious; others have come to be seen as wise and prescient.'[6]

In this chapter I hope to make the case that Huntington's inconsistency of voice, method and concept has preserved interest in his work through the post-Cold War 'unipolar moment', the formidable geostrategic consequences of the 11 September 2001 attacks, the economic crisis that opened in 2008 and a recomposition of international 'fault-lines' of transcontinental scope. I share the view of the obituarist of *The Economist* that Huntington's argument has held up '[b]oth well and badly'.[7] Whilst it is very tempting and not inaccurate to characterise him as 'slippery' and his book as 'brilliant, provocative, and utterly unconvincing', these are insufficient assessments and can edge into caricature.[8]

Equally, after 11 September many may have shared the view expressed by Fouad Ajami in the *New York Times*: 'I doubted Samuel Huntington when he predicted a struggle between Islam and the West. My mistake.'[9] However, Huntington's depiction of Islamic 'civilisation' has proved, by some margin, to be the most criticised feature of his argument, and he himself uncharacteristically backed away from claims of prescience in this connection, telling *Newsweek*: 'The causes of contemporary Muslim wars lie in *politics, not* seventh-century religious doctrine'.[10] As we shall see, this is one of several cases where Huntington's elaboration on a position effectively denies perfectly reasonable assumptions made of the original, enabling him to be simultaneously associated with contradictory stances with what Arjun Appadurai has termed 'shocking civility'.[11]

Huntington opened the third paragraph of the book with the candid admission that 'This book is not intended to be a work of social science'.[12] Very few subsequently defended it as such and many expatiated at length on its academic insufficiencies, not least because this preliminary disclaimer appeared distinctly disingenuous after reading the following three hundred pages. For Bruce Mazlish, the book's 'importance is in inverse proportion to its scholarly worth, but that is often the case with an argument that catches the public mood'.[13] Christopher Jones viewed the book less as an inquiry

than a 'manifesto', whilst for John Gray, not himself afraid of summaris-
ing the zeitgeist, 'Huntington's vision tells us more about contemporary
American anxieties than it does about the late modern world.'[14] William
Connolly identified the very conceptual core of the work as a mood-related
conceit: '[Civilisation] is a perfect term for nervous people who seek to cover
cultural defensiveness with a veneer of large-mindedness.'[15]

In a notably astute early review, Stephen Holmes noted that, 'superficially, Huntington's principal thesis, or hypothesis, is a descriptive one', but
the 'back-and-forth between hope of revival and fear of decline, between
appeals for renewed global leadership and for modest regional retreat' seriously undermined the policy implications of the book.[16] This, though, was
less important than the expressive combination of a declinist jeremiad, una-
bashed celebration of traditional Americanism and the cool survey of geopolitical objectivity that, in concert, encouraged multiple readings. For Holmes,
Huntington had advertised a great deal more than he could deliver: 'After
posting eye-catching but implausible headlines ... Huntington introduces
his reasonable and even uncontentious arguments in smaller typeface ...
Seldom has so much old wine been poured into a new paradigm.'[17]

The issue of tone was not, in reality, a surprise for Harvard professors
on the lecture/television circuit with a big message to propagate. Although
Huntington did occasionally resort to a short-cut in the vulgate – 'The
essence of Western civilization is the Magna Carta not the Magna Mac'[18] –
his register did not vary appreciably in level or confidence from those of
Robert Putnam, Lawrence Summers, Jeffrey Sachs, Niall Ferguson and other
contemporaries and successors, including, indeed, those, like Amartya Sen,
who would devote entire volumes to criticising the Huntington thesis.

The matter of timing is worth more specific consideration, especially
when linked to the publication of the magnum opus of Huntington's doctoral student Francis Fukuyama, whose *The End of History and the Last
Man* had been published in 1992. In a joint review of that book, *Clash
of Civilizations*, and John Mearsheimer's *The Tragedy of Great Power
Politics*, which appeared in 2001 and was written before 11 September,
Richard Betts observed: 'In times of change people wonder more consciously about how the world works. The hiatus between the Cold War
and 9/11 was such a time; conventional wisdom begged to be reinvented.'
Each of these three books 'presented a bold and sweeping vision, that
struck a chord with certain readers, and each was dismissed by others
whose beliefs were offended ... although Fukuyama's rang truest when the
Berlin Wall fell, Huntington's did so after 9/11, and Mearsheimer's may do
so once China's power is full grown'.[19]

For Betts, 'Fukuyama's solution was Huntington's problem', and in view
of Fukuyama's subsequent promotion of his mentor's work as well as his

later industrious efforts to minimise the differences between them, it is worth recalling the stridency of his own position, which, like Huntington's, began as a journal article before being 'promoted' into a book. In the summer of 1989, before the fall of the Berlin Wall, Fukuyama, who had left Harvard a decade earlier, wrote in the *National Interest:* 'What we may be witnessing is not just the end of the Cold War, or the passing of a particular period of post-war history, but the end of history as such; that is, the end point of mankind's ideological evolution and the universalization of Western liberal democracy as the final form of human government.'[20]

Huntington's article, at least, can be seen as a response not just to Fukuyama's piece but also to the burgeoning 'Endist' triumphalism of the following two years. For John Gray the retort was well made in that Huntington was 'right to note that the individualist values embodied in Western understandings of liberal democracy do not command universal assent ... This is an incisive criticism of Fukuyama's neo-Wilsonian certainty that Western values are universal'.[21] Huntington himself initially responded to Fukuyama with a certain magisterial brusqueness: 'This argument suffers from the Single Alternative Fallacy. It is rooted in the Cold War assumption that the only alternative to communism is liberal democracy, and that the demise of the first produces the universality of the second ... It is sheer hubris to think that because Soviet Communism has collapsed the West has won the world for all time.'[22]

Three years later, however, the tutor was notably more restrained in his critique, and it is only at the very last chapter of *Clash of Civilizations* that we encounter a barely coded admonition: 'History ends at least once and occasionally more often in the history of every civilization. As the civilization's universal state emerges, its people become blinded by what Toynbee called "the mirage of immortality" and convinced that theirs is the final form of human society.'[23]

Huntington was decidedly not buying into any unforced variation of the 'peace dividend' so prevalent in geopolitical debates of the early 1990s. On the contrary, the Soviet collapse represented a challenge unknown for three generations, as he later quoted Gorbachev's adviser Georgi Arbatov: 'We are doing something really terrible to you – we are depriving you of an enemy.'[24] The matter, though, extended beyond an extreme case of goal deprivation, and it is easy to forget the rapid onset of new challenges at the time when Huntington was, first, moving to ask whether the new order was one of civilisational conflict – his initial article title carried a question mark – and then asserting that such was, indeed, the most useful paradigm through which to understand the new state of the world.

What were the international circumstances prevailing when Huntington hardened up his thesis (presumably as much for commercial purposes urged by his publishers Simon and Schuster as in response to the critiques encouraged by *Foreign Affairs* in the subsequent issue) between 1993 and 1995?

Undoubtedly, a certain geostrategic echo of Fukuyama's triumphalism persisted in terms of bilateral agreements over the nuclear arsenal that the newly inaugurated Bill Clinton endowed with a genial patina of equity as distinctly one-sided negotiations with Boris Yeltsin advanced. However, the post-Soviet conflicts in Abkhazia and Chechnya would have urged a caution to offset the reassuring 'velvet divorce' that terminated Czechoslovakia. And if Western Europe seemed to be combining into a much more cogent regional liberal partner through the Maastricht Treaty and the establishment of the European Union, the deepening Bosnian War and the Srebrenica massacre of July 1995 in the face of a United Nations mandate placed a very serious question mark over the capacity of multilateral peacekeeping in a new era of murderous nationalisms.

Equally, Africa, a continent for which the United States government had not developed great strategic interest, was providing equally 'mixed messages', with the collapse of the South African apartheid state and the election of Mandela being matched by the Rwanda genocide and ignominious retreat of US forces from Somalia. With Eritrean independence from Ethiopia, the Horn of Africa was being transformed into an arena of conflict that would not abate for two decades.

For an author newly alert to cultural sources of conflict, the civil wars in Sri Lanka, the Yemen, the Balkans and the Caucasus formed something of a piece with bombings in India, and the campaign from Tehran to Bradford against Salman's Rushdie's *Satanic Verses*. There might be little pattern to isolated instances of terrorism, but there was precious little ideological succour to be gained from sarin poisonings on the Tokyo metro, let alone the killing of 168 people in the Oklahoma City bombing of April 1995. Perhaps, bereft of a paradigmatic Cold War discipline, US nativism might test the tensions within the hegemonic compact of the United States itself?

Even in terms of the underlying political economy of liberalism, matters were scarcely as smooth as might be suggested by the transformation of the General Agreement on Tariffs and Trade (GATT) into the World Trade Organization, the exceptional health of the US domestic budget and the rapidly emerging commercial applications of the internet. At the end of 1994 the collapse of public finances in Mexico, within a year of the ratification of the North American Free Trade Area (NAFTA), required a US Federal Reserve bail-out of some US$50 billion and opened a phase of commercial, security and migration crises that would preoccupy Huntington so sharply that they dominated the final chapter of his book. The intervening need for the US Marine Corps to invade a badly destabilised Haiti in September 1994 signalled the threat of a new migratory threat well within the traditional US sphere of influence.

Samuel Huntington was never a linguist or 'area studies' specialist, but he had a very keen interest in the potential for the minutiae of international affairs to mutate from isolated events into serious processes. His knowledge was certainly uneven – he would soon be criticised for a wilful misreading of Islam and the Middle East, as well as a weak grasp of Chinese culture and politics – but he sought to provide empirically informed evidence for his evolving thesis from the start. That was something that Fukuyama, almost by definition, felt now to be unnecessary.

Civilisation and its critics

Huntington's essential difference with Fukuyama was over the future, not about the balance of world power prevailing immediately after the fall of the Berlin Wall. Both men essentially agreed with Charles Krauthammer's declaration of a 'unipolar moment', and in this regard Huntington's style in his 1993 article possessed an assurance that could be read by some as actually endorsing the Fukuyama thesis:

> The West is now at an extraordinary peak of power in relation to other civilizations … Global political and security issues are effectively settled by a directorate of the United States, Britain and France, world economic issues by a directorate of the United States, Germany and Japan, all of which maintain extraordinarily close relations with each other to the exclusion of lesser and largely non-Western countries. Decisions made at the UN Security Council or the IMF that reflect the interests of the West are presented to the world as reflecting the desires of the world community.[25]

Such a predominance, however, could not endure without a major and energetic adaptation to the new post-Cold War world, which the book portrays in much fuller terms and in which it had to be recognised that:

> [the] unity of the non-West and the East–West dichotomy are myths created by the West. These myths suffer the defects of Orientalism which Edward Said appropriately criticised for promoting the 'difference between the familiar (Europe, the West, "us") and the strange (the Orient, the East, "them")' and for assuming the inherent superiority of the former to the latter.[26]

Huntington's volume is divided into five parts. The first makes the case that, for the first time in history, global politics is both multipolar and multi-civilisational; modernisation is not the same as westernisation, and is not producing a universal civilisation or the westernisation of the non-West. Huntington identifies a number of civilisations, but with a varying degree of assurance and somewhat variable criteria: the Sinic (Chinese); Japanese; Hindu; Muslim; Orthodox Christian; Latin American; the West; and, perhaps, Africa. This latter doubt rests on the fact that 'most scholars of Civilization except Braudel do not recognise a distinct African civilization',[27] not least because of the historical cultural and linguistic exceptionalism of Ethiopia. However, since in the mid-1990s it had seemed possible that South Africa might mutate into a 'core state', one of Huntington's key categories, the issue of identity, remained inconclusive.

The second part argues that the balance of power is already shifting, to the detriment of the West (here the tone contrasts with the original article); Asian civilisations are expanding in economic, military and political strength; Islam is exploding demographically; and non-Western civilisations are increasingly confident in reaffirming their own cultural values. As the argument builds, Huntington supplies a range of empirical evidence, which by the third part is already cluttering the picture somewhat as reportage and factual digression build in momentum. However, the thesis here is still identifiable: the parameters of the civilisation-based world order are hardening, cultural exchange is resisted, and intra-civilisation countries are perceived to be grouping themselves under lead or core states.

Part Four is entitled 'Clashes of Civilizations', and introduces an interpretative element that was to become one of the most contentious aspects of the book. Here Huntington perceives the West's universalist pretensions as increasingly bringing it into conflict with the other civilisations, particularly Islam and China. The prime expression of such clashes are 'fault line wars', often between Muslims and non-Muslims. Part Five, the most openly polemical, argues that the survival of the West depends upon Americans strenuously reaffirming their Western identity at home whilst equally firmly resisting imposing it abroad in the recognition that their civilisation is 'unique, not universal'.[28]

Threaded through these expansive and controversial assertions are a number of observations that complicate any characterisation of Huntington's thesis as comfortably supremacist. Perhaps the most notable in this respect was: 'The West won the world not through the superiority of its ideas or values or religion … but rather by the superiority in applying organised violence. Westerners often forget this fact; non-Westerners never do.'[29] Equally, Huntington ends his book with a call for global multiculturalism every bit as strong as his promotion of domestic monoculturalism: 'Western intervention in the affairs of other civilizations is probably the single most dangerous source of instability and potential global conflict.'[30]

The immediate foreign policy implications of this panorama need no elaboration. The Huntington thesis provided a comprehensive, supra-pragmatic critique of the 'liberal interventionism' so closely associated with that other

Ivy League institution Princeton, as well as with a Clinton administration that he felt increasingly free to berate. But the historical interpretation, strategic analysis and conceptual underpinnings of the book provoked a far wider popular and academic debate. At times this derived directly from the slippage in Huntington's use of terms; sometimes it emanated from his critics' zeal in attributing to him positions that he had left behind; at other times it resulted from his marked reluctance to trespass into the realm of theory; and occasionally, of course, the employment of some blunt dismissals of author and work owed as much to personal exasperation as to intellectual diligence.

One group of critics took Huntington's use of the concept of 'civilisation' itself as their central target. For Amartya Sen, Huntington's basic concept was parasitical upon his insistence that civilisations must collide; according to Bruce Mazlish, he was engaged in an eccentric emulation of Spengler and Toynbee in attributing some naturalist life-cycle to civilisations, conceiving them as essentially closed; Dieter Senghaas found that, empirically, the frontiers between civilisations were often unsustainable, and Huntington's thesis of conflict was likewise insecure and 'unthematized'.[31] Arshin Adib-Moghaddam's view of the text was that it was merely a further, albeit scandalously underinformed, link in a long chain of 'othering' clash versions of history with Islam now providing a surrogate for the USSR.[32] Edward Said, himself the most prominent critic of 'Orientalism', was an early and equally pugnacious critic of Huntington's 'shut-down, sealed off identities', regretting that he had felt the need to develop on the original article: 'all he did … was confuse himself and demonstrate what a clumsy writer and inelegant thinker he was.'[33]

That might, indeed, have been the case, but Huntington had anticipated such criticism in two ways. First, he introduced the concept of 'cleft countries' straddling two civilisations,[34] a category that is much larger than might be expected – Canada is included, despite both its sections being part of the 'West' – and that, to Huntington's evident disappointment, might even include the United States itself. Second, Huntington provided a characterisation of 'civilisation' that is evidently not impermeable or unchanging, even if it simultaneously opened a back-door charge of imprecision:

> Of all objective elements which define civilizations … the most important usually is religion … civilizations are comprehensive … none of their constituent elements can be fully understood without reference to the encompassing civilization … A civilization is the broadest cultural entity … the highest cultural grouping of people and the broadest level of cultural identity people have short of that which distinguishes humans from other species … Civilizations have no clear-cut boundaries and no precise beginnings and endings.[35]

The usefulness of such an expansive characterisation largely evaporated for critics when in subsequent empirical sections Catholic Latin America was distinguished from equally Catholic southern ('Western') Europe; when Muslim Iran was found to provide support for Orthodox Christian Armenia against non-Christian Azerbaijan; when Japan, which alone in the nineteenth century challenged the identification of 'civilisation' with Christianity, so assiduously 'westernised' in the twentieth century; or when Israel appears on none of the book's maps, and the matter of a Judaic civilisation both within the United States itself and in the wider world is passed over, making Jews indeterminate non-Westerners.[36] For Jacob Heilbrunn, such a failure to take seriously intra-civilisational divisions represented a significant lacuna, whereas Jonathan Benthall interpreted it as a sign of Huntington's lack of racism and independence from the US foreign policy establishment.[37] Stephen Holmes perceives another map – that depicting the United States as a 'cleft country'[38] – as effectively denoting African and Hispanic Americans as non-Western.[39] This was to prove an issue of rising concern to Huntington, and it was not resolved by his pithy response to much of the above criticism that 'you can't be both Muslim and Catholic'.[40]

Beyond the contested concept

Huntington's characteristic style is to make general – often very bold – claims in his text, and to provide them with an assortment of apparently supportive numbers and quotations as evidence; as a rule, he keeps direct discussion of other authors to a minimum and mostly in the footnotes.[41] However, in his discussion of Ukraine as a prominent 'cleft country', he explicitly contrasts his own civilisational approach with John Mearsheimer's 'statist paradigm':

> a civilizational approach ... emphasises the close cultural, personal and historic links between Russia and Ukraine and the intermingling of Russians and Ukrainians in both countries, and focuses instead on the civilizational fault line that divides Orthodox Eastern Ukraine from Uniate western Ukraine, a central historical fact of long standing which, in keeping with the 'realist' concepts of states as unified and self-identified entities, Mearsheimer totally ignores.[42]

Later in the text Huntington provides a map to show this division in terms of the results of the July 1994 presidential election contest between Leonid Kuchma (east) and Leonid Kravchuk (west).[43] This fault-line does not correspond exactly to the political and military front line of the conflict following the Maidan Uprising of February 2014 against the (nationally elected) Yanukovich regime, but it is a plausible socio-cultural approximation, and the fact that it was predicated nearly twenty years earlier must constitute one source of appreciation.

Mearsheimer, however, has a case to make as well as one to answer. In his view:

> Huntington pays serious attention to the state. It is at the heart of his theory. Furthermore, he believes that states act aggressively toward each other … Nevertheless, his book parts company completely from realism when he argues that states do not operate as independent actors … I think that Huntington is wrong when he says that 'civilization' is the principal ordering concept in the world today. In fact, nationalism, not civilization, is the most powerful political ideology on the face of the earth.[44]

When, in this same interview, Mearsheimer was asked about the criteria for deciding between two projections of a strategic scenario (in that case US military withdrawal from Western Europe), he replied: 'I would be comfortable saying that if little changed after ten years, if things were pretty much the same as they were when the United States was here [the EU], then my theory was falsified. But we cannot know who is right until we run the experiment.'[45]

Perhaps, then, Huntington and Mearsheimer may be said to possess equally valid and comparably flawed projections for Ukraine. Certainly, Mearsheimer's 1993 call for the Western provision of a nuclear deterrent to the country now seems much more ill-judged than his 2014 claim that 'the Ukraine Crisis is the West's Fault', which is made on the traditional realist grounds of geo-strategic misunderstanding/dismissal of palpable Russian national interests.[46]

Equally, Huntington, who had died long before this latest conflict, had greatly underappreciated both the fierce nationalist residues of the Second World War and secular tendencies in both Russia and Ukraine that overrode religio-cultural identity. However, he was more sensitive to contingency than many people recognise and, noting the realist aspects of the situation in 1994, he outlined three possible scenarios:

1. 'If civilization is what counts … violence between Ukraine and Russia is unlikely';
2. 'A second, somewhat more likely possibility is that Ukraine could split along fault lines into two separate entities, the eastern of which would merge with Russia';
3. 'The third and more likely scenario is that Ukraine will remain united, remain cleft, remain independent, and generally cooperate with Russia'.[47]

In fact, elements of all three options prevailed through 2014–15 and seemed likely to continue thus in the medium term. The path from a Harvard study to a Pentagon gaming session is here pretty straight. As Stephen Holmes noted in his early review, when plotting conventional geo-strategic scenarios, Huntington provided some very serviceable appraisals, regardless of the civilisational paradigm within which they were tendered.[48] Equally, Ronald Inglehart and Pippa Norris readily conceded that he was 'half right' because there is a global fault-line, but it just happens to correspond to sex, not democracy. In this case the paradigm was useful but the content is misidentified.[49]

Moreover, when Huntington was compared with the idealist tradition, his repudiation of universalism finds broad favour on both a conceptual level as a critique of Kantianism (Gray/Connolly), and for those 'not particularly intellectual' readers (Sen) needing a rationale for isolationist reflexes or journalists in search of a succinct background critique of interventionism (Abrahamian).[50] At the same time, if Huntington's high register and polemical impulses were stripped out, a 'soft version' of his thesis – one, for instance, that replaced 'enemies' with 'rivals' or provided a more pliable critique of secularisation – could trade as a non-racist, non-interventionist permutation of Benedict Anderson's 'imagined communities', which, understood as tribes, would make his vision more amenable to mainstream anthropology than political science.[51]

In terms of conceptual fashion, however, Huntington stood in rather stark distinction to what was already becoming the prevalent wind of globalisation theory – a term that appeared just once in the book.[52] Nevertheless, as Ian Roxborough has noted, civilisational conflict was often treated in Pentagon circles as a primordial response to globalisation, not least because a comprehensive adoption of globalisation theory, replete with Durkheimian *anomie* rampant in post- and sub-state arenas might deny the military the opportunity to persist with the logistical and intellectual paradigms of the Cold War.[53] Thus, in the words of US Marine Commander James L. Jones:

> Before us is a complex international security landscape, characterized by the opposing forces of globalization: fragmentation and integration. On the one hand, long-simmering ethnic, tribal, religious and nationalist pressures have erupted, splintering peoples, states and even regions. On the other hand, growing interdependence draws peoples and nations into increasingly symbiotic relationships, where even minor regional instability can reverberate across the globe. The tension between these forces produces a volatile socio-political and economic environment in which the efforts of the military are prominent.[54]

This, of course, meant preparation for 'asymmetric warfare' well before 11 September 2001, but that had scarcely been a lesser feature of the Cold War era than formal battle readiness.

At the same time, it is easy to forget how rapid were the technological advances of the 1990s, with there being fewer than two million internet hosts in 1993, when the White House and UN first went online, with internet banking arriving the next year, and there existing fewer than 500,000 websites when Huntington's book was issued in 1996. Within several years he would fully register the wider social and political impact of these innovations, but the composition of *Clash of Civilizations* took place in a distinctly transitional technological period.

Method, morality and the public intellectual

Two further academic reactions to Huntington's book deserve brief mention. Both – the first unreflexively empirical and positivist, the second conceptually sophisticated and post-structuralist – were essentially critical and negative, but, of course, within the political economy of academic life that can be every bit as promotional and rewarding as votes of esteem and policy salience. Huntington must have done as much to enhance the citation indices of successive generations of both Comteans and Foucauldians as any other post-war North American political scientist.

Even if the working assumptions behind the concepts and terminology of *Clash of Civilizations* had not been subjected to such critique, it was a quite natural response of professional social scientists to subject their use to empirical testing. The most obvious format for this was to see if conflict – measured in myriad forms but with conspicuously consistent methods – had taken place more often on an inter- or intra-civilisational basis. This Henderson and Tucker did for the formidably long period of 1816 to 1992, whilst Fox employed quantitative analysis to assess the position of ethnic minorities in all three of Huntington's categories of conflict – core state conflicts; those between different states within civilisations; and fault-line conflicts within states containing populations of differing civilisations. For Henderson and Tucker, the result was mixed but unsurprising: 'We find that civilization membership was not significantly associated with the onset of inter-state war during the Cold War (1946–1988), which is consistent with one aspect of Huntington's thesis; however, we also find that for the pre-Cold War period (1816–1945) states of similar civilizations were far more likely to fight each other.'[55]

Fox's conclusion was rather more damning in that he found absolutely no statistical basis for Huntington's grand theory.[56] In this, he too was delivering no novelty since in 1986 the Yale mathematician Serge Lang had famously impeded Huntington, then serving as president of the American Political Science Association, from becoming a member of the National Academy of Sciences on the grounds that he not only lacked statistical competence but had also manipulated figures in a thoroughly tendentious manner, on one occasion to claim that South Africa was a 'satisfied society' under the apartheid regime.[57]

The second set of objections, which often take Huntington as a proxy for mainstream empirical social science in general, relate less to his conceptual and methodological imprecisions than to their wider epistemological echoes in an inequitably empowered world. The partial exception to this is to be found in the work of Charles Jones, who does take Huntington's definitions seriously and finds them markedly deficient in terms of territorial fault-lines, with a failure to recognise a civilisational differential between core and frontier or margin, where, *contra* Huntington, there is much more cultural flexibility.[58] Others, such as Ulrich Beck, noted a deeper historical linkage back to the Valladolid debates of 1550 between Sepúlveda and Las Casas over the precise human qualities of the American Indians, a debate that spurred rationalisations of the modern world hierarchy through 'the standard of civilization', which Huntington only touches on with a marginal description.[59]

A more contemporary argument in the same vein was that Huntington's work effectively 'deterritorialised' geographical space through cultural determinism and morality. This critique sometimes edged into a claim that a notionally objective thesis had provided ammunition for racist and anti-immigrant nativism, as illustrated in Pat Buchanan's *The Death of the West*, published in 2002 with the subtitle 'How Dying Populations and Immigrant Invasions Imperil Our Country and Civilization'.[60] Huntington, whose reputation had survived not only Lang's imputations of dishonesty but also revelation of support for his work from the Central Intelligence Agency (CIA), the authorship of a 1967 study for the State Department on political stability in Vietnam – a report that had quite direct strategic influence – and his role as an adviser to the Brazilian military dictatorship, was to be even more tellingly attacked in this regard.

The final chapter of *Clash of Civilizations* clearly presages the core argument of *Who Are We?* on a number of grounds, but most distinctively in its assignation of the English language and Protestant Christianity as immovable determinants of American values (combined with the constitutional scripture of the independence period, these formed the 'American Creed'); its fear that these were under both demographic and ideational challenge; and its repudiation of two core responses – a concessionary domestic multiculturalism and an aggressive reassertion of American values abroad under the guise of their universalism. The tone of these passages is not as rigidly prophetic and aggressive as that of the ensuing book of 2004 – still less than that of Donald Trump's abusive rhetoric on the stump in 2015 – but it was sufficiently doom-laden and prescriptive to excite *ad hominem* as well as intellectual attacks.

Islam and public rhetoric

As noted earlier, Huntington's treatment of Islam proved the single most controversial aspect of his book, even before the 11 September attacks. It is, then, worth quoting at a little length his position, on the understanding, which he makes scrupulously clear, that 'the underlying problem for the west is not the *Islamic Fundamentalism*. Rather, *it is Islam*, a different society whose people is convinced of the superiority of their cultural identity and is obsessed with the inferiority of their power'.[61] Five factors explain the conflict with the west:

> First, Muslim population growth which has generated large numbers of unemployed and disaffected young people who become recruits to Islamist causes, exert pressure of neighboring societies, and migrate to the West. Second, the Islamic Resurgence has given Muslims a renewed confidence in the distinctive character and worth of their civilization and values compared to those of the West. Third, the West's simultaneous efforts to universalize its values and institutions, to maintain its military and economic superiority, and to intervene in conflicts in the Muslim world generate intense resentment amongst Muslims. Fourth, the collapse of communism removed the common enemy of the west and Islam and left each the perceived major threat to the other. Fifth, the increasing contacts between Muslims and Westerners stimulate in each a new sense of their own identity and how it differs from the other.[62]

Much of this might be – and has been – treated as a plausible appraisal, worthy of reasoned discussion. However, some forty pages later Huntington makes an unsupportable and provocative claim: 'two-thirds to three-quarters of inter-civilizational wars were between Muslims and non-Muslims. Islam's borders *are* bloody, and so are its innards.'[63] Glenn Perry summarised a widespread view in his comment that 'I believe that his readiness to attribute violence to Islam is particularly objectionable'.[64]

As we have seen, this proved to be one of the issues where Huntington backed away from his initial claim. None the less, given that Fred Halliday, in particular, had already produced empirically expert and analytically forceful rebuttal of Bernard Lewis, Huntington's principal source, as well as of Edward Said, Huntington's leading antagonist, it is something of a dereliction of scholarly duty as well as a mark of ideological commitment that he made such bold claims in the first place.[65] There followed powerful article- and book-based refutations from the likes of Farwarz Gerges and Arshin Adib-Moghaddam, whose work was regularly picked up by secondary critics of Huntington.[66] However, stripped of the incautious attribution of pathology, Huntington's socio-strategic assessments held up quite well. His statistics were less deceptive than in many cases, the notion of state weaknesses was at least debatable, and that of a lack of a core state was, if one accepted the notion, indisputable. As Paul Kington noted in 1999,

'Huntington's ideas have had particular resilience when it comes to analyses of Islam.'.[67]

Why should that be so? Until the attacks of September 2001 the reason seems rather prosaic and parochial. In the transition between the 1993 article and the 1996 book the empirical narrative on Islam had been considerably expanded, whereas the essentialism of the argument had been kept unchanged. Those who disagreed with Huntington's thesis continued to see no link with the supportive material; those who were agnostic began to discuss it more substantively. After 11 September 2001 the position changed far more drastically, befitting the new state of world politics. Now it mattered greatly, in the words of Richard Crockatt, that 'one does not have to swallow Samuel Huntington's ... thesis whole to believe that cultural difference, and in particular religious belief, is an increasingly important factor in international relations'.[68] For David Cannadine, who decried the tendency, the increasingly Manichean climate encouraged mainstream historians to publish books 'depicting a world irretrievably and violently sundered'.[69]

Much more decisively, the confusion of public rhetoric, particularly from the Bush administration in the wake of the attacks, enabled 'Clash of Civilization' to be misattributed disavowed, and misunderstood alike by supporters, agnostics and critics of the Huntingtonian thesis as well as the administration. Moreover, this continued to be the case until 2008, however emphatic and frequent were the government's protestations of amicable understanding towards the Muslim faith.[70] So much ink has been expended on this issue that we can safely keep to a couple of illustrative instances.

Bush's initial use of the term 'crusade' against terrorists was sufficiently maladroit that within a week of the 2001 attacks the French foreign minister felt obliged to declare 'we have to avoid a clash of civilizations at all costs'.[71] The fact that the French position on the US response to the attacks was to become a sharp source of difference was foreshadowed in a *Le Monde* editorial that same week: 'If this "war" takes a form that affronts moderate Arab opinion; if it has an air of the clash of civilizations, there is a strong risk that it will contribute to Osama bin Laden's goal.'[72] The replacement phrase 'War on Terror' continued to provoke objections at a number of levels, but it was now at least shorn of any specifically Christian connotations.

Yet even when Bush was under palpable pressure to disown Huntington's term as in any way animating US strategy, he struggled for clarity. In his 2002 address to West Point he came close to achieving the opposite: 'When it comes to the common rights and needs of men and women, there is no clash of civilization. The requirements of freedom apply fully to Africa, Latin America, and the entire Islamic world.'[73] Well into his second term, Bush's efforts to banish the term tended to reinforce the negativity associated with it: 'This struggle has been called a clash of civilizations. In truth, it is a struggle for civilization. We are fighting to maintain the way of life enjoyed by free nations.'[74] It would not be until late 2005 that Bush precisely identified the enemies of the US campaign as being variants of radical and militant Islam.

As an academic, Secretary of State Condoleezza Rice might have made a better distinction, but proved to be hamstrung by her reflections on the curriculum at Stanford, where she, a political scientist with a PhD on Communist Czechoslovakia, had become Provost weeks after the publication of Huntington's article in *Foreign Affairs*: 'Human history has been the story of clash of civilizations and that is the interesting part about it. I never understood the critique that you should teach only Western Civilization.'[75] Returning to Stanford to address Commencement less than a year after the 11 September attacks, she sought to instil caution: 'Some here have called this most virulent form of hatred a clash of civilizations. Taken literally, that is a very dangerous idea.' Likewise, the previous month she had declared to the American Jewish Committee: 'We cannot and must not allow the West to drift into what some have called a "clash of civilizations".'[76] However clear the disavowal, the turn of phrase was now irretrievably in the mainstream, its imprecisions multiplied.

These were the conditions under which the now frail and elderly Samuel Huntington sought to develop the arguments of the final chapter of *Clash of Civilizations*, precisely by stipulating the nature and vulnerability of 'Americanism'. The fact that the register and argument of *Who Are We?* were more politically shrill and morally despondent than the earlier volume may be related to Huntington's age and the experience of disputation over the previous decade, but it is just as likely that these attributes derived from the wartime atmosphere.

In *Clash of Civilizations* he had ventured the speculation that 'The accommodation between Anglo-American North American and Spanish-Indian Mexico should be considerably easier than between Christian Europe and Muslim Turkey'.[77] It is, then, perhaps not surprising that the *New York Times* described Barack Obama's visit to Ankara in April 2009 as steering 'away from the poisonous post-9/11 clash of civilization mythology that drove so much of President George W. Bush's rhetoric and disastrous policy'.[78] On the other side of the analogy, the original author had certainly both clarified and changed his position. The USA had now definitely become a fault-line state within North America; it was race and language, not religion, that determined civilisational boundaries. Uncontrolled immigration and a boundless internet threatened to collapse the degree of social receptivity required to uphold The American Dream, which could only be experienced in English. What Jorge Castañeda, then Mexican foreign minister, called 'intermestic issues' had driven to the heart of the US political agenda.[79] Foreign policy bi-partisanship was being eradicated well before the shoreline, and the universalism that Samuel Huntington so concertedly disowned overseas no longer prevailed peaceably at home. A decade after his death, Huntington's map of a racially cleft USA was not open to much empirical falsification, but its implicit projection of conflict had proved chillingly serious, even for an administration headed by an African American. Huntington's intellectual footprint remained visible, albeit for the wrong reasons.

Notes

1 S. Huntington, 'Hassner's bad bad review', *National Interest* (Spring 1997), p. 102.
2 S. Huntington, 'The lonely superpower', *Foreign Affairs*, 78:2 (1999), pp. 35–49 at pp. 42–3.
3 N. Dimou, 'The view from Greece', *Observer* (22 March 2015). 'Greece is not part of Western civilization, but it was the home of classical civilization which is an important source of Western civilization.' S. Huntington, *Clash of Civilizations and the Remaking of World Order* (London: Simon and Schuster, 1998), p. 162. According to a collection of essays by non-American authors marking the twentieth anniversary of the original publication, 'no article has been as often cited or hotly contested ... the clash of civilizations continues to be the reference point for a host of theoretical arguments across the entire spectrum of the social sciences.' J. P. Barker (ed.), *The Clash of Civilizations Twenty Years On* (Bristol: e-International Relations, 2013), p. 1.
4 S. Huntington, *Who Are We? America's Great Debate* (London: Simon & Schuster, 1994).
5 P. Anderson, 'Consilium', *New Left Review*, 83 (2013), pp. 113–67 at p. 125.
6 G. Hodgson, 'Samuel Huntington', *Guardian* (1 January 2009).
7 'Huntington's clash', *The Economist* (30 December 2008).
8 L. Jones, 'In memoriam: Samuel Huntington', *The Oxonian Review*, 8:1 (26 January 2009); J. Heilbrunn, 'The Clash of Samuel Huntingtons', *The American Prospect* (July–August 1998), p. 24. Heilbrunn fairly identifies the deficiencies of the text as intrinsic to its genre: 'Like so many previous efforts to devise grand theories of history and politics – from Spengler to Toynbee to Fukuyama – Huntington's collapses under the weight of its own assumptions.' *Ibid.*
9 Quoted in R. Betts, 'Conflict or cooperation? Three visions revisited', *Foreign Affairs*, 89:6 (2010), pp. 186–94 at p. 190. In response to the original article, Ajami had declared, 'Huntington is wrong. He has underestimated the tenacity of modernity and secularism in places that acquired these ways against great odds, always perilously, close to the abyss, the darkness never far.' F. Ajami, 'The Summoning', *Foreign Affairs*, 72:4 (1993), pp. 2–9 at p. 3. Michael Hunt repudiated the thesis in a rather different vein: 'Huntington's interpretation, with its stark and value-laden delineation of regions in conflict, commanded considerable attention when it appeared and has won fresh converts in the wake of September 11... This "clash" interpretation has flaws that are troubling but also familiar in American foreign policy thinking. Huntington's notion of civilization is monolithic, static and essentialist.' M. Hunt, 'In the wake of September 11: The clash of what?', *The Journal of American History*, 89:2 (2002), pp. 416–25 at p. 417.

10 Quoted in E. E. D. Aysha, 'Samuel Huntington and the geopolitics of American identity: The function of foreign policy in America's domestic clash of civilizations', *International Studies Perspectives*, 4 (2003), pp. 113–32 at p. 125, emphasis in the original. A month after the 11 September attacks, Huntington told the *Observer*: 'I don't think Islam is any more violent than other religions, and I suspect if you added it all up, more people have been slaughtered by Christians over the centuries than by Muslims.' S. Huntington and M. Steinberger, 'So, are civilisations at war?', *Observer* (21 October 2001).

11 A. Appadurai, *A Fear of Small Numbers: An Essay in the Geography of Anger* (Durham NC: Public Planet Books, 2006), p. 3. For Appadurai, the appeal of Huntington's thesis after 11 September was because it 'points to a new sort of moral outrage at work in the world today, a new willingness to conduct extreme acts of war in the name of specific ideas of moral purity and social rectitude, and it is of course foolish to deny that there is some powerful link between social forces in the Islamic world and the events of 9/11'. *Ibid.*, p. 17.

12 Huntington, *Clash of Civilizations*, p. 13.

13 B. Mazlish, *Civilization and its Contents* (Stanford: Stanford University Press, 2004), p. 115.

14 C. Jones, 'If not clash, then what? Huntington, Nishida Kitaró and the politics of civilizations', *International Relations of the Asia-Pacific*, 2 (2002), pp. 223–43 at p. 226; J. Gray, 'Global utopias and clashing civilizations: Misunderstanding the past', *International Affairs*, 74:1 (1998), pp. 149–63 at p. 147.

15 W. Connolly, 'The new cult of civilizational superiority', *Theory and Event*, 2:4 (1999), p. 1.

16 S. Holmes, 'In search of new enemies', *London Review of Books* (24 April 1997).

17 *Ibid.*

18 Huntington, *Clash of Civilizations*, p. 58.

19 Betts, 'Conflict or cooperation?', pp. 186–7.

20 F. Fukuyama, 'The end of history?', *National Interest*, 16 (Summer 1989), p. 319. In 2014 Fukuyama reflected that 'In the realm of ideas … liberal democracy still doesn't have any real competitors … My End of History hypothesis was never intended to be deterministic or a simple prediction of liberal democracy's triumph around the world.' F. Fukuyama, 'At the "End of History" Still Stands Democracy', *Wall Street Journal* (6 June 2014).

21 Gray, 'Global utopias and clashing civilizations', p. 156.

22 S. Huntington, 'If not civilizations, what?', *Foreign Affairs*, 72:5 (1993), pp. 186–94 at pp. 191–2.

23 Huntington, *Clash of Civilizations*, p. 301.

24 S. Huntington, 'The erosion of American national interests', *Foreign Affairs*, 76:5 (1997), pp. 28–49 at p. 30.

25 S. Huntington, 'The clash of civilizations?', *Foreign Affairs*, 72:3 (1993), pp. 22–49 at p. 39; C. Krauthammer, 'The unipolar moment', *Foreign Affairs*, 70:1 (1990/1991), pp. 23–33.

26 Huntington, *Clash of Civilizations*, p. 33.

27 *Ibid.*, p. 45.

28 *Ibid.*, pp. 20–1.

29 *Ibid.*, p. 51.

30 *Ibid.*, p. 312.

31 A. Sen, *Identity and Violence: The Illusion of Destiny* (London: Penguin, 2006), p. 10; Mazlish, *Civilization and its Contents*, p. xii; D. Senghaas, *The Clash within Civilizations: Coming to Terms with Cultural Conflicts* (London: Routledge, 1998); D. Senghaas, 'A clash of civilizations: An idée fixe?', *Journal of Peace Research*, 35:1 (1998), pp. 127–32.

32 A. Adib-Moghaddam, 'A (short) history of the clash of civilizations', *Cambridge Review of International Affairs*, 21:2 (2008), pp. 217–34; A. Adib-Moghaddam, *A Metahistory of the Clash of Civilizations: Us and Them beyond Orientalism* (Oxford: Oxford University Press, 2014).

33 E. Said, 'The Clash of Ignorance', *The Nation* (4 October 2001).

34 Huntington, *Clash of Civilizations*, pp. 137–8.

35 *Ibid.*, pp. 40–1.

36 G. E. Perry, 'Huntington and his critics: The West and Islam', *Arab Studies Quarterly*, 24:1 (2002), pp. 31–48 at pp. 34, 38; Gray, 'Global utopias and clashing civilizations', p. 157.

37 Heilbrunn, 'The Clash of Samuel Huntingtons', p. 26; J. Benthall, 'Imagined civilizations?', *Anthropology Today*, 18:6 (2002), pp. 1–2 at p. 2.

38 Huntington, *Clash of Civilizations*, p. 205.

39 Holmes, 'In search of new enemies', p. 14.

40 S. Huntington, 'Religion, culture and international conflict after September 11: A conversation with Samuel P. Huntington', *Center Conversations*, Ethics and Public Policy Center, 14 (June 2002), pp. 1–16 at p. 3.

41 Although referring to *Who are We?*, Miguel Centeno's criticism of Huntington's style also applies to *Clash of Civilizations*: 'He begins each section by making a very strong claim – for example, "By 2000 America was, in many respects, less a nation than it had been for a century" … He then proceeds to quote (a) one apparently primary source (often borrowed from another academic tome) (b) one quantitative source, whose sampling procedures and construction are ignored, and (c) one anecdotal journalistic illustration.' M. Centeno, 'Who are you?', *Contexts* 4:1 (2005), pp. 56–7.

42 Huntington, *Clash of Civilizations*, p. 37.

43 *Ibid.*, p. 166.

44 J. Mearsheimer, 'Conversations in International Relations: Interview with John J. Mearsheimer (Part II)', *International Relations*, 20:2 (2006), pp. 231–43 at p. 235. Aysha thinks that Huntington remained even more of a realist than Mearsheimer recognised: 'Realism … animates his whole vision of international affairs and is the basis of his analysis and recommendations, before and after the publication of *Clash of Civilizations* … The label "civilization" is just a generic term used to summarize the various ideational factors and challenges facing US primacy around the world.' Aysha, 'Samuel Huntington and the geopolitics of American identity', p. 118.

45 J. Mearsheimer, 'Conversations in International Relations: Interview with John J. Mearsheimer (Part I)', *International Relations*, 20:1 (2006), pp. 105–23 at p. 116.

46 'The United States should abandon their plan to westernize Ukraine and instead aim to make it a neutral buffer between NATO and Russia, akin to Austria's position during the Cold War.' J. Mearsheimer, 'Why the Ukraine crisis is the West's fault', *Foreign Affairs*, 93:5 (2014), pp. 77–89 at p. 87. See also Mearsheimer's comments in the *New York Times*, where he draws an analogy with the Monroe Doctrine for the Western Hemisphere. J. Mearsheimer, 'Getting Ukraine wrong', *New York Times* (13 March 2014).

47 Huntington, *Clash of Civilizations*, pp. 167–8.

48 Holmes, 'In search of new enemies', p. 6.

49 R. Inglehart and P. Norris, 'The true clash of civilizations', *Foreign Policy*, 135 (March–April 2003), pp. 63–70.

50 Gray, 'Global utopias and clashing civilizations', p. 156; Connolly, 'The new cult of civilizational superiority'; Sen, *Identity and Violence*, p. 44; Ervand Abrahamian, 'The US media, Huntington and September 11', *Third World Quarterly*, 24:3 (2003), pp. 529–44 at p. 534.

51 Benthall, 'Imagined civilizations?'

52 Huntington, *Clash of Civilizations*, p. 68.

53 I. Roxborough, 'Globalization, unreason and the dilemmas of American international strategy', *International Sociology*, 17:3 (2002), pp. 339–59 at p. 346.

54 J. L. Jones 'Strategic ability, operational reach, and tactical flexibility', *US Naval Institute Proceedings Magazine* (February 2001), p. 2, quoted in Roxborough, 'Globalization, unreason and the dilemmas of American international strategy', p. 351.

55 E. A. Henderson and R. Tucker, 'Clear and present strangers: The clash of civilizations and international conflict', *International Studies Quarterly*, 45:2 (2001), pp. 317–38 at p. 317. See also, A. Tusicisny, 'Civilizational conflicts: more frequent, longer and bloodier?', *Peace Research*, 41:4 (2004), pp. 485–98.

56 'The vast majority of evidence Huntington presents is anecdotal and this use of quantitative data can be described as the exception that proves the rule.' J. Fox, 'Ethnic minorities and the clash of civilizations: A quantitative analysis of Huntington's thesis', *British Journal of Political Science*, 32:3 (2002), pp. 415–34 at p. 419. Fox also provides a suggestive categorisation of Huntington's critics: 1. Those that argue for the continuing centrality of the nation-state; 2. Globalisation theorists who believe conflict has been progressively inhibited; 3. Those who believe that the real forces are both above and below the civilisational plane; 4. Those who deny any correspondence at all between civilisations and conflict; 5. Critics who see Huntington as excluding key variables such as conflict management techniques, rising secularism, information technology and pro-Western sentiment in the non-Western world; and 6. Those who assert that Huntington got his facts wrong. *Ibid.*, p. 417.

57 The claim was, somewhat paradoxically, made in what is generally thought to be Huntington's most original and influential book, S. Huntington, *Political Order in Changing Societies* (New Haven: Yale University Press, 1968), p. 55. However, it is only implicit and quite clearly relates to Huntington's borrowing from a data set that he himself had not originated. Thus, Louis Menand's

observation that Huntington's figures are sometimes 'improperly derived' seems more accurate than Lang's frankly obsessive scientism. L. Menand, 'Patriot Games: The New Nativism of Samuel P. Huntington', *The New Yorker* (17 May 2004). For a fair and contemporaneous view, see J. Diamond, 'Soft sciences are often harder than hard sciences', *Discover* (August 1987), p. 34. For two very different appreciations of the decisive impact of *Political Order* on modernisation and development theories, see F. Fukuyama, 'Samuel Huntington's Legacy', *Foreign Policy* (6 January 2011), and C. Leys, 'Samuel Huntington and the End of Classical Modernization Theory' in *The Rise and Fall of Development Theory* (Bloomington: Indiana University Press, 1996).

58 C. Jones, 'American civilization', *Human Figurations*, 2:1 (2013). A similar point is made by H. Kreutzmann, 'From modernization theory towards the "clash of civilizations": directions and paradigm shifts in Samuel Huntington's analysis and prognosis of global development', *GeoJournal*, 46 (1998), pp. 255–65 at p. 260.

59 U. Beck, *The Cosmopolitan Vision* (Cambridge: Polity Press, 2006). For a contemporary survey of this aspect, see B. Bowden, *The Empire of Civilization: The Evolution of an Imperial Idea* (Chicago: University of Chicago Press, 2009).

60 The thesis of deterritorialisation may be found in G. Ó. Tuathail, *Critical Geopolitics: The Politics of Writing Global Space* (Minneapolis: University of Minnesota Press, 1996); the link to Buchanan in L. Bialasiewicz, '"The death of the West": Samuel Huntington, Oriana Fallaci and a new "moral" geopolitics of births and bodies', *Geopolitics*, 11 (2006), pp. 701–24, which makes a feminist critique of anxiety over miscegenation and the projection of the defence of the West to a biological, bodily dimension.

61 Huntington, *Clash of Civilizations*, p. 217 (emphasis added).

62 *Ibid.*, p. 211.

63 *Ibid.*, p. 258 (original emphasis).

64 Perry, 'Huntington and his critics', p. 36.

65 F. Halliday, '"Orientalism" and its critics', *British Journal of Middle Eastern Studies*, 20:2 (1993), pp. 145–63. Halliday responded early to Huntington's essay in F. Halliday, *Islam and the Myth of Confrontation* (London: I. B. Tauris, 1996). His general attitude was 'once you get specific and stop engaging in Huntington's kind of grand narrative theorizing, things come into sharper focus'. F. Halliday and D. Postel, 'Who is responsible? An interview with Fred Halliday', *Salmagundi*, 150/151 (2006), pp. 221–40 at p. 231. Such a cool observation did not really reflect Halliday's visceral response to Huntington: 'Much of this is bad history, bad sociology, and bad international relations. It may also be bad ethics. What I term "faultline babble" has come to be the intellectual malaise of our time.' F. Halliday, 'Culture and International Relations', Paper presented to the University of the Basque Country, Summer Programme on International Law and International Relations (13 July 2007).

66 F. Gerges, *America and Political Islam: Clash of Cultures or Clash of Interests?* (Cambridge: Cambridge University Press, 1999); F. Gerges, *The Far Enemy: Why Jihad Went Global* (Cambridge: Cambridge University Press 2005);

Adib-Moghaddam, 'A (short) history of the clash of civilizations'; A. Adib-Moghaddam, *A Metahistory of the Clash of Civilizations: Us and them beyond orientalism* (London: Hurst, 2014).

67 P. Kington, 'Contextualising Islamic Fundamentalism', *International Journal*, 54:4 (1999), pp. 695–704 at p. 695.

68 R. Crockatt, 'No common ground? Islam, anti-Americanism and the United States', *European Journal of American Culture*, 23:2 (2004), pp. 125–42 at p. 126.

69 D. Cannadine, 'Getting Beyond the "Clash of Civilizations"', *History News Network* (5 June 2013). Cannadine, who singled out Anthony Pagden in this regard, published his self-explanatory *The Undivided Past: Humanity Beyond Our Differences* (New York: Knopf, 2013).

70 For a representative sample, see White House, 'Backgrounder: The President's Quotes on Islam' (December 2002).

71 H. Vedrine quoted in P. Ford, 'Europe cringes at Bush "crusade" against terrorists', *Christian Science Monitor* (19 September 2001).

72 *Le Monde* (16 September 2001).

73 'Text of Bush's Speech at West Point', *New York Times* (2 June 2002).

74 'Text of President Bush's Address to the Nation', *Washington Post* (11 September 2006).

75 Quoted in B. Ryan, *Condoleezza Rice: Secretary of State* (New York: Ferguson, 2004), pp. 41–2.

76 C. Rice, '"Acknowledge that you have an obligation to search for the truth"', *Stanford Report* (19 June 2002); 'Condoleezza Rice Affirms Support for Israel, Recalls Personal Battle against Intolerance, Terrorism', press release of *American Jewish Committee* (10 May 2002).

77 Huntington, *Clash of Civilizations*, p. 149.

78 'End of the Clash of Civilizations', *New York Times* (11 April 2009).

79 J. Castañeda. *Utopia Unarmed: The Latin American Left after the Cold War* (New York: Knopf, 1993).

Paul Wolfowitz and the promise of American power, 1969–2001

Paul Dundes Wolfowitz is best known for his hawkish service to the George W. Bush administration, when he pushed strongly – and by most accounts, influentially – for the invasion and occupation of Iraq. But this was merely the most recent chapter in a long foreign policy career that began in 1969, and that included service to the Nixon, Ford, Carter, Reagan and George H. W. Bush administrations. This chapter characterises this period as one in which Wolfowitz's worldview departed the fringe and settled in the mainstream. Through a series of policy initiatives, the United States sharply increased military spending, reinvigorated the democracy-promoting aspects of Wilsonianism, abjured relativism in favour of moral certainties, deployed the rhetoric of human rights and gradually focused more of its attention on the Middle East.

Wolfowitz did not guide this process single-handedly, but he was a consistently important voice throughout the period. While serving the Carter, Reagan and George H. W. Bush administrations, Wolfowitz helped to catalyse policy shifts and formulated guidance documents that influenced later presidencies. When remote from power during the 1990s, Wolfowitz and other 'neoconservatives' lambasted the Clinton administration – putting it very much on the defensive – and proposed alternative strategies to which George W. Bush would turn following the terrorist attacks of 11 September 2001. Whether advising presidents or criticising them, Wolfowitz's ideas became unavoidable points of reference. Examining his career and counsel from 1969 to 2001 helps to reveal in part the intellectual foundations of America's evolving role in the world.

The scholarly literature on Wolfowitz is surprisingly sparse. An admirer, Lewis Solomon, published a biography in 2007, which remains the only full-length study of this important figure. Its title – *Paul D. Wolfowitz: Visionary Intellectual, Policymaker, and Strategist* – gives a fair sense of the content, which praises Wolfowitz's foreign policy career, and the quality of the thought that sustained it, with metronomic consistency.[1] The best short study of Wolfowitz's career in print is Richard Immerman's chapter 'Paul Wolfowitz and the Lonely Empire', published in *Empire for Liberty*, an intellectual history of American Empire.[2] James Mann's *Rise of the Vulcans*[3] and George Packer's *The Assassin's Gate*[4] both offer insightful portraits of Wolfowitz at various stages of his career, but are necessarily episodic in their treatment. Finally, of course, there is a large literature on 'neoconservatism' that often attends closely to Wolfowitz, but in a similarly intermittent fashion.[5] It is clear that much work remains to be done, particularly on the period preceding 2001.

There is one factor that might explain why Wolfowitz has eluded sustained attention: namely, that he never held a major foreign policy position such as secretary of defence, secretary of state or national security adviser. In this respect his career followed a similar trajectory to one of his mentors and inspirations, Paul Nitze, an influential shaper of American diplomacy in the early Cold War, whose National Security Council (NSC) Report 68 expanded the parameters of US foreign policy to encompass the developing world. The careers of Nitze and Wolfowitz both showed that nudging ideas into the mainstream of policy-making did not necessarily require proximity to the White House. When ideas are timely and presented cogently, they can transcend the bureaucratic constraints placed on their authors.

Wolfowitz and Nitze both served on Team B, a group convened in 1976 to review the Central Intelligence Agency's (CIA) classified data and assess whether the agency's view of the Soviet Union's military intentions and capabilities was coloured by complacency. After completing their deliberations, Team B launched a strong attack on the CIA. Their report criticised the agency for leaning too heavily on satellite imagery and signals intelligence. They alleged that the agency paid insufficient attention to the actual speeches made by members of the Politburo – much more than mere bluster – and to the increasingly aggressive manner in which the Soviet proxies across the world, whether in Angola, Afghanistan or Vietnam, actually behaved.[6] As Nitze explained in a letter to Zbigniew Brzezinski, who became Jimmy Carter's national security adviser, 'The Soviet leaders are totally frank in saying that they believe the correlation of forces has moved dramatically in their favor over the last five to ten years. They attribute this to their growing military preparedness and to détente.'[7] The aggressiveness and certainty with which Pipes and Nitze made their case left the fresh-faced, undermanned CIA 'Team A' reeling. 'It was like Walt Whitman High versus the Redskins', said one CIA analyst of the meeting between both 'teams' in October 1976. Another recalled: 'People like Nitze ate us for lunch'.[8]

Participation in the Team B exercise was a formative experience for Wolfowitz. The group's conclusions appeared to show that the core component of Kissinger's grand strategy – that improved relations with Moscow increased America's range of diplomatic options – rested on a fallacy. The Soviet Union was as committed to the extinguishment of liberal capitalism as it had been under Josef Stalin. How does one interact with an entity subscribing to such a worldview? Team B's answer: one doesn't. As Wolfowitz later recalled: 'The B-Team demonstrated that it was possible to construct a sharply different view of Soviet motivation from the consensus view of the analysts, and one that provided a much closer fit to the Soviets observed behavior.'[9] He departed the exercise convinced that threats to the United States were often worse than they appeared, that Washington should plan on the basis of the worst-case scenario, that arms spending should be sharply increased, and that the CIA was essentially untrustworthy, conditioned by the same systemic biases – the veneration of objectively verifiable evidence, an unwillingness to cite ideology as a causal factor – that also blighted the State Department. It was all bracing stuff, although Team B's alarmist assessments turned out to be factually wrong.[10]

Team B, and Wolfowitz's geopolitical awakening, was something of a hinge moment in the history of US foreign policy. Kissingerian realism was soon to be eclipsed by moralism, stridency and instinctual certainties about American virtue and its duty to combat genuine evil. In the summer of 1976, as James Mann recounts in *The Rise of The Vulcans*, Wolfowitz invited two graduate students – one of whom was Francis Fukuyama – to assist his work on Team B as unpaid interns. At dinner at his home, Wolfowitz ruminated on the strengths and limitations of Henry Kissinger's doctoral thesis *A World Restored*. It was a well-researched and interesting book, Wolfowitz said, but Kissinger had identified the wrong exemplar. That craftsman of Realpolitik, Metternich, projected a vision that was lacking in scruple and substance; the 'peace' he helped to secure was unsustainable in the long term. Tsar Alexander I, who had advocated fierce resistance to Napoleon Bonaparte on moral and religious grounds, was the true hero of the tale. Fukuyama later recalled: 'I remember him saying the thing that's wrong with Kissinger is that he does not understand the country he is living in, that this country is dedicated to certain universalistic traditions.'[11] On Kissinger's preference for amoral, balance-of-power diplomacy, Wolfowitz was fond of quoting a sardonic Polish phrase that emphasised its insidiousness: 'the stability of the graveyard'.[12] Wolfowitz's values-led universalism marked a clear break with Kissinger and would dominate the debate about foreign policy for a generation to come.

Paul Wolfowitz was born in Brooklyn on 22 December 1943, the second child of Lillian Dundes and Jacob Wolfowitz. Like many talented, cash-poor Jewish immigrants, Jacob Wolfowitz attended the City College of New York, where he received a first-class education. He then moved to

New York University where he completed his doctoral dissertation in mathematics. Jacob's interests were myriad. He was a highly cultured man, a steadfast supporter of Franklin Roosevelt's New Deal, a dedicated Zionist and an organiser of protests against the Soviet Union's brutal treatment of minorities and dissidents. In 1951 Jacob moved the family from New York City to Ithaca, where he took a professorship in mathematics and statistics.

Paul's childhood in Ithaca – an attractive if isolated college town in upstate New York – was idyllic and directed by his father toward serious purposes. The family library was well stocked, and Paul consumed his father's histories of the Second World War and the Holocaust – of which he confessed he read 'probably too many' – George Orwell's oeuvre and John Hersey's *Hiroshima*, a visceral account of the atomic bombing of that city.[13] Paul was a precocious student at Ithaca High School. During his senior year the school gave him dispensation to attend a calculus class at Cornell in the morning before completing his school lessons in the afternoon.[14] Cornell recognised Paul as a student of uncommon ability and offered him a university place with a full scholarship; too good an opportunity for him or his family to decline. He majored in mathematics and chemistry and appeared poised to follow in his father's disciplinary footsteps.

Paul's exemplary scholastic record meant he qualified for membership of the Telluride Association, a select group of Cornell undergraduates from various disciplines united only by their smarts. Telluride was a self-governing entity founded in 1910 with seed money from an unorthodox Colorado businessman named Lucien Lucius Nunn. Telluride encouraged the free exchange of ideas and compelled a large degree of self-reliance and responsibility. It was the students, not administrators, who hired kitchen and cleaning staff, organised basic maintenance, invited guest speakers and oversaw admissions. And it was at Telluride in 1963 that Wolfowitz first encountered Professor Allan Bloom, a charismatic classicist and political theorist who had moved to Telluride as a faculty adviser.[15] Bloom's tutoring style was Socratic, the classical philosophers were his lodestars and his pleasures tended toward the Bacchanalian – he lived a full and joyful life. Bloom was close to Alexandre Kojève, Raymond Aron, Leo Strauss, Susan Sontag and the great novelist Saul Bellow, a fellow graduate of the University of Chicago, who later wrote a novel around him, *Ravelstein*, in which a thinly disguised Wolfowitz (named Philip Gorman) also makes a cameo appearance.[16]

Wolfowitz changed direction at Cornell, moving away from natural science and toward political science. By Wolfowitz's own admission, Bloom had a role in inspiring this shift: 'He had a lot to do with my coming to appreciate that the study of politics could be a serious business, even though it wasn't science in the sense that I understood science to be. That was an important eye opener.' Sensing the appearance on the scene of a dangerous influence, Jacob Wolfowitz took a rather dim view of Bloom's grandiose philosophising; indeed, both were suspicious of the other's subject areas. 'On the one hand', Wolfowitz remembered, 'Bloom was somewhat disdainful of hard science in general because it left out the philosophical dimension.'[17] His father, likewise, viewed the social sciences as inferior disciplines: that their presumption to be a science – and thus deliver verifiable truth – was unconvincing.

Jacob was fighting a losing battle with his son. It was not just Bloom's charisma and passion for political theory he had to counteract, but momentous world events that drew Wolfowitz closer to those disciplines that promised to make sense of them. 'I was a Cuban Missile kid', Wolfowitz said later, 'I was a sophomore in college when all that happened. There were other things in it as well. It was kind of a passion for history and politics even though I was good at math and science.'[18] The combination of Bloom and the Cold War conspired to frustrate a father's hopes for his son. Paul applied and was accepted to the prestigious PhD programme in biophysical chemistry at Massachusetts Institute of Technology (MIT). Unbeknownst to his father, however, he had also applied to doctoral programs in political science at Harvard and the University of Chicago. When both offered him places, Wolfowitz chose Chicago largely because Leo Strauss, a major thinker with close links to Bloom, was on the faculty. 'I told my father I had to try political science for a year', Wolfowitz said. 'He thought I was throwing my life away.'[19]

But the professor at Chicago that Wolfowitz cited as his true mentor was not Strauss, but his PhD supervisor Albert Wohlstetter, who worked at the RAND Corporation through the 1950s where he developed a global reputation in the field of nuclear strategy.[20] Wohlstetter moved to the University of Chicago in the 1960s where he taught political science. Here he developed a strong focus, which remained throughout his career, on the best means to forestall the proliferation of nuclear weapons. One visit to Israel in the late 1960s left him fearful that its hostile neighbours were hell-bent on acquiring a nuclear capability, and that America's duty to Israel (and the world) was to use whatever means were necessary to prevent this from happening.[21] Wohlstetter's influence was clearly evident in Wolfowitz's doctoral dissertation, which examined and critiqued Israel's desire to develop nuclear-powered desalination stations near its borders with Egypt and Jordan. Desalination served a laudable function, Wolfowitz conceded, but he also feared that the plutonium by-product of such plants could find its way into the wrong hands and eventually pose an existential threat to Israel itself.

Paul Wolfowitz's first foray into real world politics occurred in 1969, in the midst of his doctoral research. Wohlstetter advised him to set his thesis aside for a while and take a job with him in Washington DC conducting research for the Committee to Maintain a Prudent Defense Policy, a pressure group established by Paul Nitze and Dean Acheson to protect the development of an anti-ballistic missile system from Congressional sequestration. Wolfowitz was more than willing to cease doctoral work for a while. Nitze and Acheson were significant individuals and both warmed to the energetic Wolfowitz. The Safeguard ABM system was saved by a vote of 51 to 50 in the Senate (as the vote was tied the extra vote came from Vice President Spiro Agnew). No wonder that Wolfowitz's return to his doctoral research was something of a comedown. Even after Wolfowitz accepted a tenure track position at Yale in 1970, his default career focus tended toward job opportunities in Washington DC rather than journal articles, teaching and grant applications. In 1973 he joined the Nixon administration and remained there throughout Nixon's protracted waltz with oblivion, Gerald Ford's ascension to the Oval Office and Ford's defeat in November 1976 by Jimmy Carter. At that point Wolfowitz faced a stark choice: leave with Ford or remain in post and work for Carter.

Jimmy Carter rose to political prominence as the governor of rural Georgia, and his presidential campaign was driven by this well-cultivated outsider status, by the purity that supposedly accrues through avoiding Washington DC.[22] Carter was a born-again Christian, and a clear sense of right and wrong informed his worldview. Carter lambasted Kissinger, Nixon and Ford for too narrowly defining America's national interests, and insisted that the nation's foreign policy should pay greater heed to human rights. Carter pointedly exchanged warm letters with Andrei Sakharov, encouraged post-Helsinki dissidents across the Soviet bloc, and established a Bureau of Human Rights and Humanitarian Affairs at the State Department that graded each nation on how well they treated their citizens. During his inaugural address in 1977, Carter declared: 'our commitment to human rights must be absolute.'[23]

The new president's words and actions reassured an admiring Wolfowitz, who accepted the position of deputy assistant secretary for defense for regional programs. It was a mid-level position that invited Wolfowitz to contemplate and identify future trends, a function he was pleased to perform. Wolfowitz identified the Persian Gulf as a particularly nettlesome region for Washington, and Baathist Iraq – the pan-Arab Baathist movement was driven by nationalism and a variant on socialism, dedicated to achieving an Arab renaissance, thus reducing the region's susceptibility to the whims of larger nations – as a likely future threat. The vast oil reserves based in the region, combined with dwindling US domestic capacity, made the Persian Gulf economically a vitally important region, one where Wolfowitz suspected the Soviet Union would attempt to make mischief. Yet even without direct adventurism on the part of Moscow, an assertive and nationalist Iraq – implacably opposed to Israel, flush with high-tech Soviet weaponry – posed a clear threat to regional stability.

Wolfowitz presented his report – titled 'Capabilities for Limited Contingencies in the Persian Gulf', or more commonly known as the 'Limited Contingency Study' – to Secretary of Defense Harold Brown in 1979. It was a fascinating and prescient piece of futurology:

> The emerging Iraqi threat had two dimensions. On the one hand, Iraq may in the future use her military forces against such states as Kuwait or Saudi Arabia (as in the 1961 Kuwait crisis that was resolved by timely British intervention with force). On the other hand, the more serious problem might be that Iraq's *implicit* power will cause currently moderate local powers to accommodate themselves to Iraq without being overtly coerced. The latter problem suggests that we must not only be able to defend the interests of Kuwait, Saudi Arabia and ourselves against an Iraqi show of force, we should also make manifest our capabilities and commitments to balance Iraq's power – and this may require an increased visibility for U.S. power.[24]

What looks far-sighted today, however, appeared quirkier in 1979. The military brass did not favour a partial redeployment of its assets to the Persian Gulf; Harold Brown worried that Wolfowitz had created a threat where none existed. A confident young Baathist named Saddam Hussein was at that juncture outmanoeuvring his rivals to consolidate power at the apex of Iraqi politics. Fearful that Wolfowitz's report might be leaked, and Saddam recklessly and needlessly antagonised, Brown ordered that the Limited Contingency Study be buried deep in the Pentagon's archive. Iran was America's primary regional ally in the Middle East, and the Nixon doctrine held that surrogates such as the Shah should bear the preponderant burden of safeguarding the region. Further down the line, Wolfowitz could not resist a little sarcasm: 'Well, we don't plan forces for the Persian Gulf. The Shah of Iran takes care of the Persian Gulf for us.'[25]

During his service to the Carter administration, Wolfowitz was given the opportunity to engage in ambitious blue skies thinking – if not the power to execute those ideas. Yet even as Wolfowitz mulled over the future, the Carter present frustrated him. After assuming the presidency, Carter had needled Moscow with his human rights emphasis – which Brezhnev viewed as an aggressive intrusion into Soviet domestic affairs – but he was dedicated to achieving a second, more comprehensive nuclear arms control agreement with the Soviet Union: SALT II. In August 1978 Carter had vetoed a US$37 billion arms bill because it provided for a US$2 billion nuclear aircraft carrier that the president deemed unnecessary. A member of Carter's White House staff correctly predicted that his veto would 'make you look weak on defense issues at a time when public attitudes are shifting to the right'. On 18 November Carter's pugnacious national security adviser Zbigniew Brzezinski identified 'a growing domestic problem involving perceptions [of foreign policy] … To put it simply and quite bluntly, it is seen as "soft".' To re-establish his *bona fides* as a resolute cold warrior, Brzezinski advised the president to do something that 'has a distinctively "tough" quality to it'.[26]

On 25 December 1979 the Soviet Union invaded Afghanistan; a desperate attempt to prop up a Marxist–Leninist government struggling to quell an Islamist insurgency riled by secular attempts to reduce the influence of political Islam on Afghan society. President Carter's response was fierce. He withdraw the SALT II Treaty from consideration in the Senate, increased defence spending, reinstituted registration for the draft, embargoed grain and technology shipments to the Soviet Union and ordered an American boycott of the 1980 Olympic Games in Moscow. The president also authorised the CIA to begin funnelling arms and supplies to the Afghan insurgent movement, the mujahideen, although Zbigniew Brzezinski later allegedly claimed that covert support commenced as early as July 1979, predating the invasion by some six months.[27]

Wolfowitz viewed the Soviet invasion of Afghanistan as the inevitable consequence of Kissinger and Nixon's détente policy, which had encouraged Soviet adventurism. Brezhnev was actually surprised when Carter withdrew the SALT II Treaty from Senate consideration. That is how comfortable the Politburo had become in its 'normalised' relationship with Washington – Moscow believed it could invade another nation and assume the continuation of business as usual. The Iranian Revolution, meanwhile, reinforced Wolfowitz's view that the Persian Gulf would become a major area of crisis and contestation. And again, it laid bare the Nixon-era fallacy of recruiting regional powers to serve American interests. During Jimmy Carter's 1980 State of the Union address Wolfowitz could have been forgiven for claiming vindication for the contentious logic presented in his Limited Contingency Study. In a pugnacious speech, the president warned that 'an attempt by any outside force to take control of the Persian Gulf region will be regarded as an assault on the vital interests of the United States of America, and such an assault will be repelled by any means necessary, including military force'.[28] The Carter Doctrine was the Wolfowitz Doctrine melted down and recast. The Persian Gulf was now deemed a vital area of American concern.

At the close of 1979, as Carter reeled from this three-part succession of bad news, Fred Iklé called his former staffer and advised him to leave the administration with all due haste. Iklé had taken a position advising Ronald Reagan's presidential campaign and anticipated a decisive victory for his man in the next election. 'You've got to get out of there', Iklé warned Wolfowitz. 'We want you in the new administration.'[29] In remaining in an administration whose policies he disliked through a misguided sense of loyalty, Wolfowitz ran the clear risk of sabotaging a future job in a more accommodating administration. He did not need telling twice. At the beginning of 1980 Wolfowitz resigned from the Carter administration and took a job as a visiting associate professor at the Paul H. Nitze School of Advanced International Studies – the institution Nitze had founded with Christian Herter in 1943.

In 1976 Paul Nitze and Eugene Rostow had formed a pressure group called the Committee on the Present Danger (CPD). The group was hostile to détente and positive that the Soviet Union was building an ominous strategic superiority in the field of nuclear weapons. Its membership included former treasury secretaries like Henry H. Fowler and Charles Walker, and national security hawks like Jeane Kirkpatrick, Norman Podheretz, Richard Pipes and Nitze himself. The CPD became a bane of Carter's presidency. After Carter and Brezhnev signed the SALT II Treaty in June 1979, Nitze quickly mobilised the Committee to block its ratification in the Senate. One concerned Carter adviser confided to the *Washington Post* that 'Paul Nitze is worth 100 bureaucrats'. Another staffer gamely observed: 'Henry Kissinger we will have to stroke; Paul Nitze we will have to beat.'[30]

Some chance. While the Soviet invasion of Afghanistan torpedoed SALT II, Nitze's deftly managed lobbying effort had already mortally weakened the bill. The CPD was a highly effective advocacy organisation, a shadow foreign policy establishment in many respects, making it unsurprising when Reagan made so many national security appointments with a CPD affiliation. Richard Allen became national security adviser, William J. Casey became the director of Central Intelligence, Jeane Kirkpatrick became the US Ambassador to the United Nations and Richard Pipes became a senior staff member on the National Security Council. Nitze returned to policy prominence as an arms control negotiator. The hawks had finally found their roost.

But finding a job for Wolfowitz proved problematic. He had worked for the Carter administration for too long and was viewed by some as guilty by association – just as Iklé had feared. Richard Allen again headed the president-elect's foreign policy advisory team and Wolfowitz's résumé worried him. 'He was a goner, as far as I was concerned', Allen later remembered. 'He'd just been at the Pentagon. He had worked for Carter. I thought he was a Carter guy.' John Lehman, a friend who had worked with Wolfowitz in the Nixon administration, urged Allen to look beyond happenstance, meet with Wolfowitz in person, and form his own opinion. Allen agreed, met with Wolfowitz, reversed course, and never again doubted his foreign policy credentials.[31] He suggested that Wolfowitz become chair of the policy planning council and Wolfowitz gladly accepted.

On the Senate Foreign Relations Committee, Jesse Helms raised the same objections to Wolfowitz as he had to Nitze – that he was a Democrat, and hence soft on national security. Helms's colleagues convinced the elderly senator otherwise, however, and Wolfowitz assumed his position, hiring promising young scholars from America's elite universities, including Francis Fukuyama from Cornell and Zalmay Khalilzad, another former Telluride student, from Chicago. He also reached out to one of his former students at Yale, a conservative lawyer named I. Lewis 'Scooter' Libby, and to the conservative African American activist (and Telluridian) Alan Keyes. While Wolfowitz's team also included moderates like Dennis Ross, who later served in the Clinton administration, and Stephen Sestanovich – yet another Cornell contemporary – there is no doubt that Wolfowitz, and the majority of his twenty-five-person staff, were on the hawkish, neo-Wilsonian end of the spectrum.

Wolfowitz's first year certainly proved as much. He led studies that challenged 1970s orthodoxies: the value of détente with Moscow, engagement with China and the vital importance of resolving the Arab–Israeli conflict. So Wolfowitz argued that the United States did not need any arms control agreements with the Soviet Union *and* that their absence actually improved Washington's strategic position. He attempted with some success to stall a growing momentum in the State Department toward interacting meaningfully with the Palestinian Liberation Organization (PLO). He was a steadfast supporter of Israel and was strongly opposed to providing new military hardware to Saudi Arabia – such as the Airborne Warning and Control System – that might undermine Israeli military dominance. Finally, Wolfowitz repudiated Kissinger's assertion that the existence of a multipolar world made it essential that Washington engage respectfully with Beijing. Wolfowitz viewed the People's Republic of China as a repressive state devoted to upending the status quo in East Asia that America had devoted so many resources to underwriting. President Reagan's announcement of a massive arms build-up negated the supposed requirement that Beijing be cultivated as a counterweight against the Soviet Union. Even in the most hawkish presidential administration of the Cold War, Wolfowitz's policy planning staff stood apart in its bellicosity and desire to challenge conventional wisdom.

On the issue of China, Wolfowitz clashed bitterly with Secretary of State Alexander M. Haig Jr, who had previously served as Kissinger's deputy at the National Security Council and who held no doubts about China's strategic importance to the United States in the Cold War. In the spring of 1982 Wolfowitz drafted a memo that strongly criticised Haig's State Department for making unnecessary concessions to China on the subject of arms sales to Taiwan. As Wolfowitz's biographer Lewis Solomon writes: 'In view of growing friction between the two, the Secretary of State snubbed other proposals for Wolfowitz's policy planning staff and attempted to cut them out of the information loop.'[32] Wolfowitz's willingness to push the envelope had turned out to be counterproductive – he lacked the bureaucratic guile of a Kissinger or Nitze. Scooter Libby later recalled that Wolfowitz's assemblage of conservative talent achieved virtually nothing that was concrete and enduring. In March 1982 the *New York Times* reported that Secretary of State Haig had informed 'Paul D. Wolfowitz, the director of policy planning, that he will be replaced ... Associates reported that Mr. Haig found Mr. Wolfowitz too theoretical.'[33]

The *New York Times* was a little ahead of the mark, though it had accurately characterised Haig's basic view. But Haig's own problematic relationship with President Reagan – his high self-regard and thinly disguised desire to aggregate power at Foggy Bottom – led to the Secretary of State's downfall in June. Reagan appointed George P. Schultz to replace him. Schultz in turn promoted Wolfowitz to become Assistant Secretary of State for East Asia and the Pacific. Through sheer good luck Wolfowitz had survived another day. 'Paul, this is an administrative job', Schultz cautioned. 'It's not just thinking. It's a big area. You've got to get around, get to see a lot of people.'[34] Wolfowitz had been given a wonderful opportunity to manage relations with a pivotal region. The job also required him to sharpen his bureaucratic acumen and relational skills, and to better understand when the gap between theory and reality is unbridgeable.

Eschewing the protocol diplomacy of civility and moderation, President Reagan departed from his predecessors in excoriating the Soviet Union as 'the focus of evil in the modern world' during a speech to the National Association of Evangelicals in 1983. More substantively – and vexingly from Kennan's Atlanticist perspective – Reagan offered military support to any insurgent group in the developing world dedicated to overthrowing a leftist government: the initiative that became known as the 'Reagan Doctrine'.[35] Rather than 'containing' communism within the Iron Curtain, Reagan sought to extinguish it far beyond the European theatre through supporting insurgencies in Nicaragua, Afghanistan, Angola, Cambodia, Mozambique and Ethiopia.[36]

Allied to this rhetorical and proxy-supporting escalation of the Cold War was a vast increase in America's defence expenditures. In collaboration with Secretary of State Caspar Weinberger, Reagan set his first annual defence budget at US\$220 billion, the largest ever in peacetime. Reagan planned for annualised increases in the budget of 7 per cent per annum, which ultimately led to the 1987 defence budget weighing in at a colossal US\$456.5 billion. He devoted significant resources to the B-1 stealth bomber, F-14 and F-15 fighter jets, and the new generation of MX intercontinental nuclear missiles.[37] And then in March 1983 Reagan announced the development of the Strategic Defense Initiative (SDI), a satellite based, laser-armed system designed to shoot down incoming nuclear missiles that was soon dubbed 'Star Wars' by incredulous critics. Wolfowitz's friend and ally Richard Perle embraced the nickname: 'Why not?' he asked. 'It's a good movie. Besides the good guys won.'[38]

Wolfowitz applauded Reagan's rapid defence build-up and his willingness to lambast the Soviet Union on moral grounds – evil it assuredly was, so why the fuss? But the aspect of Reagan's foreign policy that pleased him the most was his clearly stated desire to spread democracy. In a speech to the UK House of Commons, greeted enthusiastically by Prime Minister Margaret Thatcher and her cowed front bench, but more cautiously by the rest of the chamber, Reagan observed that democracy-promotion was one of America's principal goals, proposing a concerted effort to 'foster the infrastructure of democracy' the world over. One passage on the world's limitless capacity for democratic enlargement was music to Wolfowitz's ears:

> This is not cultural imperialism, it is providing the means for genuine self-determination and protection for diversity. Democracy already flourishes in countries with very different cultures and historical experiences. It would be cultural imperialism, or worse, to say that any people prefer dictatorship to democracy … Let us now begin a major effort to secure the best – a crusade for freedom that will engage the faith and fortitude of the next generation. For the sake of peace and justice, let us move toward a world in which all people are at least free to determine their own destiny.[39]

In this speech, Reagan was deploying the Wilsonian language of democracy-promotion – but applied without exception. According to Lou Cannon, a Reagan biographer: 'The Westminster speech expressed more cogently than any address of his presidency Reagan's belief that the forces of freedom would triumph over communism.'[40] His words set off a chain of events that included the creation of the National Endowment for Democracy in November 1983 – a non-governmental organisation devoted to supporting democratic institutions overseas – and to a hardening of policy toward undemocratic but steadfast allies such as the Philippines, South Korea and Taiwan.

This democracy-promoting yin was counterbalanced to some degree, however, by a pseudo-realist yang. In 1979 Jeane Kirkpatrick, a noted professor of international affairs at Georgetown University, published an influential article in *Commentary* magazine titled 'Democracy and Double Standards'. While her preference in ideal conditions was the Wilsonian proliferation of pure and virtuous democracies, Kirkpatrick cautioned that the Cold War world was not so simple. The article launched a strong attack on the Carter administration for pushing autocratic leaders, such as the shah in Iran and Anastasio Somoza in Nicaragua, to liberalise and democratise their governments too quickly. Kirkpatrick faulted Carter for encouraging far-reaching changes only in nations 'under pressure from communist guerrillas. We seem to accept the status quo in Communist nations (in the name of "diversity" and national autonomy) but not in nations ruled by right wing dictators or white oligarchies [such as South Africa].' Here was the double standard of Kirkpatrick's title. Instead of pursuing laudable but self-defeating pipe dreams, she recommended that political leaders be more patient with authoritarian governments that support US policy. These regimes were more likely to evolve gradually in the direction of liberal-democracy than Marxist–Leninist 'totalitarian' varieties. Allied to this was Kirkpatrick's contempt for ahistorical wishful thinking. Wilsonianism was clearly the intended target:

> Although most governments in the world are, as they have always been, autocracies of one kind or another, no idea holds great sway in the mind of educated Americans than the belief that it is possible to democratize governments, anytime, anywhere, under any circumstances ... Decades, if not centuries, are required for people to acquire the necessary discipline and habits [of democracy].[41]

Kirkpatrick's article made an immediate impression on Reagan, who read it soon after publication and sent her a note expressing admiration for her logic. After assuming the presidency, Reagan appointed Kirkpatrick to become his ambassador to the United Nations, the first woman to ever serve in that position.

In 1983 Secretary of Defense Caspar Weinberger and CIA director William Casey both urged Reagan to appoint Kirkpatrick his national security adviser, which would have been another first for a woman. Secretary of State Schultz persuaded Reagan otherwise, however, later observing: 'I respected her intelligence, but she was not well suited for the job. Her strength was in her capacity for passionate advocacy.' Schultz remarked that the role of national security adviser required the temperament of a 'dispassionate broker', which he believed did not describe Kirkpatrick.[42] He may have been right. But then again, few national security advisers have historically resembled 'dispassionate brokers', a criterion that certainly would have excluded Walt Rostow, Henry Kissinger and Zbigniew Brzezinski from service. Perhaps the more likely explanation is that the path-breaking Kirkpatrick hit a glass ceiling. She later remarked: 'I can't think of any advantages to being a woman in US politics, frankly.'[43] Yet while Kirkpatrick was prevented from hitting the heights, her distinction between useful right-wing and irredeemable left-wing versions of authoritarianism had a significant

American foreign policy

influence on the policies pursued by the Reagan administration, much to Wolfowitz's chagrin.

One of Wolfowitz's primary goals at the State Department was to deploy US influence in East Asia to compel various authoritarian governments – in the Philippines, South Korea and Taiwan, most notably – to transition to democracy. In collaboration with Richard Armitage, based at the Pentagon, and Gaston Sigur, on the NSC staff – the so-called 'troika' – Wolfowitz began to consider how democratic change might be effected. They began with the Philippines, where Ferdinand Marcos had led the nation in dictatorial style since 1965 – and whose wife, Imelda Marcos, was known globally for her extravagant tastes, which included a collection of shoes that numbered in the thousands. They had quite a task ahead of them. When Vice President George W. Bush visited Manila in 1981, he told a glowing Marcos: 'We love your adherence to democratic principles and democratic processes', a statement that rather underplayed his tendency to declare martial law whenever his regime was electorally threatened. When Jeane Kirkpatrick visited Manila a few years, the savvy Marcos quoted verbatim from 'Democracy and Double Standards' during a banquet toast. He thanked her ostentatiously for providing such a compelling rationale for continued US support for anti-communist regimes such as his.[44]

Yet slowly but surely, aided by the support of Secretary of State George Schultz – who viewed the removal of Marcos as a strategic victory for Washington regardless of Wilsonian niceties – US policy toward the Marcos regime hardened. In January 1985 Wolfowitz, accompanied by his aide Scooter Libby, travelled to Manila, where they met and encouraged Marcos's principal political opponents. During Congressional testimony, Armitage and Wolfowitz stated their clear preference for policies that would apply pressure on Marcos to liberalise the political system of the Philippines. In late 1985 the opposition leader Corazon Aquino appeared to win a snap general election, but Marcos refused to accept the result. Washington soon learned that Aquino was the fair winner and that Marcos was clinging onto power through the traditional recourse to electoral fraud. Schultz urged Reagan to threaten to cut off military aid to Marcos if he continued to refuse to accept the popular verdict and step down.

Reagan agonised over this for a while – such a move certainly contradicted Jeane Kirkpatrick's views on useful dictators – before following his secretary of state's counsel and dispatching the ultimatum. This led inevitably to the end of Ferdinand Marcos, who was flown out of the Philippines with his wife on an American Air Force plane. A precedent had been set. A year later massive street demonstrations demanded the removal of Chun Doo Hwan's authoritarian government in South Korea. Reagan again urged the leader of a flailing, unloved autocracy to step aside and allow history – marching toward a liberal-democratic endpoint – to run its course.[45]

Henry Kissinger was distressed to witness the repudiation of yet another of his strategic maxims. Détente was a dead accented letter, balance-of-power diplomacy had been dismissed as anachronistic and contrary to American values, and now 'the better the devil you know' principle had been rent asunder. He attacked the Reagan administration for its democracy-promotion agenda: 'Are there no other overriding American interests?' he asked despairingly. What would other American allies with an authoritarian colouring (and there were many) make of Reagan's shabby treatment of Marcos? 'Whatever else may be said about the Marcos regime', wrote Kissinger, 'it contributed substantially to American security and had been extolled by American presidents for nearly two decades.' Kissinger closed his column by recording 'grave concerns' about this Wilsonian resurgence.[46]

Wolfowitz held Kissinger's logic in contempt for it highlighted a damaging paradox: 'You can't use democracy, as you appropriately should, as a battle with the Soviet Union, and then turn around and be completely hypocritical when it's on our side of the line.'[47] Values and morality were an integral part of the struggle with the Soviet Union; the Cold War was nothing if not an ideological struggle. The United States had to be on the side of the angels as often as possible.

Wolfowitz's aspirations were of course laudable, but they were also applied inconsistently by the administration he served. In Chile, the Reagan administration continued to lend Augusto Pinochet's brutal regime its material and political support. US policy toward El Salvador, Guatemala, Costa Rica, Honduras and Nicaragua was sullied by egregious human rights abuses perpetrated by insurgent groups challenging leftist governments. These were ignored by the Reagan administration in the name of a wider anti-communist good, and people certainly noticed.[48] Wolfowitz's assertion that 'the best antidote to communism is democracy' was catchy, but it failed to capture the totality of the Reagan administration's foreign policies, which were often just as callous and amoral as those pursued during the Nixon–Kissinger era.[49]

Secretary of State Schultz appointed Wolfowitz to serve as the US ambassador to Indonesia in 1986. It was a position Wolfowitz coveted for personal reasons; his wife, Clare, was an anthropologist with research interests there. But this was also an important nation in world affairs. Indonesia was the world's most populous Muslim country and had been a steadfast ally to the United States following the bloody rise of Suharto in 1967, who ruled the nation until 1998 as a repressive anti-communist. Suharto was precisely the type of leader whom Jeane Kirkpatrick viewed as essential to US interests. There was never any danger of the United States applying political pressure on Suharto à la Marcos – the strategic stakes were much higher. Nonetheless, Wolfowitz politely chided Suharto for failing to encourage greater 'openness in the public sphere' and established a bond of friendship with Abdurrahman Wahid, a critic of Suharto who led one of Indonesia's largest Muslim political parties. One of the most notable aspects of Wolfowitz's stay in Jakarta, however, was the degree to which he imbibed Indonesian culture. As historian Richard Immerman writes: 'Over the next three years he learned the language; he studied the culture; he toured the neighborhoods. He even won a cooking contest.'[50]

The three-year stint in Indonesia was an enriching period for Wolfowitz, clearly, but there was also a downside – he was far removed from the momentous events that occurred throughout the final two years of Reagan's presidency. In 1985 Mikhail Gorbachev became the general secretary of the Communist Party of the Soviet Union. His youth (he was fifty-four) and vigour cast Gorbachev in vivid contrast to the decrepit gerontocracy – Leonid Brezhnev, Yuri Andropov and Konstantin Chernenko – that preceded him. Indeed, Ronald Reagan once joked: 'How am I supposed to get anyplace with the Russians if they keep dying on me?'[51] In 1986 a hale and hearty Gorbachev announced a new policy of perestroika, roughly translated as 'restructuring', designed to liberalise the Soviet economy and remedy deficiencies in regard to supply and demand. Gorbachev followed this up in more radical fashion in 1988 in announcing a new policy of glasnost, or openness, which delivered on the promise of the Helsinki Accords, extending political freedoms, including freedom of speech, to the Soviet citizenry.

George Kennan was thrilled by Gorbachev's ascension, but fretted that the Reagan administration was incapable of grasping this opportunity, just as Eisenhower had failed to act decisively following the death of Stalin in 1953. In October 1986 Kennan recorded a diary entry that imagined him in conversation with this new leader: 'You could give in to us on every point of our negotiations; you would still encounter nothing but stony hostility in official government circles; and your concessions would be exploited by the president as evidence that he had frightened you into compliance; that the only language you understood was the language of force.'[52]

Kennan was correct in one sense. Many conservatives did indeed attribute Gorbachev's shift in direction to the pressure Reagan applied on Moscow through the radical hike in US defence spending and the launch of the SDI. But he was wrong in another. Reagan's actual response to Gorbachev's ascension was far removed from the 'stony hostility' that Kennan feared inevitable.[53]

Over the course of a brief but historic encounter in Reykjavik, Iceland in October 1986, Reagan and Gorbachev established sufficient trust to propose the elimination of *all* nuclear weapons by the year 2000.[54] The suggestion was quickly scuppered – to the relief of Prime Minister Margaret Thatcher and many within the administration – by Reagan's refusal to shelve the SDI program, which Gorbachev fairly pointed out was not in the spirit of things. That such an idea was even seriously discussed was remarkable all the same, and it paved the way for nuclear arms negotiations of a more substantive nature than SALT I. The 1987 Intermediate-Range Nuclear Forces Treaty (INF) was the first ever to deliver a real cut in the superpowers' nuclear arsenal: Moscow dismantled 1,836 missiles and the United States 859. This caused a predictable outcry among conservatives, among them Richard Perle, William Buckley and Jesse Helms. Howard Philips of the Conservative Caucus derided Reagan as 'a useful idiot for Soviet propaganda'.[55]

The year 1988 closed in remarkable fashion. On 7 December 1988 Gorbachev delivered a hugely significant speech at the United Nations. He began by conceding that Moscow – and thus Marxism–Leninism – had no monopoly on wisdom and truth, which was akin to the Pope suggesting the same of the Bible. He followed this remarkable admission of ideological doubt by declaring that the Soviet Union would not deploy military force as a means to achieve its aims, and observed that his goal was much more modest than his predecessors – to attain 'reasonable sufficiency for defense', which in practical terms meant demobilising half a million troops from the Red Army. He ended by promising that Moscow would henceforth respect the right of all the constituent nations of the Warsaw Pact to self-determination: 'the principle of freedom of choice is mandatory', Gorbachev declared.[56] With remarkable grace and efficiency, Gorbachev had ended the Cold War – so far as he was concerned, at least.

So what had happened? Who deserved the acclaim? In a 1993 essay for the *National Review*, Wolfowitz identified Reagan's confrontational tactics as the catalyst for Gorbachev's radical reforms and Moscow's military retreat: 'It is interesting how many of Russia's new democrats give Ronald Reagan much of the credit for the collapse of the Soviet Union.'[57] George Kennan believed that such extrapolations, common amongst Reagan's hawkish supporters, were illusory and indeed dangerous; the connection between cause and effect was impossible to establish. As he observed to his friend, the historian John Lukacs: 'The suggestion that any American administration had the power to influence decisively the course of a tremendous political upheaval, on another great country on another side of the globe is intrinsically silly and childish.'[58]

The election of 1988 pitted Reagan's experienced, cautious and uncharismatic Vice President, George H. W. Bush, against Michael Dukakis, a similarly stilted communicator whom the Bush campaign damned as the stereotypical Massachusetts liberal: weak on crime and foreign policy, with an unsteady grasp of economics. The election was a blowout: Bush won

53.4 per cent of the popular vote to Dukakis's 45.7 per cent, which translated into a 426–111 victory in the Electoral College. The fact that Bush won in Vermont, New Jersey and Connecticut says it all.

For his part, Paul Wolfowitz lamented Reagan's departure and was ambivalent about Bush's ascension. The new president nominated Dick Cheney, a colleague from the Ford administration, to serve as his Secretary of Defense. Cheney recalled Wolfowitz from Indonesia to serve as his Undersecretary of Defense for Policy. In his memoir *In My Time*, Cheney recalled: 'Paul had the ability to offer new perspectives on old problems. He was also persistent. On more than one occasion, I sent him on his way after I had rejected a piece of advice or policy recommendation, only to find him back in my office a half hour later continuing to press his point – and often he was right to do so.'[59] They made a close and like-minded duo, but a clear ideological gap divided Cheney and Wolfowitz, the two most hawkish members of the Bush administration, from the rest of the national security team.

President Bush appointed Brent Scowcroft, a former deputy to Henry Kissinger who shared much of his former boss's worldview, to serve as his national security adviser. Bush nominated another Realist-inclined figure, James A. Baker III, to serve as his Secretary of State. For these staffing reasons, Wolfowitz deliberated for a while before accepting Cheney's job offer. The man who gave Wolfowitz his first job in Washington, Fred Iklé, observed that his friend 'hesitated for a long time. He couldn't make up his mind. He talked about going back to academia.' Perhaps he remembered his marginality during the incommodious Nixon–Ford years and did not want to repeat the experience in his prime with another 'moderate' Republican. Regardless, Wolfowitz's friends and colleagues convinced him to accept the job; the administration needed more men of conviction to counter the renascence of Kissingerian realism. His new job asked Wolfowitz to turn away from the multicultural vibrancy of Indonesia and refocus his intellectual energies on the regions and issues that had consumed him during the 1970s: arms control, forward planning, the Persian Gulf and the wider Middle East.

The foreign policy crisis that defined Bush's presidency for posterity was the Gulf War, which was either a model of diplomatic *élan* or a missed opportunity depending on taste.[60] On 2 August 1990 Saddam Hussein ordered the invasion of Kuwait to forcibly wrest back a territory – and the oil reserves and access to the sea it provided – that he viewed as historically belonging to Iraq. Saddam did not anticipate a strong American response, which perhaps was understandable. Eight days prior to the invasion April Glaspie, the US Ambassador to Iraq, told him directly: 'We have no opinion on your Arab conflicts, such as your dispute with Kuwait … I have direct instructions from President Bush to improve our relations with Iraq. We have considerable sympathy for your quest for higher oil prices, the immediate cause of your confrontation with Kuwait.'[61]

The chairman of the Joint Chiefs of Staff, Colin Powell, appeared to confirm Saddam's confidence as well founded the day after the invasion. He told General H. Norman Schwarzkopf, head of US Central Command, 'I think we'd go to war over Saudi Arabia, but I doubt we'd go to war over Kuwait.' Powell was wrong. When he counselled caution during the first National Security Council meeting called to discuss the crisis, Dick Cheney slapped him down: 'Colin. You're chairman of the Joint Chiefs. You're not secretary of state. You're not national security adviser. And you're not secretary of defense. So stick to military matters.'[62] Twelve years later Colin Powell *was* secretary of state. And his call for caution in Iraq was similarly ignored, trailing off into the vacuum of inconsequence that separates Foggy Bottom from the White House.

Paul Wolfowitz's Carter-era prophecies, meanwhile, had apparently been vindicated in dramatic fashion. Saddam Hussein was fulfilling the early bellicose promise that Wolfowitz had identified before anyone. With Powell the sole dissenting voice within the administration, some form of military intervention was never in doubt. 'This will not stand', President Bush declared, 'this aggression against Kuwait.'[63] Sensing the worst, as was his wont, George Kennan wrote on 16 December: 'Mr Bush continues to entangle us all in a dreadful involvement in the Persian Gulf to which no favorable outcome is visible or even imaginable … At the moment, it is hard to see anything ahead but a military-political disaster.'[64]

Operation Desert Storm was launched on 16 January 1991 in dramatic style, with a devastating salvo of Tomahawk missiles, and laser-guided bombs dropped by Stealth F-117 aircraft, that targeted Iraq's air bases and electrical and communications networks. This aerial bombardment lasted until 24 February, when forces from the US-led coalition entered Kuwait from Saudi Arabia and engaged Iraqi troop concentrations. The land invasion spanned just one hundred hours, the time it took for the demoralised Iraqi army to cut, run and concede defeat in the face of overwhelming odds – Goliath won this particular match-up. American fatalities amounted to just over one hundred, Iraqi losses numbered between 20,000 and 35,000. It was as one-sided a war as any in American history, similar in its decisiveness to the United States' crushing defeat of Spain in 1898.

In advance of the ceasefire, tens of thousands of Iraqi troops fled Kuwait down the so-called 'highway of death'. Colin Powell urged Schwarzkopf, for reasons of honour and civility, not to destroy these fleeing troops, as easy and as injurious to Saddam Hussein's rule as that would have been.[65] Secretary of State James Baker had a vivid recollection of Powell's objections to continuing the slaughter: 'I remember Colin Powell saying with a trace of emotion, "We're killing literally *thousands* of people".'[66] Deputy National Security Adviser Robert Gates remembered 'very clearly Colin Powell saying that this thing was turning into a massacre. And that to continue it beyond a certain point would be un-American, and he even used the word "unchivalrous".'[67] President Bush heeded Powell's advice and ordered the coalition forces to stand down.

Wolfowitz was unhappy that the war ended so swiftly, having fewer qualms than Powell – his lack of military experience might have limited his imagination – about strafing the departing Iraqi troops. He was certainly correct to a point in believing that a medium-scale slaughter might have prevented a larger one later. Wolfowitz's deputy, Scooter Libby, recalled: 'We objected to it. I was floored by the decision. Neither of us liked it.'[68] But neither party was close enough to the action to make a difference. A few days after hostilities ceased, the CIA reported that many of Saddam's elite fighting forces, the Republican Guard, had escaped Kuwait with significant supplies: at least 365 Soviet T-72 tanks crossed back into Iraq and an entire division, the Hammurabi, also remained intact. General Schwarzkopf also granted a foolish concession to Iraq when it permitted its helicopters to fly in order to transport officials across Kuwait and Iraq. Saddam ruthlessly exploited this loophole, ordering helicopter gunships to crush Shiite and Kurdish forces that were assembling to launch a revolution, encouraged by the earlier words of President Bush and Secretary Baker suggesting that they rise in revolt.

Wolfowitz later observed: 'Simply by delaying a ceasefire agreement – without killing more Iraqi troops or destroying more Iraqi military assets – the United States might have bought time for opposition to Saddam Hussein to build and to act against him..[69] But while delay appeared a savvy option with the benefit of hindsight, it was never actively considered at the time. Scowcroft and Baker believed that civil war in Iraq would have negative unintended consequences, including a substantial strengthening in the position of Iran. Employing a rationale that Kissinger and Kennan would have cheered, Powell later wrote: 'Our practical intention was to leave Baghdad enough power to survive as a threat to an Iran that remained bitterly hostile to the United States.'[70]

As for the invasion of Iraq and the ouster of Saddam Hussein, this was viewed at the time as implausible: vexing in design and execution, and unknowable in consequence. As Bush wrote in his memoir, co-authored with Scowcroft: 'Had we gone the invasion route, the United States could conceivably still be an occupying power in a bitterly hostile land. It would have been a dramatically different – and perhaps barren – outcome.'[71] Many hawkish Republicans, including the president's own son, would challenge this classically realist interpretation. Donald Rumsfeld, to give one such example, presents a strong case against Bush–Scowcroft pragmatism: 'For his part, Saddam Hussein came to believe that the United States lacked the commitment to follow through on its rhetoric. He saw America as unwilling to take the risks necessary for an invasion of Iraq.'[72] But public opinion at the time in the United States and across the world saw things rather differently – the Gulf War was a resounding success for America and the coalition. Clear-cut aggression, the crossing of an established international border, had been met with a resolute response, sanctioned by the United Nations and carrying the crucial support of Moscow, Cairo and Damascus. It was a remarkable achievement all considered. Rumsfeld's assessment was not so much written as bloated with hindsight. Nonetheless, Cheney, Rumsfeld and Wolfowitz all learned a lesson that they applied to the Second Iraq War: Colin Powell and similarly risk-averse generals had to be detached from the decision-making fulcrum.

On 19 August 1991 hardline communists launched a coup against Mikhail Gorbachev, placing him under house arrest at his dacha in the Crimea and ordering tanks and infantry to assume strategic positions in Moscow. Boris Yeltsin became the focal point of resistance, famously standing atop a tank across from the White House of Russia in a catalysing act of defiance. The coup collapsed in the face of popular antipathy and Gorbachev returned to Moscow, though not in triumph. On 21 August Yeltsin requested that Gorbachev read a statement outlining details of the coup against him – a request that was hard to turn down in the circumstances. The following day Gorbachev resigned as general secretary of the Soviet Communist Party, though he retained his position as the Soviet Union's titular president. Over the course of the next few months Ukraine, Armenia, Georgia and Moldova moved swiftly to secure their independence from Moscow. On 8 December political leaders from Russia, Ukraine and Belarus met at Belovezh Forest, near Minsk, to form a Commonwealth of Independent States (CIS) – others would soon join. On 25 December Gorbachev resigned as president of the Soviet Union. The hammer and sickle was lowered from the Kremlin and the blue, white and red tricolour of the Russian Federation was raised to take its place. Boris Yeltsin was now assuredly in charge.

Gorbachev departed office by warning that something terrible had just happened to the United States – it had been deprived of an enemy.[73] Its departure certainly created a huge vacuum in the enemy column. It fell to Paul Wolfowitz, as undersecretary of defense for policy, to launch an effort to ascertain which nations were most likely to step up and take Moscow's place as the bad guy. In a speech in early 1992 Wolfowitz vowed to learn from the aftermath of earlier conflicts, when Washington downsized its military capabilities too quickly. 'We've never done it right in the past', complained Wolfowitz. After securing victory in 1945, for example, the Truman administration had erred in cutting defence spending – Nitze's NSC-68 was prescient but arrived too late to swiftly repulse North Korea, resulting in a painful, protracted war: 'It only took us five short years to go from having the strongest military establishment in the world, with no challengers, to having a force that was barely able to hang onto the Korean Peninsula against the attack of a fourth-rate country.'[74] Wolfowitz's assessment vastly underestimated the Red Army – enough of a 'challenger' for Washington to essentially give up on Eastern Europe – but the gist of his message was clear. The lessons of history teach that the cashing of a 'peace dividend' is invariably premature. The United States should remain vigilant by normalising the high levels of defence spending introduced by Reagan.

Like NSC-68, the Defense Policy Guidance (DPG) document of 1992 was a seminal statement of intent. Wolfowitz directed the study but delegated its drafting to Zalmay Khalilzad, who in turn took advice from Richard Perle, Albert Wohlstetter and Scooter Libby.[75] The DPG resembled NSC-68 in that it was a collective enterprise inspired by the vision of one individual. It also assumed worst-case scenarios: emphasising the necessity that the United States maintain an insurmountable lead in military and power-projection capabilities. Someone in the Pentagon, desirous of a wider debate, leaked the document to the foreign affairs journalist Patrick Tyler, who published excerpts in an article for the *New York Times* on 8 March 1992. Tyler reported that the 46-page document stated: 'America's political and military mission in the post-cold-war-era will be to insure that no rival superpower is allowed to emerge in Western Europe, Asia, or the territory of the former Soviet Union.'[76]

The DPG offered a clear-cut repudiation of the collectivist aspirations of the United Nations – 'ad hoc coalitions' was the preferred alliance model. This was the principal policy area where Wolfowitz disagreed fundamentally with Woodrow Wilson. The former feared that America's enemies would use a well-intentioned but dangerous institution like the UN to curtail the nation's freedom of action. Wilson was more hopeful that the proclivities and interests of nations could harmonise, instilling vitality and unity of purpose into his cherished League of Nations; more optimistic, ultimately, than Wolfowitz that the world could have a peaceable future. The DPG identified a whole series of threats to American interests, whether they were 'European allies, Arab dictatorships, Muslim terrorists, resurgent Russians, Chinese and North Korean communists, weapons proliferators', as George Packer described them.[77]

In reference to the ominous threat posed by hostile nations with weapons of mass destruction, the DPG detailed the potential necessity of 'preempting an impending attack with nuclear, chemical or biological weapons'. The report jarred with Colin Powell's more sanguine state of mind – he joked

during a contemporaneous interview with the *Army Times*: 'I'm running out
of demons. I'm running out of villains, I'm down to Castro and Kim Il-Sung.
I would be very surprised if another Iraq occurred.'[78]

Tyler's article provoked outrage among America's allies, who were
not thrilled at the vassal status bestowed on them by Wolfowitz and his
colleagues. The reaction from old-school Republicans and mainstream
Democrats was similarly hostile. Patrick Buchanan, a retrenchment-inclined
Republican who struggled to identify many 'good' wars in American history,
observed that the DPG was 'a formula for endless American intervention
in quarrels and war when no vital interest of the United States is remotely
engaged'. He urged President Bush, whom he was challenging for the
Republican Party (also known as GOP, Grand Old Party) presidential nomination, to disown it. George Stephanopoulos, an influential adviser to the
fast-rising Democrat Bill Clinton, described the draft as 'one more attempt
to find an excuse for big budgets instead of downsizing'. Bush's national
security adviser Brent Scowcroft later remarked of the DPG: 'That was just
nutty. I read a draft of it. I thought, "Cheney, this is just kooky". It didn't
go anywhere. It was never formally reviewed.'[79] Scowcroft is correct on the
absence of presidential imprimatur, but wrong to observe that it 'didn't go
anywhere'. It went through various drafts and emerged as a remarkable and
durable strategy document. On 5 May 1992 Wolfowitz sent the final draft
to Dick Cheney and added a PS: 'We have never had a defense guidance this
ambitious before.'[80] While the document fell into partial abeyance for the
next eight years, the next President Bush resuscitated it. And this administration would reintroduce the idealistic Wilsonian dimension that Wolfowitz
felt was lacking in the original DPG drafts: a strong emphasis on America's
role in fostering democratisation.[81]

The election of 1992 pitted the incumbent Bush against Bill Clinton, a
charismatic and politically gifted former governor of Arkansas. For James
Carville, a key Clinton adviser, the election was about one thing: 'It's the
economy, stupid';[82] and his reductionism was apposite – Clinton won the
election largely on those terms, aided by the candidacy of a centre-right
third-party candidate Ross Perot, who siphoned votes from the unfortunate Bush. But foreign policy did figure significantly in the campaign – how
could it not, just one year after the collapse of the Soviet Union? – and many
Wilsonians on both sides of the political aisle found that there was much to
like about Clinton. For starters, Clinton criticised Bush's narrow realism on
multiple fronts. He accused Bush of issuing a weak, un-American response
to the Tiananmen Square massacre of 1989, when Chinese troops attacked
pro-democracy demonstrators in Beijing and across the nation, killing hundreds and injuring thousands. He attacked Bush for failing to engage seriously with the looming crisis in the former Yugoslavia, where Slobodan

Milosevic's Serbia posed a serious threat to regional stability, and whose army had Bosnia's Muslim population in its sights. Clinton believed that James Baker's callous assessment of the crisis in the Balkans – 'we don't have a dog in that fight'[83] – revealed a distressing truth about the Bush administration's human rights deficiencies.

Wolfowitz was quite sympathetic to the sweep of Clinton's critique of Bush, as his appraisal of the Bush administration attests:

> [T]hat impressive victory [in Iraq], coming on top of the victory in the Cold War, contributed to a widespread feeling that the United States no longer faced serious dangers in the world or else that the problems we faced could be handled by a newly invigorated United Nations. Rhetoric from the administration about 'A New World Order' – or comments that we had 'no dog' in fights such as those in the former Yugoslavia – did nothing to counter that complacency.[84]

But while he found Bush's foreign policies largely wanting, Wolfowitz had learned a painful lesson from the Carter era: it was difficult to work for a Democrat without burning bridges with the GOP. And besides, Clinton could criticise Bush's timidity all he wanted on the campaign trail. The real test was how he would act in office. Wolfowitz doubted with good reason that Clinton was nearly as hawkish and values-led as he appeared. So he left the Pentagon and took up the position of Dean of the Johns Hopkins School of Advanced International Studies. The policy school that Paul Nitze had cofounded was an appropriate place for Wolfowitz to begin his assault on an irresolute Democratic president. He began assailing Clinton's foreign policies on largely the same grounds as Clinton had attacked those of Bush.

For Wolfowitz, Madeline Albright was the redeeming feature of the Clinton administration. During Clinton's second term Secretary of State Albright declared herself comfortable 'with the projection of American power'. She pointedly observed that the historical analogy that motivated her worldview took place in the 1930s, not the 1960s: 'My mind-set is Munich; most of my generation's is Vietnam. I saw what happened when a dictator was allowed to take over a piece of a country and the country went down the tubes. And I saw the opposite during the war when America joined the fight. For me, America is really, truly, the indispensable nation.'[85]

Wolfowitz thrilled to Albright's words, observing that she 'represents the best instincts of this administration on foreign policy'.[86] Indeed, the Clinton administration appeared to be closely following the recommendations presented in the controversial 1992 DPG. Defence spending scarcely dipped in real terms from the Reagan-era levels, the maintenance of primacy remained the principal goal, and the United States reserved the right to undertake unilateral action when necessary to protect its interests or right wrongs.

These sentiments were borne out in practice. In 1999, for example, the United States spearheaded NATO airstrikes against Slobodan Milosevic's Serbia to defend Kosovo against a brutal assault motivated by ethnic cleansing. The UN was not willing to authorise such an action due to Russian objections, but Clinton paid no heed, operating through NATO instead. Serbia eventually desisted and Milosevic's odious regime collapsed – a win on multiple levels. But the United States had indeed acted as 'the indispensable nation' in side-stepping the UN when it deemed action necessary. And most allies, such as Great Britain's Prime Minister Tony Blair, recognised and encouraged this reality. Much of Clinton's foreign policy vindicated a document that roused such ire upon its publication in 1992. The playing was different – Clinton favoured pianissimo, Wolfowitz forte – but the notation was largely the same.

His admiration for Albright notwithstanding, Wolfowitz did identify serious flaws in the Clinton administration's policies toward certain regions. First among them was Saddam Hussein's sullen and resentful Iraq, where Clinton's containment strategy comprised the enforcement of 'no-fly zones' through intermittent air strikes and the maintenance of stringent UN sanctions. Wolfowitz viewed this combination as not up to the task of applying sufficient pressure on Saddam Hussein. In a widely discussed article authored in 1996 for the *Wall Street Journal*, under the attention-grabbing headline 'Clinton's Bay of Pigs', Wolfowitz accused Clinton of neglecting the growing threat posed by Saddam. This was manifested in Iraq's invasion of a Kurdish 'safe zone' in northern Iraq in August 1996 and a dishearteningly weak US military response in the form of ineffectual cruise missile strikes. Wolfowitz lambasted the 'pinprick' Tomahawk cruise missile attacks favoured by Clinton and accused the administration of 'betraying the Kurds' in permitting Iraqi forces to strike northward against that restive region with impunity.

This was clearly bad news for America's reputation as a guarantor, and for its hard-won reputation as a military power without equal, but it also emboldened Saddam, whose military might pose a threat to the United States itself. Wolfowitz believed the stakes in Iraq could scarcely be higher: 'Saddam is a convicted killer still in possession of a loaded gun – and it's a pointed at us.' Here was one of the first public references to Saddam's chemical and bacteriological weapons programmes, and the potential that he may either use them against the United States or sell or gift them to a terrorist organisation to do the same. To prevent the realisation of such a horrific possibility, Wolfowitz urged Clinton to 'go beyond the containment strategy and confront the Iraqi dictator once and for all'.[87]

In the general election of 1996 Wolfowitz served as an adviser to the aged Republican candidate Bob Dole. Iraq turned out to be one area where clear daylight could be detected between the candidates. While campaigning for Dole, Wolfowitz remarked to a reporter: 'The US has virtually abandoned its commitment to protect a besieged people from a bloodthirsty dictator.'[88] But Dole and Wolfowitz struggled to land any meaningful blows on Clinton. Dole's campaign staked out positions that were considerably more hawkish than those of George H. W. Bush – on the need for developing a missile defence system and on his implacable hostility to the United Nations. But in the realm of foreign policy, Clinton's first term had been largely devoid of Carter-like disasters.

Wolfowitz was profoundly disappointed that Dole had lost the election, his defeat hastened by the peripheral part that foreign affairs played in the overall outcome. He and Dole had certainly found it difficult to land significant blows on Clinton for being weak on national security in the absence of serious geopolitical threats. US elections are not won or lost on the fate of the Kurds, Rwandans, Bosnians or Kosovars. During the Cold War the draft-dodging Clinton would likely have been easy prey for a decorated Second World War veteran like Dole, who had only narrowly avoided death in 1945 after being seriously wounded by German machine gun fire. But times had changed, as the GOP foreign policy establishment well understood.

The problem may have been complexity. The bipolar Cold War era often rewarded leaders with a Manichean sensibility. The unipolar post-Cold War world did not. Gorbachev's warning that he had done a terrible thing to the United States, depriving it of an enemy, lacked specificity. It turned out that the GOP was the damaged party. A relatively placid international environment certainly helped Clinton to defeat George H. W. Bush – also a decorated Second World War veteran, and with a formidable foreign policy record – and Dole in successive elections. Voters traditionally favoured the GOP over the Democrats to better protect national security. The end of the Cold War had neutralised this advantage.

Wolfowitz responded to this challenge by focusing most of his energies on a single enemy, Iraq, and by broadening the range of his ambition. In 1997 he published a chapter in an edited book, *The Future of Iraq*, in which he detailed three possible ways to deal with Saddam Hussein: containment, engagement or replacement. Wolfowitz argued strongly for the final option, though did not spell out what this might entail.[89] He followed this up with an article co-authored with his long-standing collaborator Zalmay Khalilzad, succinctly titled: 'Overthrow Him'. In a strongly worded article Wolfowitz and Khalilzad identified the primary strategic lesson of the Gulf War – 'military force is not enough' – instead stating that a broad and effective US policy toward Iraq 'must be part of an overall political strategy that sets as its goal not merely the containment of Saddam but the liberation of

Iraq from his tyranny'.[90] In the absence of the Soviet Union, overthrowing Saddam Hussein and liberating Iraq became Wolfowitz's *idée fixe*.

That same year Wolfowitz joined other hawkish Republicans declaring intellectual allegiance to the Project for the New American Century (PNAC), a think tank founded in Washington DC by William Kristol and Robert Kagan. It released its 'Statement of Principles' on 3 June 1997. The statement revealed a political party in deep dialogue with itself – rattled by Clinton's success in winning two consecutive elections – about its future foreign policy direction:

> American foreign and defense policy is adrift. Conservatives have criticized the incoherent policies of the Clinton Administration. They have also resisted isolationist impulses from within their own ranks. But conservatives have not confidently advanced a strategic vision of America's role in the world. They have not set forth guiding principles for American foreign policy ... We seem to have forgotten the essential elements of the Reagan Administration's success: a military that is strong and ready to meet both present and future challenges; a foreign policy that boldly and purposefully promotes American principles abroad; and national leadership that accepts the United States' global responsibilities.[91]

The statement of principles was a rousing declaration of allegiance to the style and substance of Ronald Reagan's first term in office, although it was short on policy specifics. Among the statement's signatories were Elliot Abrams, Dick Cheney, Eliot A. Cohen, Francis Fukuyama, Fred Iklé, Zalmay Khalilzad, Scooter Libby, Donald Rumsfeld and Paul Wolfowitz – the shadow foreign policy establishment.

Some of the specifics were fleshed out on 26 January 1998, when PNAC published an open letter to President Bill Clinton, urging a change in US policy toward Saddam Hussein's Iraq. The signatories rendered their concerns in simple prose, writing that the 'current policy, which depends for its success upon the steadfastness of our coalition partners and upon the cooperation of Saddam Hussein, is dangerously inadequate'. President Clinton needed to open his eyes to the fact that Iraq was working assiduously to develop weapons of mass destruction, which could destabilise the region and indeed the world. 'It hardly needs to be added', stated the authors darkly, 'that if Saddam does acquire the capability to deliver weapons of mass destruction, as he is almost certain to do if we continue along the present course, the safety of American troops in the region, of our friends and allies like Israel and the moderate Arab states, and a significant portion of the world's supply of oil will all be put at hazard.'[92] After the letter was published a small selection of its signatories, including Wolfowitz, Richard Perle and Donald Rumsfeld, travelled to the White House to discuss Iraq with Clinton's national security adviser Sandy Berger. After departing the meeting, Perle declared that he was 'appalled at the feebleness of the Clinton administration'.[93]

The clock was ticking on Bill Clinton's presidency, however. During 1998 the GOP foreign policy brains trust began surveying the field in earnest to identify (and tutor) the Republican most likely to defeat Al Gore – Clinton's Vice President, who was all but certain to win his party's nomination – in 2000. In the spring of 1998 the Governor of Texas, George W. Bush, visited Stanford University's Hoover Institute to discuss foreign policy with an illustrious group that included George Schultz and Condoleezza Rice, Stanford's provost, who had worked for Bush's father and who had co-authored a well-received book on the reunification of Germany with the University of Virginia's Philip D. Zelikow.[94] A follow-up meeting was scheduled in Austin a few months later. Joining Bush, Rice and Schultz in the heat of July were Dick Cheney – then head of the Halliburton Corporation, a vast oilfield services company with a staff in excess of 50,000 – and Wolfowitz. Bush informed the gathering that he was planning to run for the presidency and that he wanted their help. Impressed by Bush's humility and sincerity, Wolfowitz agreed to help. And the rest, as they say, is history.

George W. Bush's foreign policies were inspired in part by a set of ideas that had been gestating for twenty-five years. It was during the Carter administration that Wolfowitz first identified Saddam Hussein as a potential threat, and the Persian Gulf as a region of vital concern to US interests. Indeed, Wolfowitz displayed remarkable consistency in his foreign policy career from 1969 to 2001. His commitment to projecting US power into the Middle East and belief in the potentially transformative impact of democracy-proliferation are consistent themes. There is nothing mercurial about Paul Wolfowitz – for good and for worse.

Andrew Bacevich certainly found Wolfowitz to be an impressive thinker and strategist when he first encountered him. When Wolfowitz became Dean of the School of Advanced International Studies (SAIS) at Johns Hopkins University in 1993, he had hired Bacevich as a 'minor staff functionary'. In an open letter to Wolfowitz, published by *Harper's* in March 2013, Bacevich recalled how disappointed he had been in SAIS, but how impressed he had been by its Dean:

> From five years of listening to these insiders pontificate, I drew one conclusion: people said to be smart – the ones with fancy résumés who get their op-eds published in the *New York Times* and appear on TV – really aren't. They excel mostly in recycling bromides. When it came to sustenance, the sandwiches were superior to the chitchat.
>
> You were an exception, however. You had a knack for framing things creatively. No matter how daunting the problem, you contrived a solution. More

important, you grasped the big picture … Where others saw complications, you discerned connections. Where others saw constraints, you found possibilities for action.[95]

Wolfowitz was the consummate grand strategist: a University of Chicago PhD; a devotee of Albert Wohlstetter; a detector of immutable patterns across history. Following Wilson, Wolfowitz's worldview was undergirded by a single principle: substantive geopolitical stability is contingent upon the spread of democracy. Wolfowitz begins by imagining what a peaceable world looks like and works backward to realise that utopian aspiration. The abstraction is the starting point in matters of import; the primary goal is often vaulting and unprecedented.

Such ambition clearly has virtue. But it also resembles the self-righteousness shared by Wolfowitz's fiercest critics on the left. Who is more confident than the individual who understands the *true* nature of world affairs? Noam Chomsky and Paul Wolfowitz share many common traits; among other things, they both overstate America's actual or prospective ability to shape the world. The Second Iraq War emphasised the limits of American power rather than the potentialities. Like Vietnam, this lesson has salutary value; but only if it is heeded.

In his open letter, Bacevich encouraged Wolfowitz to re-examine the assumptions that informed his foreign policy views:

> Why did liberation at gunpoint yield results that differed so radically from what the war's advocates had expected? Or, to sharpen the point, *How did preventive war undertaken by ostensibly the strongest military in history produce a cataclysm?* … To be sure, whatever you might choose to say, you'll be vilified, as Robert McNamara was vilified when he broke his long silence and admitted that he'd been 'wrong, terribly wrong' about Vietnam. But help us learn the lessons of Iraq so that we might extract from it something of value in return for all the sacrifices made there. Forgive me for saying so, but you owe it to your country.[96]

Bacevich might be overly optimistic on that front, for the prospects for a Wolfowitzian self-reckoning do not appear to be promising. In an interview in June 2014 Wolfowitz suggested that America had actually 'won' the Second Iraq War by 2009, but that this hard-earned victory had been squandered by President Obama in his headlong rush to withdraw.[97] Paul Wolfowitz's self-belief remains absolute.

Notes

1 L. D. Solomon, *Paul D. Wolfowitz: Visionary Intellectual, Policymaker, and Strategist* (Westport: Praeger Security International, 2007).

2 R. H. Immerman, *Empire for Liberty: A History of American Imperialism from Benjamin Franklin to Paul Wolfowitz* (Princeton: Princeton University Press, 2010).

3 J. Mann, *The Rise of the Vulcans: The History of Bush's War Cabinet* (New York: Viking, 2004).

4 G. Packer, *The Assassins' Gate: America in Iraq* (New York: Farrar, Straus and Giroux, 2005).

5 See for example, S. Halper and J. Clarke, *America Alone: The Neoconservatives and the Global Order* (New York: Cambridge University Press, 2004); J. Vaïsse, *Neoconservatism: The Biography of a Movement* (Cambridge MA: Harvard University Press, 2010); J. Velasco, *Neoconservatives in U.S. Foreign Policy Under Ronald Reagan and George W. Bush* (Washington DC: Woodrow Wilson Center Press, 2010); and J. F. Drolet, *American Neoconservatism: The Politics and Culture of a Revolutionary Idealism* (London: C. Hurst and Co, 2011).

6 Immerman, *Empire for Liberty*, p. 203.

7 Library of Congress, Washington DC (hereafter LOC), Box 70, Papers of Paul H. Nitze, Letter from Paul H. Nitze to Zbigniew Brzezinski, 26 March 1976.

8 N. Thompson, *The Hawk and the Dove: Paul Nitze, George Kennan, and the History of the Cold War* (New York: Henry Holt and Company, 2009), p. 259.

9 Mann, *Rise of the Vulcans*, p. 74.

10 See Chapter 6 of J. Rovner, *Fixing the Facts: National Security and the Politics of Intelligence* (Ithaca: Cornell University Press, 2011).

11 Mann, *Rise of the Vulcans*, pp. 75–6.

12 Immerman, *Empire for Liberty*, p. 202.

13 Packer, *The Assassins' Gate*, p. 25; Immerman, *Empire for Liberty*, p. 199.

14 Solomon, *Paul D. Wolfowitz*, p. 10.

15 Bloom's best-known work is *The Closing of the American Mind* (New York: Simon and Schuster, 1987), which offers an impassioned defence of the teaching of philosophy through a 'canon' and denigrates the woolly, relativist direction of US higher education.

16 S. Bellow, *Ravelstein* (New York: Viking, 2000).

17 Transcript of Paul Wolfowitz Interview with Sam Tannenhaus, *Vanity Fair* (9 May 2003), http://archive.defense.gov/Transcripts/Transcript.aspx?TranscriptID =2594 (accessed 6 February 2017).

18 Transcript of Paul Wolfowitz interview with Nathan Gardels, *Los Angeles Times* (29 April 2002), http://archive.defense.gov/transcripts/transcript.aspx? transcriptid=3435 (accessed 6 February 2017).

19 J. Cassidy, 'The Next Crusade: Paul Wolfowitz at the World Bank', *New Yorker* (9 April 2007), www.newyorker.com/reporting/2007/04/09/070409fa_fact_cassidy (accessed 20 August 2012).

20 For a selection of Albert and his wife Roberta's writings on nuclear strategy see R. Zarate and H. D. Sokolski (eds), *Nuclear Heuristics: Selected Writings of Albert and Roberta Wohlstetter* (Washington DC: Strategic Studies Institute, 2009).

21 Mann, *Rise of the Vulcans*, p. 30.

22 On Carter's presidency see G. Smith, *Morality, Reason and Power: American Diplomacy in the Carter Years* (New York: Hill and Wang, 1986); B. Glad, *An*

Outsider in the White House: Jimmy Carter, His Advisors, and the Making of American Foreign Policy (Ithaca: Cornell University Press, 2009); and S. Kaufman, *Plans Unraveled: The Foreign Policy of the Carter Administration* (DeKalb: Northern Illinois University Press, 2008).

23 J. E. Zelizer, *Arsenal of Democracy: The Politics of National Security – From World War II to the War on Terrorism* (New York: Basic Books, 2010), p. 275.

24 M. R. Gordon and B. E. Trainor, *The General's War: The Inside Story of the Conflict in the Gulf* (Boston MA: Little Brown, 1995), p. 480 (original emphasis).

25 Solomon, *Paul D. Wolfowitz*, p. 26.

26 Zelizer, *Arsenal of Democracy*, pp. 283, 286.

27 N. Hamilton, *American Caesars: Lives of the Presidents from Franklin D. Roosevelt to George W. Bush* (New Haven: Yale University Press, 2010), pp. 329–30.

28 Quoted in Solomon, *Paul D. Wolfowitz*, p. 26.

29 Mann, *Rise of the Vulcans*, pp. 97–9.

30 *Ibid.*, p. 273.

31 *Ibid.*, p. 109.

32 Solomon, *Paul D. Wolfowitz*, p. 46.

33 F. X. Clines and W. Weaver, 'Briefing', *New York Times* (30 March 1982), p. 12. See also Mann, *Rise of the Vulcans*, p. 115.

34 *Ibid.*, p. 116.

35 See Speech by Ronald Reagan, 8 March 1983 in *Public Papers of the President of the United States, Ronald Reagan, 1983* (Washington DC: Government Printing Office, 1983), pp. 363–4.

36 See J. M. Scott, *Deciding to Intervene: The Reagan Doctrine and American Foreign Policy* (Durham NC: Duke University Press, 1996) and R. Garthoff, *The Great Transition: American-Soviet Relations and the End of the Cold War* (Washington DC: Brookings Institution Press, 1994).

37 G. Schneider and R. Merle, 'Reagan's Defense Buildup Bridged Military Eras', Washington Post (9 June 2004), www.washingtonpost.com/wp-dyn/articles/A26273-2004Jun8.html (accessed 26 August 2016). Also see James Mann, *The Rebellion of Ronald Reagan* (New York: Viking, 2009).

38 F. Fitzgerald, *Way Out There in the Blue: Reagan, Star Wars, and the End of the Cold War* (New York: Touchstone, 2000), p. 29.

39 Quoted in Immerman, *Empire for Liberty*, p. 29.

40 L. Cannon, *President Reagan: The Role of a Lifetime* (New York: Public Affairs, 2000), p. 272.

41 J. Kirkpatrick, 'Dictatorships and Double Standards', *Commentary*, 68:5 (1979), pp. 34– 45 at pp. 41, 37.

42 George Schultz, *Turmoil and Triumph: My Years as Secretary of State* (New York: Charles Scribner's Sons, 1993), p. 320.

43 'Jeane Kirkpatrick Admits Sex Discrimination Apparent', *Oklahoman* (20 December 1984), http://newsok.com/jeane-kirkpatrick-admits-sex-discriminati on-apparent/article/2092075 (accessed 11 January 2017).

44 Mann, *Rise of the Vulcans*, pp. 130, 92.

45 See *ibid.*, pp. 132–4.

46 H. A. Kissinger, 'What Next When U.S. Intervenes', *Los Angeles Times* (9 March 1986).
47 Solomon, *Paul D. Wolfowitz*, p. 36.
48 See W. LaFeber, *Inevitable Revolutions: The United States in Central America*, Second Edition (New York: W. W. Norton and Company, 1993).
49 Mann, *Rise of the Vulcans*, p. 136.
50 Immerman, *Empire for Liberty*, p. 207.
51 R. Reagan, *An American Life: The Autobiography* (New York: Simon and Schuster, 1990), p. 611.
52 J. L. Gaddis, *George F. Kennan* (New York: Penguin Press, 2011), p. 668.
53 See J. G. Wilson, *The Triumph of Improvisation: Gorbachev's Adaptability, Reagan's Engagement, and the End of the Cold War* (Ithaca: Cornell University Press, 2014).
54 See K. Adelman, *Reagan at Reykjavik: Forty-Eight Hours that Ended the Cold War* (New York: Broadside Books/Harper Collins, 2014).
55 Cannon, *President Reagan*, pp. 779–81.
56 G. C. Herring, *From Colony to Superpower: U.S. Foreign Relations since 1776* (New York: Oxford University Press, 2008), pp. 898–9.
57 P. Wolfowitz, 'How the West Won', *National Review* (6 September 1993), p. 62.
58 J. Lukacs, *George Kennan: A Study of Character* (New Haven, London: Yale University Press, 2007), p. 181.
59 D. Cheney, *In My Time: A Personal and Political Memoir* (New York: Threshold Decisions, 2011), p. 162. For a study of the relationship between Cheney and George W. Bush see P. Baker, *Days of Fire: Bush and Cheney in the White House* (New York: Doubleday, 2013).
60 On the conflict and aftermath see L. Freedman and E. Karsh, *The Gulf Conflict, 1990–1991: Diplomacy and War in the New World Order* (Princeton: Princeton University Press, 1993) and Gordon and Trainor, *The General's War*.
61 Immerman, *Empire for Liberty*, p. 214.
62 Mann, *Rise of the Vulcans*, p. 184.
63 Herring, *From Colony to Superpower*, p. 909.
64 G. F. Kennan, *The Kennan Diaries*, ed. F. Costigliola (New York: W. W. Norton and Co., 2014), p. 616.
65 Mann, *Rise of the Vulcans*, p. 192 (original emphasis).
66 J. A. Baker III, *Politics and Diplomacy* (New York: G. P. Putnams, 1995), p. 194.
67 R. Gates, 'The Gulf War: Oral History', *Frontline*, PBS, first broadcast 9 January 1996, www.pbs.org/wgbh/pages/frontline/gulf/oral/gates/1.html (accessed 26 August 2016).
68 Mann, *Rise of the Vulcans*, p. 191.
69 *Ibid.*, p. 192.
70 C. Powell and J. E. Persico, *My American Journey* (New York: Random House, 1995), p. 531.
71 G. H. W. Bush and B. Scowcroft, *A World Transformed* (New York: Alfred A. Knopf, 1998), p. 489.
72 D. Rumsfeld, *Known and Unknown: A Memoir* (New York: Sentinel, 2011), p. 414.

73 J. L. Gaddis, 'Grand Strategies in the Cold War' in M. Leffler and O. Arne Westad (eds), *The Cambridge History of the Cold War: Volume II, Crises and Détente* (Cambridge: Cambridge University Press, 2010), p. 43.

74 Mann, *Rise of the Vulcans*, p. 198.

75 Immerman, *Empire for Liberty*, p. 217. For the various drafts of the DPG see the website of the National Security Archive based at George Washington University: www.gwu.edu/~nsarchiv/nukevault/ebb245/index.htm (accessed 26 August 2016).

76 P. E. Tyler, 'U.S. Strategy Plan Calls for Insuring no Rivals Develop', *New York Times* (8 March 1992), www.nytimes.com/1992/03/08/world/us-strategy-plan-calls-for-insuring-no-rivals-develop.html?pagewanted=all&src=pm (accessed 26 August 2016).

77 Packer, *The Assassins' Gate*, p. 21.

78 Mann, *Rise of the Vulcans*, p. 203.

79 D. Chollet and J. Goldgeier, *America Between the Wars: The Misunderstood Years Between the Fall of the Berlin Wall and the Start of the War on Terror* (New York: Public Affairs, 2008), p. 45.

80 Memorandum from Paul Wolfowitz to Secretary of Defense Dick Cheney (5 May 1992), www.gwu.edu/~nsarchiv/nukevault/ebb245/doc14.pdf (accessed 26 August 2016).

81 Immerman, *Empire for Liberty*, p. 218.

82 L. Vavreck, *The Message Matters: The Economy and Presidential Campaigns* (Princeton: Princeton University Press, 2009), p. 134.

83 Bacevich, *American Empire*, p. 68.

84 P. Wolfowitz, 'Shaping the Future: Planning at the Pentagon' in M. T. Leffler and J. W. Legro (eds), *In Uncertain Times: American Foreign Policy after the Berlin Wall and 9/11* (Ithaca: Cornell University Press, 2011), p. 46.

85 C. Preble, *The Power Problem: How American Military Dominance Makes Us Less Safe, Less Prosperous, and Less Free* (Ithaca: Cornell University Press, 2009), p. 31.

86 Mann, *Rise of the Vulcans*, p. 395, footnote 40.

87 P. Wolfowitz, 'Clinton's Bay of Pigs', *Wall Street Journal* (27 September 1996). I Chollet and Goldgeier, *America Between the Wars*, p. 188.

88 Solomon, *Paul D. Wolfowitz*, p. 69.

89 P. Wolfowitz, 'The United States and Iraq' in J. Calabrese (ed.), *The Future of Iraq* (Washington DC: Middle East Institute, 1997), p. 111.

90 Z. Khalilzad and P. Wolfowitz, 'Overthrow Him', *Weekly Standard* (1 December 1997), p. 14. In Mann, *Rise of the Vulcans*, p. 236.

91 Statement of Principles (3 June 1997), https://web.archive.org/web/20050205041 635/ http://www.newamericancentury.org/statementofprinciples.htm (accessed 26 August 2016).

92 Letter to Bill Clinton (26 January 1998), https://web.archive.org/web/2005020 4091959/www.newamericancentury.org/iraqclintonletter.htm (accessed 26 August 2016).

93 Mann, *Rise of the Vulcans*, p. 24.

94 C. Rice and P. D. Zelikow, *Germany Reunified and Europe Transformed: A Study in Statecraft* (Cambridge MA: Harvard University Press, 1995).

95 A. J. Bacevich, 'A Letter to Paul Wolfowitz', *Harper's* (March 2013), p. 48, http://harpers.org/archive/2013/03/a-letter-to-paul-wolfowitz/ (accessed 7 July 2016).
96 Bacevich, 'A Letter to Paul Wolfowitz', p. 50 (original emphasis).
97 K. Wong, 'Wolfowitz: We "won" the Iraq War', *The Hill* (6 August 2014), http://thehill.com/policy/defense/214453-wolfowitz-we-won-the-iraq-war#.U-Ifzl4Wmfs.twitter (accessed 26 August 2016).

Index

EU authorised representative for GPSR:
Easy Access System Europe, Mustamäe tee 50,
10621 Tallinn, Estonia
gpsr.requests@easproject.com

www.ingramcontent.com/pod-product-compliance
Lightning Source LLC
Chambersburg PA
CBHW052005270326
41929CB00015B/2798